Steelers
Takeaways

Player Memories
Through the Decades

by
Ron Lippock

Steelers Takeaways

by

Ron Lippock

Blue River Press • **Indianapolis, Indiana**

Dedication
A couple of quick thank you's. First, to the players, for being so open, honest, and willing to discuss often very personal issues. The game is full of glory from the fans' perspective, but we rarely see what many of these players go through to get there, and to recover mentally and physically once their time in the NFL is over. And secondly, to my family for their support, even as you put up with the myriad of calls and interviews over the past few years that broke up our days and evenings.

Author: Ron Lippock
Editor: Morgan Sears
Cover Design: Phillip Velikan
Interior Design: Regina Rexrode
Cover Photograph: Shutterstock #79902145

ISBN-13: 978-1-68157-007-5

Published by Blue River Press
http://www.brpressbooks.com

Distributed by Cardinal Publishers Group
Tom Doherty Company, Inc.
www.cardinalpub.com

Contents

Foreword by Terry Hanratty

I grew up in Butler Pennsylvania, just a few miles from Steeler headquarters, then in the Roosevelt Hotel. Little did I know in 1969 I would play for the Rooney Family. I can remember as a kid going to Slippery Rock College to watch the Steelers' training camp practices. Bobby Layne, Big Daddy, Tom the Bomb, and all the other great names. One thing I noticed was how slow they practiced. I learned years later it was what they did the night before that caused the slow movement in practice. The Steelers did not win many games back then, but they were OUR Steelers.

Enter Chuck Noll.

Chuck Noll taught the team, Rooneys and the City of Pittsburgh how to WIN. People throughout the country sort of knew where Pittsburgh was, but when Chuck was finished everyone knew where the Steel City was - you had to go through there to try to win a championship.

Chuck had a plan and he was going to stick with it. Back in the day everyone was trading their draft picks for old vets with a couple of years left. Not Chuck, he was going to build through the draft. He didn't want someone he had to break of their bad habits and teach the Steeler way. I was a rookie with Chuck in 1969, which was a long year, we were 1-13. That was the last year anybody in the country chuckled when they talked about the Steelers from Pittsburgh.

I, like most players, was blessed to have played for the Rooney family. Where else could you walk into a locker room after a game and have Mr. Rooney there to shake your hand, win or lose. I laugh when I see how some of today's owners act – thank you Chief! Three coaches since 1969 - again credit the Rooney family.

So, I thank Ron Lippock and the *Pittsburgh Sports Daily Bulletin* for allowing myself and others to keep up with all of those guys that played before, during and after I played. Those stories take me back to those times spent with my colleagues – both on the field, and most importantly, the times spent off the field – as friends. Many of these stories I've forgotten over the years – and some I didn't even know. How he got us to open up about some of this stuff, I'll never know!

Many of these guys he spoke to weren't household names either – but they were Steelers - and all had unique stories getting to the NFL and of their time as players. Those stories are great reads –personal, funny, some sad – but they opened up for Ron and gave honest accounts of their time in Pittsburgh.

I can say that when I was interviewed by Ron I had no idea what an effect it would have on my daily life. I look forward to reading the interviews. I think Ron's book is a must read for all past, present and future Pittsburgh sports fans.

-Terry Hanratty, Steelers Quarterback 1969-1975

Intro

I was asked when I first conceived of this book: "Why another book on the Steelers? What makes this one….different?"

Fair question – one I asked myself as well. The answers were surprisingly easy for me to come by. At first, I leaned on the fact that I had interviewed over three-hundred former players – from those that played in the 1950s, to those just recently retired. More well-known names like Lynn Swann, Hines Ward, Andy Russell, and L.C. Greenwood, sure. But just as importantly, the literally hundreds of role players and practice squad guys that rarely got the chance to tell their stories before, but whose perspectives on the team, issues and viewpoints were often very different from those of the "big name" players. Many of their stories were extremely personal, interesting, and unique because of those different perspectives and experiences.

The other answer that came to mind though, was that this isn't intended to be another "Story of the Steelers" book, though you get a strong understanding of the team's history through the stories and quotes given by all of the players. Rather, this is more the "Stories of the player's experiences" – of the hundreds that wore the Black and Gold. Not just stories as players. But as *people,* who struggled and grew as men– succeeded and failed - both on and off the field. Who were driven by humor, financial needs, anger, camaraderie, competition and fear…and who were affected positively and negatively by coaches and peers, race, and religion. And by the physical nature of the game itself.

There are stories never told before. And I think as I step back from them and all of the interviews, I understand now why the Steelers appeal so much to their fans. The Steelers players are not larger than life - not bigger than their fans. In fact, their lives and motivations mirror those of their fans. They are the guys next door…easy to identify with, because most never tried to be larger than life. They never tried to be more important than their fans or teammates. All they wanted to do was succeed. To earn a living. To be great at what they did. And to be accepted and remembered. Just like you and me. You'll see what I mean, I think, as you read these stories and quotes from players.

It Starts at the Top

The Steelers had been a team in flux for a couple of decades prior to the 70s, nothing like the model of consistency we identify them as being today. While the Chief was well-liked and cared for by the players he treated so well, numerous coaching changes, unwise trades, poor drafting – these were the cornerstones of the Steelers in the 50s and 60s. This led to poor seasons, disgruntled players, and ultimately, a change in direction for ownership.

Which is not to say there wasn't a great deal of talent on the team. But a complete organizational and cultural change was required for the team to succeed. And while the Rooney family struggled at first to learn the "business of football", they did in fact do so. They learned from their mistakes, learned patience, and hired Chuck Noll to build the team – the right way.

Coach Noll, with the support and encouragement of the Rooney family and hard-nosed staff, instilled innovation, accountability, leadership, and a culture of winning that required players to support as well as compete with one another.

The Rooneys:

Where to start, when discussing the stories that players told about their time in Pittsburgh? Where else…but with the Rooneys, and the rest of the front office. And it's not that I had to ask the players about their thoughts on the Rooneys over the years. In fact, I'd often refrain from doing so at first because it would consume the conversation. And frankly, to be honest, I was skeptical. So much has been written on the charity and kindness of the Rooney family. To me, it sounded like a kernel of truth that had grown to mythical proportions. Not that I doubted the fact the Rooneys were good, charitable people. But I doubted the extent

– the depth – of that kindness attributed to them. Simply because as owners of a rugged business in a blue-collar city, one expects more gruffness, and less, well, *sweetness*.

But the players dispelled my skepticism. They clearly felt compelled to discuss the impact of the Rooneys on their lives. Because it wasn't just about football with the Rooneys. It was about family. Players were *family*. And as you'll see with the interview excerpts to follow, it didn't matter if you were a Hall of Fame player or taxi squad player – if you were a Steeler, you were treated with respect, sincere interest, and care by the organization. And not just as an active player. You became part of the Steelers legacy.

Below, you'll read about the Chief's involvement in player's personal lives, his tendency to help players financially, disregard for racial concerns of the time, the time he spent with players to get to know them, and more.

You'll also find that there were some players who had experiences with the Rooneys that weren't as pleasant. Not that these occurrences were numerous, but they serve as a good reminder that, for as good as they were, they were still business owners. They still had an obligation to put the team's needs above those of an individual player's, when there were conflicts between those two principles. And those didn't always go over well with players.

Joe Gordon, Former Quteelers Director of Communications:

The Rooney family – the respect they received from all entities in society – their commitment to the community rubbed off on the players. It was a big factor in Noll's success – his character was consistent with the Rooneys and that created high-character teams.

There were few problems then and generally not of the same magnitude of the problems you see today. There were no drugs and steroids were just coming into play. Because of the examples set by Rooney and Noll, there were few issues. When we did have problems, we addressed them to help the player. Very few problems like that happened though. The biggest problems were things like fights in bars – nothing like the problems that exist in sports today.

Society is different too. Athletes weren't as independent like today and were much more respectful of authority than they are today as well.

"Red" Mack, Steelers Wide Receiver, 1961-1963, 1965:

Art Rooney got one pick every draft. I was his pick.

I lived on the North Side of Pittsburgh as a kid – four to five blocks from Mr. Rooney. My parents got divorced and I was living in St. Paul's Orphanage. We had a team and played St. Mary's – a big school with brand new uniforms. We were a rag-tag team with torn up uniforms, but we kicked their ass.

After the game a fellow came up to us and took us all out to dinner. The next year we went to football camp and that guy was there again. He bought us all new uniforms.

That guy was Art Rooney.

I don't know if he remembered me and that's why he drafted me? I should never have been drafted. I had two bad knees – I had surgeries on both in college.

Mr. Rooney came to practice every day. He knew about your family – if your kids or wife was sick, he knew. I don't know who gave him that information.

Gene Breen, Steelers Defensive Lineman, 1965-1966:

I was unhappy being sent to Pittsburgh. I came from Lombardi – the greatest team and coach – to a floundering team. We had beer bottles thrown at us by fans – one hit me in the head after I took my helmet off. We practiced in mud, had one shower head in the locker room and no weight equipment.

I was from Pittsburgh – born and raised. Unfortunately, playing for Pittsburgh was my worst experience. Losing was tough for me. After two years in Pittsburgh, I was cut from the team.

I was a military student at Virginia Tech and I got orders to report to Vietnam. Lombardi hired a lawyer for me and got Lou Anderson to get me to attend classes to get my Masters. This got me a two-year deferral.

Then I was traded to Pittsburgh. After the two years were up, the Rooneys wouldn't help me. They didn't care about me at all. The military was knocking on my door so I told Rooney I want out – "I'm done with you" I told him. So they cut me.

My paperwork was all in Pittsburgh. I got picked up by George Allen and the Rams and played for the Rams an additional two years. My lawyer saw the cast on my knee that I got from an injury while in Pittsburgh and I wasn't going to be accepted for active duty after that. During my career I had six knee operations but never missed a game but in the offseason. I rehabbed in the Steelers offices – my leg had actually atrophied. Ralph Berlin and the Rams trainer both were supposed to oversee the rehab but Berlin wouldn't sign me in to the building. "I'd probably sue him" he said. I was shocked.

Nancy, my wife, just reminds me to stay positive. But I did experience the negative that I have talked about. I don't want the Rooneys to read this and think I hated them – but my experience in Pittsburgh with them just wasn't good.

Dick Hoak, Steelers Running Back 1961-1970, Steelers Coach 1972-2007:

My last year as a player for the Steelers I suffered a concussion with four games left. I got another concussion the next week. I told my wife I was going to retire and spent two weeks in the hospital.

Every day the Chief came to see me to make sure I was all right.

In 1968, my best year, I was having a good year but the team was not so good. We practiced on the South Side then but got our checks in a hotel where the offices were in Pittsburgh. When I went to get my check I was told the Chief wanted to see me. I went up and he gave me a substantial check and said he knew we're not having a good year, but take this check.

In the last game, after I made the pro bowl, I separated my shoulder a week before the pro bowl. The secretary said Dan [Rooney] wanted to see me. He gives me another check. I told Dan the Chief already gave me one last week. Dan said he knew, but the Chief wanted me to have this one too.

"Red" Mack, Steelers Wide Receiver, 1961-1963, 1965:

The Steelers were a very poor team [in the early 60s] But the Rooneys were good people – very good people.

Mr. Rooney was too nice – he had to get out of the business of running the team. He and George Halas [Chicago Bears] were friends and kept trading and loaning players back and forth until Dan Rooney took over and the team started drafting much better players

I was there in the forgotten years. In '61, there were three teams you didn't want to be drafted by: Washington, Chicago, and Pittsburgh. They were still owned by the original owners and were the cheapest teams in football. Until Art got out of the business and his son took over and Chuck Noll came in – that's when they became a modern team. They got new facilities and paid players. But until then, it was the forgotten years.

Art Rooney was the greatest guy in the world. It just wasn't a viable franchise then. I remember we went to an exhibition game in Richmond, Virginia. They split us up on two DC-3's. The airplanes were patched up – not painted. Buzz Nutter was standing on the steps talking to Coach Parker. He didn't want to get on the plane. He finally got on and asked everyone where the parachutes were!

Lou Michaels, Steelers Kicker and Defensive End, 1961-1963:

I got to meet the finest owner in the U.S. – ever. I also met the secretary who worked at the Steelers front office and married her!

No owner was greater than Art Rooney was.

He took me to the Kentucky Derby, Preakness, and to his farm in Maryland. When I played for Baltimore and kicked four field goals for them against Pittsburgh, he called the owner and told them, "See, I told you, you got a great football player!" He took me for dinner after that game.

He loved people – he'd help anybody and had respect for everyone. I have yet to hear one bad word about Mr. Art Rooney. He was a great man, and I'll hold that opinion to my dying day.

Brady Keys, Steelers Cornerback, 1961-1967:

I started in 1968 with a fried chicken franchise. It grew to 135 restaurants – which then grew into Kentucky Fried Chicken and Burger King franchises.

It was a concept I developed – my own fried chicken batter – when I played for the Steelers. I called Art Rooney in the off-season from Los Angeles and told him what I did – about the idea and asked if he'd help me with money to start the business. All I heard was silence on the line. I had to ask if anyone was still on the line. Mr. Rooney answered back "I am. I'm just trying to figure out how fast to get you the money!"

He gave me ten thousand dollars – which was like one million dollars in those days. And in 1969 people just didn't loan that kind of money – especially to a Black man trying to start a business. I built my first two restaurants with that money.

I just want readers to know the Pittsburgh Steelers and the Rooneys – I owe them everything I am today. They gave me ten thousand dollars and never let me pay it back. They gave me one charge – to be successful. It's been on my mind ever since.

Clendon Thomas, Steelers Safety, 1962-1968:

I played for the best owner in the league – Art Rooney. I appreciated the way he treated me, not only as a boss but as an interested friend. He had a substantial horse farm in Maryland and I had a small operation in Oklahoma so we had a common interest.

After playing Baltimore he took me to his farm on Monday to see his yearlings. While driving back to Pittsburgh, Art shared many stories covering many subjects, our Irish heritage, his amazing history starting the Steelers. I cherish the attention and friendship I received from this gentleman. He also took the time to introduce me to Del Miller, his close friend who won the Hamiltonian harness race with a horse named "Adios" and built the Meadows harness track just outside of Pittsburgh.

Frank Lambert, Steelers Punter, 1965-1966:

Mr. Mara said that, after I got to Pittsburgh and was sure that we had incurred all the expenses we could expect, to send him a note with a total of our expenditures. He required no itemized list. He did not have to do that.

As for Art Rooney, I join the many former players who remember him as a player's owner. He was at most practices. He always had time to chat with players. His signature hat, topcoat, and cigar are part of an enduring and fond image I have of him.

Before my second season, I pulled a muscle and missed the first three preseason games. I could not punt in practice and was really antsy. I guess he sensed that and one day took me aside and told me that I was the team's punter and I should worry about nothing but healing.

Our strong suit was a tough defense. But, in those years, the Steelers did not yet have a winning culture. I remember that in 1965 we lost several games in the last two-to-three minutes. It got to the point that we wondered if we could hold onto a lead.

I remember visiting with Mr. Rooney in the 1970s and he told me how he wished that I could have played for Chuck Noll. He said that Noll had built an outstanding team primarily through the draft and that he had instilled a winning expectation. Those guys expected to win every game.

Ken Kortas, Steelers Defensive Lineman, 1965-1968:

Dan Rooney was given control of the team...sort of. Art was mellowing. Danny wanted to make something out of it. He was more of a ramrod kind of guy.

After the quarterback debacle, Danny spent money to get a quarterback. They drafted Hanratty but found out he was a rollout quarterback with a weak arm. They said uh oh...So they drafted Bradshaw next year and spent a lot of money. Art would never have done that.

They had no other business on the side. This was their business.

Rocky Bleier, Steelers Running Back, 1968-1980:

When I got back [from Vietnam] Dan Rooney was President and was running the team. He gave me an opportunity and put me on injured reserve. He bought me a year. I made the Taxi Squad the following year – they wanted me to get bigger and stronger. I was then activated in '71. I put on strength and weight, and made the team on my special teams play in '72. We had a terrific year and won the division. In '73 I made the team again with my special teams play. Then in '74, during the fifth game, there was an injury and I went in and played. We went to the Super Bowl, more afterwards, one thousand yards.

Warren Bankston, Steelers Fullback, 1969-1972:

The Rooney family was so very special. The "Chief" (Art Rooney, Sr.) would call us into his office, give us tickets to the Pirates games, and visit with us as if we were his own kids. Playing at Three Rivers Stadium was a bit rough on the body (hey, artificial turf has come a long way), but now that the stadium is gone, no one can take away the electricity that the great fans of Pittsburgh brought each week.

Chuck Allen, Steelers Linebacker, 1970-1971:

My second year, when I returned to our apartment from training camp, I found out that Roberto Clemente and his family were our upstairs neighbors.

The Rooneys let my wife and I use one of their boxes at the stadium to attend the World Series game. Art Rooney Sr. lived only a couple of blocks from the hospital where I had my knee surgery. I had sent my family home to Washington and Mr. Rooney brought me books to read about past Steelers greats.

Mr. Rooney asked my opinion of Coach Noll. My response was just "Give him a little more time, he just needs a few more players." Jack Lambert was Noll's pick two years later. Little did I know the turnaround would be so soon.

Anyway, when I was to get out of the hospital, Mr. Rooney said he would have someone drive me to the airport to return me home. He did – it was his brother who was a priest! How many owners would do this today?

Gordon Gravelle, Steelers Offensive Lineman, 1972-1976:

My time in Pittsburgh was very beneficial to my growth and development as a person and future businessman. I learned more life lessons from the Rooney family, the Steelers management team and the Steelers coaching staff than I had before or have since those few years I spent there.

I was exposed to and learned (through no fault of my own) how a first class organization was run and how the Rooney's had established a culture of "people first" where all of the employees, including the players, were treated with dignity and respect. I also learned quite quickly after I was traded that it was not the same at other teams.

Dick Conn, Steelers Cornerback, 1974:

The Rooney family is the best owner in the game. Mr. Rooney (Art) would come around the locker room with that cigar in his mouth and shake hands with every player from Joe Green down to me. He sent me a one hundred dollar check for my wedding and I still have the stub where he wrote me a personal note. I was proud to be a part of the funding for the Art Rooney Statue back in 1990. He was another great influence on my life.

Brad Cousino, Steelers Linebacker, 1977-1978:

I reflect on my NFL career and with the Steelers quite often. I learned so much about the concept of being on a team. Like how to commit to do your job no matter what...and then to trust and expect that your teammates are going to do their job no matter what. I learned an important lesson that it is critical to understand that not everyone can be the star, but that every facet of being on a team is critical to the end result whether you are a starter, a backup, a role player, a practice player, a trainer, equipment manager, coach, ball boy, etc. Very few get the recognition but every aspect is critical to making a group of individuals transform to becoming a world class champion.

I can still remember my first team meeting with the Cincinnati Bengals in 1975 and it was Paul Brown's last year as the head coach. At that meeting there was a major discussion about how the goal was to beat the Steelers. Two years later, the mindset of the Steelers was "how to win another Super Bowl"...it was so obvious that the Steelers ownership, management, coaching, etc. had a completely different mindset as compared to the Bengal organization at the time. In addition, the Steelers ownership and coaches treated their players as family, respecting them and instilling in them the desire to be the best they could be and giving them the necessary tools to succeed.

Not one of the players thought they were a super star and expected star treatment and no one person was above the team.

As a group, virtually everyone was fun to be around. The players, coaches and management treated everyone with respect, including the ball boys.

Joe Bushofsky, Former Steelers Scout:

The Steelers are a great organization and the Steeler Nation all rally around the success of the Steelers. Art Rooney Jr. and Jack Butler played a big part in the Steelers success and although Art Jr. never talks about his accomplishments, he is responsible for many of the good players that the Steelers drafted because he had the guts to stand up and fight for the players that the scouting department felt could help the team.

Just knowing Art and Jack Butler is a privilege and an honor.

Art Jr. was on the road when he first started and after he was named Director of Scouting, he always came to the all-star games (Senior Bowl, etc.) and he and Jack Butler also were present at many games of top prospects.

Tim Rooney, the cousin, spent many hours evaluating the pro players and also studying films of college prospects. The Steelers sent their coaches to work out and evaluate some top prospects at their respective positions if the team scouts had graded the player to make their team…They also studied film, talked with the position coach and checked on injuries, character, etc.

Tunch Ilkin, Steelers Offensive Lineman, 1980-1992:

Even in '87 during the strike, when Rooney heard I was looking for a field to practice on, he called me and told me "There's a key on Marianne's desk that unlocks the gate to the practice field." Marianne was his secretary. He said "You didn't get it from me."

He never threatened me as a player rep during the strike. Many reps were worried about getting cut but I never had to worry about that. He always used to come up to me and ask me "Tunch my boy, how are things in Turkey? Still killing each other each other, just like Ireland?"

Everyone in the organization are all just down-to-earth guys. The humility they have is unbelievable.

Calvin Sweeney, Steelers Wide Receiver, 1980-1987:

When Art Rooney Sr. brought the four of us top picks in to meet the press and coaches. He came up to me and asked me my name. I told him "Calvin," He said "Calvin? That's not a good Irish name. I'll call you Mikey."

And he never called me Calvin again. He'd come up to me in practice and say "Hey Mikey – how are you doing?"

Frank Pollard, Steelers Running Back, 1980-1988:

I remember after my second season, I just finished packing up my car and was leaving my apartment when I got a phone call from The Chief. He told me about how good he thought my second season was and said that he wanted me to go see his son before I left. Well, I thought he was going to release me. What else could it have been?

Well, I went to Mr. Rooney – and he said he appreciated my effort and that it was a good year for me. That's the difference with the Steelers – a big difference, to show that kind of appreciation.

Brian Blankenship, Steelers Offensive Lineman, 1987-1991:

In 1991, in the fourth game of the season against the Patriots I injured my neck. On the following Monday I went to Joe Maroon's office for an MRI and later that morning I found out I could no longer play.

I called my agent and told him the news. He asked me if I had signed my new contract that we had verbally agreed on Saturday before the New England game. I told him I had not and he said get over there and sign it before they found out about the injury.

I told him I was going to see Dan Rooney before I sign anything. I knocked on Mr. Rooney's door and informed him of my prognosis and he was very kind and gave me praise for my short five year career. He said that he was sorry and would do whatever he could to make sure I was ok. He asked me about the new contract and I told him the deal was agreed to on Saturday – so he told me to get my butt across the hall and get it taken care of.

That was my proudest moment as a Steeler.

Lorenzo Freeman, Steelers Defensive Lineman, 1987-1990:

The Steelers were a family organization. Art always came in to the locker room during the week. It was amazing. As he got older, he'd still come in and talk to all the players and knew who everyone was. He knew where I played in college and would talk to me about the prior game and would converse with all of us about ourselves and the team.

So, we missed that [when he passed away]. We enjoyed seeing his face. We knew he cared about us…it was just sad. No everyone talked about it but it impacted a lot of players. I don't want to say it had anything to do with our record, but it was sad.

John Jackson, Steelers Offensive Lineman, 1988-1997:

I met Art Rooney Sr. when the draft picks came in. It was an unbelievable experience sitting down and having dinner with him. He knew who everyone was – he picked them himself. And he was sharp as a tack.

I was really impressed that he knew who I was. We talked about horses – he knew I was from Kentucky I guess. I wasn't a big horse fan like the Chief though – he was naming horses and was just a lot more knowledgeable than me. It was a really good experience.

Eight guys in that class made the team that year – it was a special class. Dermontti and I played together for eight years, and six of us played for five years together. That just doesn't happen now.

I didn't know the history of the Rooneys when I got there. After he died, all the stuff about what he did for the community came out. Paid for funerals for those that couldn't afford them. He used to walk around the North Side at night when he couldn't sleep. People knew who he was but wouldn't touch him.

Rick Strom, Steelers Quarterback, 1989-1993:

I will always remember meeting Art Rooney, Sr., "The Chief." One day before my first mini-camp, I re-introduced myself to him a week after initially meeting him. He told me he knew who I was and "to remember I was just as good as those other boys." It was just the thing a local undrafted rookie quarterback needed to hear to help me believe I could compete at that level.

Coaching:

The Steelers have had only six head coaches since the 60s – fewest of any team in the NFL over that stretch of time. Each coach was unique – from the more flamboyant Bill Austin, the technical and stoic Chuck Noll, to recent coaches Bill Cowher and Mike Tomlin, who fell somewhere in between their predecessors in terms of their emotional approach to the game.

Every Steeler fan understands Chuck Noll's arrival heralded a new era of winning football in Pittsburgh. And most realize his technical approach to the game was a driving force behind that success. But Coach Noll brought more than technique. For all of that stoic approach, few coaches brought more innovation and dared to bring more change to a team than Noll had. And that, as much as his ability to recognize talent and individual competitiveness, enabled the team to succeed.

But what led to that need for change and innovation? You'll read quotes below from players who played under Noll's predecessors. On the polarizing and strictness of Coach Bill Austin, and Nixon's insecurity.

You'll also get a good understanding of what made Coach Cowher and Coach Tomlin so appreciated by players – how their intensity, honesty, and passion for the game motivated their teams.

However, there were conflicts as well. Especially with the coaching staff prior to Coach Noll. Those coaches were often more disciplinarian, more "direct" in the way they worked with players. This created some ill feelings between a number of the players I spoke to and their coaches.

And let's not forget the assistant coaches – the ones that players worked most closely with. They also had profound effects on players– both positive and negative, accepting and sometimes confrontational. From Dick LeBeau and Dan Radakovich to Kent Stephenson, Lou Riecke and Mike Archer – they were then ones who were best able to help the players understand their abilities, limitations, and roles on the team.

Art Michalik, Steelers Linebacker, 1955-1956

[Head Coach Walt] Keisling was a good man, but he was old school. We'd practice for two and a half hours in the morning and in the afternoon. They wanted to try me out at center in Pittsburgh. I came into camp early – a week before the veterans all came in. I came in at 228 pounds, at the time all we had was a skeleton crew – quarterback, receivers and centers. By the end of the first week I was down to 212 pounds!

Dick Haley, Steelers Cornerback, 1961-1964, Steelers Director of Player Personnel, 1971-1990:

Buddy Parker was a good coach – he was just different. The Steelers organization was very different than it is today – the culture, the conditions.

Buddy was a bright coach, but he didn't have enough discipline. He had better players in Detroit than he did in Pittsburgh too, but we had some good guys – Lipscomb, Bobby Layne – it just wasn't working.

Big Daddy, Ernie Stautner....we had guys that were in the league a while. Guys that had been around. Buddy didn't want many first and second year players – Parker was known to want experienced guys. Not like the 70s – those 70s teams didn't have many guys that played on other teams.

Lou Michaels, Steelers Kicker and Defensive End, 1961-1963:

Buddy was full of intensity. He told me I would be his right defensive end and kicker right away. With Parker, all you had to do was win. Nothing counted except winning. If you lost, you walked on egg shells.

He was a tough man, but hey, it worked. We almost won a division title – we had three ties that year. We lost that last game in Yankee Stadium or we would have gone to the championship. We were unlucky – we should have won. We made mistakes – lots of mistakes we usually didn't make. When we lost we went from first place to second because of those three ties.

That first season was bad, but by the second season, after he brought in Lipscomp and others, we almost won it all.

If we won, we never had a curfew. But if we lost, we better be in by eleven! That's the way it was. If we lost, he'd blame his tie, coat, shirt....he cut off his tie on a plane after a loss and threw his shirt in the garbage.

Art Pappy Lewis once came down to a Tuesday practice with the team and walked back to the locker room with Parker. That week we won, so Parker called Lewis and told him to come down to the next Tuesday practice. We won again, so Parker called him again to come down.

The fourth time, we lost. So Buddy called Art and told him he didn't have to come back that Tuesday!

We also never practiced on Friday the thirteenth. Buddy was just very superstitious.

He threw so many coats and shirts in the garbage. He was a coach you wanted to play for – he wanted to win and that's what you wanted in a coach. No matter what anyone says, it's no fun if you are losing.

Dick Hoak, Steelers Running Back 1961-1970, Steelers Coach 1972-2007:

Chuck [Noll] got things done quietly – he didn't do a lot of speaking. He didn't speak to you every day. Maybe the day before the game and the day after he'd talk about the game.

Chuck was a person that acted the same if we won or lost.

A good example was one season where we started off against Cleveland and lost 51-0. The second game we played Cincinnati and they beat us 41-10. The next game was against a very good Vikings team – on the Tuesday morning before the game Chuck came in and just started talking about how we would beat the Vikings – like we won the first two games!

Chuck had an even keel about him – he wasn't too high or too low.

Now, Bill Cowher got upset about things and would rant and rave some – and get elated about things too.

Bill also had more of an open door policy – Chuck had an open door policy too, but players were afraid to use it (laughs). Bill would also call players into his office more.

There are a lot of ways to skin a cat. The biggest thing about coaching – and I saw that with a lot of Pittsburgh coaches – is you have to be yourself. Players will know if you aren't – they'll sense the BS and not accept you.

Theron Sapp, Steelers Fullback, 1963-1965:

Buddy Parker was tough. He didn't say a whole lot. He did like to take a short drink now and then!

We had a good year in 1963, Ed Brown was the quarterback that season and that was after Big Daddy Lipscomb overdosed. We would have had a chance to win it all if that didn't happen.

We lost to the Giants in a terrible weather game that last game or we would have won the division. We beat them earlier in the year before I got there. Ed Brown went the whole week without a beer – he said he wanted to concentrate on the game. Well, I think that threw his timing off because he had a bad game.

Chuck Logan, Steelers Tight End, 1964:

Buddy Parker was a very knowledgeable football coach. However, I think that he was surrounded by some incompetent assistant coaches. Some of them could barely speak. My one memory of Buddy is seeing him on the ground (Thanksgiving weekend) with three or four irate Steeler fans trying to push a St. Louis Cardinal pennant in his face while pummeling him. The fans were disappointed in having lost to the Cardinals at home. They were probably steel workers, having paid fifteen dollars for their ticket, and having too many Iron City's to drink.

I felt terrible for Buddy and none of the fans were coming to his rescue.

Marshall Cropper, Steelers Wide Receiver, 1967-1969:

Coach Austin was an outstanding individual. I enjoyed my experience with him. He was like any other coach, he just wanted to win.

The biggest struggle and the root of the struggle for those 60s teams was that we needed to play together enough to establish teamwork. We needed to spend enough time together to make good decisions.

Whenever there's a new coach, it always means a big change. Coach Noll was one who came in and made the necessary adjustments and changes that best suited the team. He always had good work ethics, and he really worked us. He made us work, and we knew the end result would be good because we put in the work.

Clendon Thomas, Steelers Safety, 1962-1968:

Bill Nixon made a serious mistake with our team prior to a scrimmage at St. Vincent College training camp. He made a comment to our team that he was aware of some of the terrific defensive play of the Steelers. And, he wanted to see it. I couldn't believe he said it! That's the equivalent of waving a red cape in front of a fighting bull. He saw it!

I think three of my starting teammates were injured for the year in the scrimmage without quality replacements, and our chance for a winning season was done.

Ken Kortas, Steelers Defensive Lineman, 1965-1968:

Buddy Parker, I loved him. I said I like this guy the moment I got there.

We did not have a good year my first year. We couldn't score – we needed a quarterback. They tried to trade Ben McGee for Norm Snead in Philadelphia. There was an argument though between the Rooneys and Parker and Parker was fired two weeks into training camp. Philadelphia was willing to do the trade but the Steelers didn't want to trade McGee – they thought he'd be a good defensive lineman.

Then came the ill-fated Bill Austin. He showed up and ruined Pittsburgh football, I think.

Hiring him was a mistake – he was a strange person.

I can't elaborate. I didn't get along with him at all – he tried to aggravate me. The whole team knew he was strange. The final straw was when he was in his third year of his contract. We were scrimmaging at St. Vincent's and he was getting so mad that the offense wasn't clicking. He was just going overboard.

The defense was just too good – the offense couldn't score against us. But Paul Martha got a concussion and he was carried off in the station wagon. The next play, linebacker Bill Saul gets piled on and his knee gets bent the wrong way, and now he's out. The very next play I get hit in the ankle – I didn't move away in time from a block – and that put me out a month with a severe sprain. I told the wagon as it was pulling away to hold on!

We got three starters hurt in one practice because he overdid it. We all said that guy was crazy.

There were other issues too. It was just a bad mistake. What was weird was that he got a job afterwards with Lombardi in Washington. Lombardi died and they kept him on. When I was picked up on waivers by Washington after playing in Chicago I said oh no, he's here.

Roy Jefferson, Steelers Wide Receiver, 1965-1969:

Bill Nunn was the conduit for those guys coming to the team from the smaller, Southern Black colleges. Those guys were more intimidated by the coaches than I was, I grew up in California and wasn't intimidated.

That's where Coach Austin and I didn't see eye-to-eye. He was a dictator and I wasn't mild-mannered in my reaction to him. He'd curse at me and I'd curse him back. He was just one of those guys that wanted you to be afraid of him…that's my thought on his coaching technique, anyway.

I was a high-strung, young guy. I thought I was smart – I knew the offense and would not be intimidated. You can't put fear into me. I was also a guy that liked to go out at night and had curfew problems, and Coach Noll and I argued about that.

I remember we played the Giants in Toronto and I was out after curfew. He sent me home and suspended me for a week.

Then, it all came to a head in training camp in 1970. Noll was running back-to-back passing drills, 7-on-7s then 11-on-11s. I had a cough and the trainer told me I was not allowed to practice. I said I was okay and I kept asking to practice, but the trainer said no.

Well, it was ninety-four degrees, and for some reason most of the receivers were hurt that day. I told [Receivers coach] Lionel Taylor that those guys were going to kill themselves in that heat. There were just two guys, one being Hubie Bryant, to run plays and they were both young guys trying to make the team.

I asked Taylor to let me run some patterns – that the young guys will kill themselves to make the team. He finally said to let him check with Chuck. But he never did.

I was pissed. Incensed. So I went and listened in the huddle, tapped the other receiver and told him I was going to run for him that play. Hanratty threw me the ball, then on the next play he threw it to me again, and Coach Noll saw it that time. Noll was hot – he yelled at me to get off the field – that I was not supposed to be out there practicing. So I yelled at him back and got off the field.

Well, later in the locker room they bring Hubie Bryant in packed in ice – sweat was literally popping off of him – I never saw anything like it. It actually hit me in the face. I never saw that before – I started crying. They took him away in an ambulance.

Someone came in then and told me Chuck wanted to see me. He said "Roy, I'm tired of you usurping my authority." I explained what I was doing – that I thought those guys would kill themselves. I said those kids could have died out there and that someone should get on you for allowing that to happen. I said I didn't want to play for him – that I didn't care if he traded me.

The next thing you know, I was traded.

Gene Breen, Steelers Defensive Lineman, 1965-1966:

In 1965, I was traded to Pittsburgh for a draft pick. When I arrived, Buddy Parker had been fired. They didn't have a head coach then. Mike Nixon was the interim head coach.

Nixon was quiet. He didn't have the charisma that Lombardi had. He was knowledgeable but just didn't have the personality. He was an assistant coach, not a head coach.

Austin was the special teams coach in Green Bay. He was a great football player for the Giants, but as a head coach, he wasn't very good.

He didn't believe in himself. He drafted poorly – a few number one picks didn't work out. And I remember Larry Gagner as a rookie came in with an issue he wanted to talk to Austin about. They talked, and then in practice, the team was in a circle and Austin brought Larry into the circle and talked to the entire team about Larry's issue. I mean, what kind of coach does that?

He was not my favorite coach, let's put it that way. Dan Rooney Jr. even once said he didn't know why Lombardi recommended him so highly to us.

When I played for the Rams after Pittsburgh, I remember running past Austin and him yelling at me, giving me crap. That's the kind of guy he was.

Bill Asbury, Steelers Running Back, 1966-1968:

Austin was curiously a good position coach, but not what I would call a team leader. It seemed at times he was torn between trying to be himself and an imitation of Vince Lombardi. There were times when he was the "players coach" and other times when he was outright mean-spirited.

I remember one team member saying about him "I was here when he got here, and I'll be here when he's gone." Another comment about two-thirds through our last season together (1969) someone said, "Let's get it up for New Orleans" that being the last game of the season. He and I were not close.

Larry Gagner, Steelers Offensive Lineman, 1966-1969:

I liked Bill Austin. He was Lombardi's offensive line coach for those glory years. He knew that particular aspect of the game well.

Unfortunately, for him and us players at the time, that wasn't enough knowledge for complete success. I trust he would have had more success being himself than mimicking Vince Lombardi. A lot of the Austin Steeler players felt like they had little left for the games because of those grueling practices. But in all fairness to Bill Austin, he and his Steeler teams never had the opportunity of taking advantage of the state of the art facilities that the building of Three Rivers Stadium offered.

Chuck Noll's first year's record wasn't as good as the poorest of the Austin years, but through the crafting drafting by Chuck Noll things turned around quickly. Noll's practices were much less physically punishing, especially in training camp, than Austin's, but Noll was the complete teacher in all aspects of the game. That was his forte.

John Brown, Steelers Offensive Lineman, 1967-1971:

The guys said he [Bill Austin] was a cross between Steve McQueen and Vince Lombardi, which made him hard to figure out. He wasn't a great coach, in my opinion.

Chuck Noll came and put order to the team. Chuck did not tolerate a lack of discipline. He actually recruited me in college when he was a coach in San Diego.

Remember, I had Paul Brown as a coach in Cleveland. He was a stately older gentleman. He tolerated nothing. I remember he would stand up in front of the team and tell guys that he heard about what they did last night, and if they did it again he'd tell their wife! Even Jim Brown listened to him.

Bill Austin was laissez faire. He was not a strict disciplinarian – it was a different culture.

Bruce Van Dyke, Steelers Offensive Lineman, 1967-1973:

Bill Austin wanted to be one of the guys. He had some funny quirks. He wanted all of his guards on special teams – as wedge busters. We only had four on the team and we had to go run down the field on punts and kicks and then play. We were big, slow guys running down the field and all the teams knew we weren't fast guys.

He also had this reverse psychology idea. When we won, he'd run us to death on Tuesdays after the game. When we lost, he would take it easy on us. I think his plan worked the opposite way. We'd be losing games and he'd tell us that at least we wouldn't have to run on Tuesdays!

He also always wanted to go drinking with the guys and had a prejudiced streak in him as well.

The biggest thing Chuck Noll did was to bring a highly intellectual perspective to the game. He knew all the fundamentals about every position. No other coach I played for knew that. At some point throughout the year he'd pull us aside and teach us about the fundamentals and techniques – what we were doing wrong, foot positions and things like that.

After a time it gave us a lot of confidence in him as a coach. The team accepted him fairly well – the problems with Roy Jefferson was the only real one but he was a Coach Austin carryover. The coaches before had always tried to motivate you – but Coach Noll was very matter-of-fact.

Kent Nix, Steelers Quarterback, 1967-1969:

When Coach Noll came in…he took over the offense, defense, and special teams. He was more of a teacher of the game, not highly excitable and installed a new offense. The offense was totally new to me as we had been running the Green Bay Packer offensive scheme under Bill Austin. Compared to the former one….this had twice as many plays and nuances than Coach Austin had used.

In the end, we had the feeling as a team he was going to be successful in his goals and visions for the franchise. I loved his offense…it complimented my passing abilities and wished I could have stayed to learn more about his successful system.

Ralph Berlin, Steelers Trainer, 1968-1993:

One of the first things Noll did was get them all together and he told them that they weren't a good bunch of players and that not many would be there when he was done. He weeded many of the guys out, and the ones he kept played – guys like Russell and John Brown.

I was new. Noll came in a year after me, so it was a process for all of us getting used to a new regime. But he brought in a winning team and because of that he could do what he wanted to do.

The scouting department deserves a lot of the credit. That '74 draft was the best in the history of the league. There were four Hall of Famers in that class. With no free agency then, the team was able to keep the nucleus in Pittsburgh. You couldn't have kept that team together today.

I remember there was a sportswriter then who said that if you paid the players what they were worth then, it would cost fifty-seven million dollars just to put the defense on the field. That was a lot of money back then! The minimum signing bonus then was ten thousand dollars. If you talked to the agent of a third or fourth round pick today, they'd laugh at a one million dollar bonus.

Mike Taylor, Steelers Offensive Lineman, 1968-1969:

Chuck Noll was a damn good coach! He started changing out the roster and drafted Joe Greene, L.C. Greenwood and others that ultimately turned things around in Pittsburgh.

I remember a great compliment that Chuck Noll paid me in front of my Steeler teammates during the film session after our game with the Chicago Bears in 1969. He said, "If we had more effort put out by others, as Mike Taylor did against the Bears, we would win a few more games here in Pittsburgh." It was a nice pat on the back from Chuck Noll, even though the next week my bags were packed and I was on my way to New Orleans. And so goes the life of an NFL football player.

Coach Kolb was a technician and very detail oriented. We played really good defense in those years as well but we never won the big one or got to a Super Bowl. We played hard though and we were still respected as a tough team. Despite the departure of some future Hall of Famers, guys like Ham, Stallworth, Webster, Shell, and other great players still remained on that team in 1982.

Dick Shiner, Steelers Quarterback, 1968-1969:

Bill Austin was a heckuva football coach. Under different circumstances, his success could have been different. He was like Van Brocklin. I played for Van Brocklin in Atlanta and he should have been one of the greatest coaches in the NFL, but was his own worst enemy. He couldn't forget that he wasn't playing. The way he was on the sidelines – he got so many penalties. And if you looked at him the wrong way, he'd call you in the office for three straight days and read you the riot act. You could smile at him and he'd think you were up to something bad. But there was no one more knowledgeable than him. He just fought himself and the players for no reason!

Austin – I learned a lot from him on offensive line play He applied Lombardi's strategy and I learned a lot from that. Keep it very basic…and possession passing.

Austin settled us into an offense. We got better. We didn't win, but we improved. I felt bad when he was fired. He gave me my chance to start and I learned a lot from him.

I remember he instituted the hitch route – the five yard stop. It had just started then. I'll never forget – Austin told me to start throwing that stuff. I didn't do and would come to the sidelines and he'd tell me again to do it. After a couple of times, he grabs my arm and says, "Look you bleepity-bleep, either you start throwing those passes or you bleeping rear end is on the bench!"

I started throwing them then – the message got across.

We beat Atlanta that year – I think we completed eight of those passes. Two years later when I got traded to Atlanta, Van Brocklin says to me, "Hey, we don't throw that midget-league shit around here. We go down the field!"

Rocky Bleier, Steelers Running Back, 1968-1980:

Bill [Austin] was in his third season of a three year contract. I didn't know what to expect when I got drafted, I didn't know anything about the organization. I just wanted to make the team. My rookie season as like most then – we just wanted to make the team. I was the 417th person picked in the draft. I looked at my competition on the team. The coaching was secondary. As the season went on though, you could see he lost his leadership. He lost control of the players – there were arguments and confrontations in meetings between players and coaches. We were 3-11. That was the end of it...Bill I think was just out of his realm as a head coach. He was a great assistant coach at Green Bay. But he was rough and edgy as a head coach. He played football in the military...I think my experience is that losing after a while creates a losing attitude...and it all starts to go downhill.

Jon Kolb, Steelers Offensive Lineman, 1969-1981:

I remember getting ready to go up against Klecko one week. He had fourteen games in a row where he had a sack. I was nervous – I hadn't given up a sack all season and the media got wind of the matchup. Lambert was making my life miserable in practice – he and Perles. Lambert would tell me that "It was a good thing you aren't playing against me!"

The defense weren't the kind of guys that prayed for you and wished you the best. They were the opposite. Later on in the week I had had enough and dared Lambert to line up against me in two-minute drills. They came at the end of practice when guys went after each other at full speed, after being tired from a full day of practice.

Jack lined up at defensive end. I thought he would try to beat me with a speed rush and he caught me leaning and ran right over me. He hit Bradshaw from the blind side – hard and knocked him to the ground. There was no letup. Chuck went and patted Lambert on the back and turned around and yelled at me.

Chuck was a good example of the way the world really is. I could have shot him I was so mad. But I had two choices – pout or get better. We had a mature team that didn't pout – we just learned and got better. Sometimes you got beat but you tried. Roosevelt had the saying, "My place will never be with those souls that never know either victory or defeat."

Terry Hanratty, Steelers Quarterback, 1969-1976:

Chuck got the best out of everyone except Roy though. He had a quiet strength about him. I never remember him raising his voice – even in the locker room. He was a "thought man" – there was always a reason for everything.

It's interesting. Back then quarterbacks called their own plays. Chuck gave me as a rookie full reign – I thought that was great. Now, quarterbacks get the plays sent in their helmets. They may watch film, but they don't call their own plays and don't watch the film like we did.

Me, Terry, and Joe would all watch film and game plan together with Chuck and the quarterback coach. There were no offensive coordinators. We all got involved.

Don Alley, Steelers Wide Receiver, 1969:

Chuck Noll was the defensive coordinator in Baltimore the whole time I was there. He brought Don Shula's offensive playbook, verbatim, with him to Pittsburgh. It was a rather complicated offense and I was just beginning to get a handle on it after two seasons and three training camps.

I arrived in Pittsburgh right after our last pre-season game and a week before the first regular season game, and I recall that nobody including the assistant coaches knew the plays. We were practicing at the fairgrounds on a field that my high school team wouldn't have practiced on, Three Rivers stadium was under construction, and we were to play our home games at Pitt stadium, and I really felt that I had taken a really big step backward coming from a Super Bowl team in Baltimore to a rather dis-organized situation in Pittsburgh.

Bob Adams, Steelers Tight End, 1969-1971:

Chuck Noll was the youngest coach in the league that year, and a natural, gifted teacher. Teaching was in his bones. I admired him for his organizational skills and ability to communicate concepts. He controlled everything and had tremendous knowledge about many areas of life.

In the beginning, and perhaps forever, he was always teaching someone, or so it seemed. He was structured, organized, and professional as could be. He seemed to know everything about every position on the team including special teams.

For instance, while walking back to the dorm at St. Vincent's, one evening, Warren Bankston and I were passing by the practice field after dinner. A local guy was down on the field with his golf bag and was practicing chip shots. We saw Chuck approaching the golfer from fifty yards away. He said a few words to him and then turned him around and wrapped his arms around him holding his arms and took him through the motions of chipping the ball up to an imaginary pin. Warren and I looked at each other in amazement. Here was the head coach of the team, taking the time to instruct a local resident on chip shots. We agreed this man was a teacher from the soles of his feet to the depth of his soul. He loved it.

However, one thing he taught me and the other tight ends in our 1969 camp was a highly dangerous blocking technique he learned earlier in his career that almost got my head knocked off by All Pro defensive end, Ben McGee. The technique was called, ominously, "leg whipping." This involved diving in front of the opponent down the line with the upper body blocking his forward motion, then swinging the hips and legs around cutting his legs out from under him or tripping him. However, not only did the technique bruise the defender, it bruised the shins of the blocker. It hurt.

The technique was limited as it was dangerous and later outlawed. One day in practice I leg whipped Ben and I hurt him. I lay on the ground looking up at this menacing six foot, six inch giant. He grabbed hold of me, pulled me up to his chest and said, "Rookie, if you ever do that again I'm gonna kill ya!" Stress on "kill." Looking into Ben's eyes I had no doubt what he said was true. Life and careers are too short and I was convinced I would need to find a substitute for the leg whip technique. That too was a lesson all by itself.

Chuck taught me a valuable lesson concerning "luck." After a stunning upset of Detroit in our opener at Pitt stadium in '69, we suffered a complete string of losses for the rest of the season.

Well, we were in our ninth or tenth loss, I think it was to Dallas, and following the game Chuck came in to talk to the players. We were wet and muddy, quite downtrodden, looking at the floor, only glancing in his eyes. I thought he was going to fire us all, except Andy Russell, Dick Hoak, and Joe Green of course. He stood up on a stool, hands on hips, sternly but not menacingly. He then said in a hoarse but terse voice these words and no others, "An old coach of mine once told me, in a time such as today, that luck is…preparation meeting opportunity." He stepped down and left the room not saying another word. Those words were etched in my soul.

L.C. Greenwood, Steelers Defensive Lineman, 1969-1981:

Chuck did a great job of bringing the right people in and giving them a chance. He didn't have a lot of players from big schools. Hanratty, Lynn, Franco…a few, but not many. Most were from the small Southern schools.

Most of us had a hunger to show what small school guys could do. Chuck honed our skills. That hunger was what made us successful – so many guys came and went on that team.

Lee Calland, Steelers Cornerback, 1969-1972:

I learned about Chuck right away. Chuck Hinton and Ben McGee were still there when I got there. Chuck called a meeting with the team in '72 and told us he did the hardest thing he ever had to do in releasing them both. I knew right there, that was the place for me. He had compassion. There was more to him than x's and o's.

Warren Bankston, Steelers Fullback, 1969-1972:

Simply put, he knew what he wanted to do by setting a high standard of professionalism for himself and demanding the same from the players and coaches. After the 1972 season, the seeds had been planted, and the players responded with desire, dedication and determination. Once you know you can win, it is just a matter of performance on the field-execution-that wins games. None of the coaches suited up. Their job was to prepare the players, mentally, physically, and psychologically. They did a great job.

Chuck used to say two things I remember: First, "if you want to know who lost the game, go look in the mirror." Second, "luck is preparation meeting opportunity." He would lose his temper occasionally, but his demeanor was business-like, straightforward, consistent, and honest. No sucker punches and no withholding the facts. He told us like it WAS.

Warren Bankston shows off receiving skills versus the Chargers.
Photo courtesy of Warren Bankston

Hubie Bryant, Steelers Wide Receiver, 1970-1971:

I do remember Roy Jefferson blaming me for getting him traded! We had a bunch of injured wide receivers in camp so I was out there running every turn – was just not many backups healthy enough to go.

Roy went over to Chuck and told him he was going to kill me in practice. The two got into an argument about it, and shortly after Roy was traded. Roy said sticking up for me got him traded!

Lionel Taylor was also big in that. Lionel Taylor saw something in me. He told me to give me something to fight for you with. Even though all of us receivers were fighting for the same job, he created a team feeling for us – when one of us did well we all did. He wouldn't allow any animosity between us.

He also made sure we weren't prima donnas. When he saw the backs blocking, he'd bring us over and tell us we can block hard too. He made sure we were a great blocking group, and we were.

Dennis Hughes, Steelers Tight End, 1970-1971:

I had a hip pointer in '70 that set me back. I also did not have a good relationship with Coach Lionel Taylor. I was a Southerner and he didn't like that one bit. He wouldn't talk to me. He wanted nothing to do with me.

He took me out of the game against Philadelphia because I was called for a clipping penalty. The referee was wrong – was at the wrong angle. Well, he jerked me out of the game and chewed me out right there on the sidelines. I said wait a minute! I'm not a boy – I'm a man and you don't talk to me that way. He apologized to me later during the game and even said it wasn't a clip.

You don't do that – you have to keep your faculties about you. He bad-mouthed me to Chuck and benched me even though I was the team's leading receiver.

Babe Parilli, Steelers Quarterback Coach, 1970-1973:

Chuck wanted me to groom Bradshaw. To tell you the truth, they didn't know a lot about the passing game when I got there. I played with Chuck in Cleveland. The running game was used to set up the passing game – the opposite of today. Even as a player, Chuck was smart. He wasn't real big but he was always where he was supposed to be. He played offensive guard and linebacker – he played two ways.

Hanratty was an outgoing guy with the players. Bradshaw was so uptight and hyper. Hanratty was a happy-go-lucky guy and players loved him for that.

Bradshaw was so uptight we had to hypnotize him three times. Lou Riecke – the weight lifting coach – would room with me sometimes at the hotel for a couple of days. He knew hypnosis and hypnotized Bradshaw the night before the game for three games. That helped him to relax. We'd tell him to relax and be calm…it actually helped him. If I see him again I will tell him that we never actually brought him out of it. He went from being quiet and not outgoing to the opposite now. He's done a great job – everyone loves him now!

I used to take them out for beers. Especially Bradshaw – to help him relax. It was a serious business. I had a deal going with Chuck Noll. He was the bad guy and I was the good guy. I told Chuck that it made it easier for me. He'd yell at Bradshaw a lot. That bothered Bradshaw – he'd scream at Bradshaw to get ready and on the field when we were going over techniques.

It was all planned but it went too far sometimes – it got on Bradshaw. Chuck was hard on him. I got Bradshaw in his second year, but his first year he wasn't good. He only completed about thirty-eight percent of his passes his first year – and that went up to over fifty percent his second.

Bob Leahy, Steelers Quarterback, 1970-1971:

I was captivated by Chuck Noll. All he said and did, I was inspired with. He made such an impression on me. It made me relish coaching. Bradshaw and I used to joke about how we were both from small colleges. I made an All American team and the guy I threw to broke all of the college receiving records until Jerry Rice came along. But when I showed up at the Steelers camp, I didn't know man versus zone. I knew nothing about the strategy of football. I was exposed to that first in camp. The five quarterbacks and the coaches would all meet, and the first two days all we talked about was how defenses played. Nothing about offense at all. I learned that getting to know what the defense is doing is necessary if you are going to be successful on offense.

Chuck Allen, Steelers Linebacker, 1970-1971:

Coach Noll went on to Baltimore then Pittsburgh. He traded for me before the start of the 1970 season. He told me that he was a little concerned about my past injuries but I might be able to help him out and help turn things around in Pittsburgh.

He wanted players who would pay the price mentally physically. He wanted players who would put the team first.

Coach Noll was smart and intense and had little time for players who showed any resistance. In other words, "My way or the highway." Noll believed in the draft. Joe Greene, Bradshaw, L.C. Greenwood, Jack Ham, Franco Harris, and Mel Blount. He also knew the value of seasoned veterans like Andy Russell, Rocky Bleier, Ray Mansfield, and Dick Hoak.

Noll had good training from his playing days and his early coaching experiences with coaches like Paul Brown, Sid Gilman, and Don Shula.

Dan Radakovich, Steelers DL & OL Coach, 1971, 1974-1977:

I changed the way they blocked. I invented the full-arm extension to avoid holding. They questioned if it was legal but it was and it saved us a lot of holding calls.

I also tailored all the jerseys. I wouldn't let defensive linemen get a hold my linemen! I wanted the jerseys to be skin tight, so I had Parisi's mother-in-law tailor them. Then we re-tailored them ourselves to make them even more skin-tight. But guys could *still* hold on to the jerseys, so we double-taped the shoulder pads under their jerseys – even Joe Greene couldn't grab hold of them.

I'm not sure if the team is still taping pads now – it's legal to do it. I remember Haley of the 49'rs used to put silicon on his jersey – they were red but he put so much on the jersey turned black. We complained but the refs never did anything. Oakland used to put grease on their jerseys – we complained about those all the time.

I was a linebacker coach in college so I had the defensive line do linebacker drills! I had them do different things – moving laterally and working on their pass rush techniques. I told them if they were quick as linebackers they would have it made.

I remember years later George Allen of the Redskins even said it – that those Steelers defensive linemen were as quick as linebackers. I took a lot of pride in that!

Chuck kept to himself. It was hard for me to talk to him then. We talked more after we both retired then we did when we were in Pittsburgh. Once a week we'd meet with the doctor and talked about who was hurt and who could play. But that was about it.

Gordon Gravelle, Steelers Offensive Lineman, 1972-1976:

Coach Noll was more of a teacher than the stereotypical coach in the NFL. He had an uncanny ability in keeping us humble. One of my favorite Coach Noll saying went something like this: In life and football you can never reach the peak and stay there by resting on your laurels. There is no plateau, you need to improve even if you have reached the top. If you don't you will be going downhill because your competitors are working harder than you and therefore will be better than you.

Randy Grossman, Steelers Tight End, 1974-1981:

The Steelers, by luck, were the best team I could have possibly signed with because of Chuck Noll. Perhaps because Chuck was an undersized offensive guard, he didn't care what a player looked like, he was only concerned with a player's ability to execute. Game plans were designed to take advantage of opponent's weaknesses not so much our strengths.

It was a given that you could execute what the coaches wanted done. I never saw my size as a disadvantage in getting done what the assignment was. If I couldn't do what they wanted done I wouldn't have made Chuck's team.

Mike Collier, Steelers Running Back/Return Specialist, 1974-1977:

We had the best preparer in the game in Chuck Noll. He was the best at making us ready to win a championship. He never got enough credit. You always hear people talking about Belichick and other guys as the greatest coaches. You rarely hear about Noll. That upsets me greatly. He was one of the greatest coaches ever in that timeframe.

He knew how to motivate. We fed off of his enthusiasm and tenaciousness on the sidelines, and his hard work. We all fed off of that.

John Banaszak, Steelers Defensive Lineman, 1974-1981:

All of the assistants believed, like Coach Noll, in the fundamentals of the game and drilled them. Chuck loved to teach. He broke the game down to the fundamental level and taught it. He is famous for introducing the thought process that each of us would go through pre snap.

In looking back on those teams and what we accomplished I would have to say the Chuck's philosophy of the game of football was pretty simple, work hard, have fun, and win.

From Chuck Noll I learned that you have to find young men that are disciplined and motivated, from George Perles I learned that the game demands toughness and from my college coach Dan Boisture I learned that you can coach and still develop a personal relationship with your players.

Sydney Thornton, Steelers Running Back, 1977-1982:

I have yet to find out why they drafted me! Under Chuck Noll's philosophy, if you are a good football player, there's a job for you. He didn't discriminate when it came to football players. He only had hangups about attitudes and the way you carried yourself. But if you were a football player you were Chuck's man.

They put me behind Franco my rookie year and I had my ups and downs learning the system. The next season they put me behind Rocky and I had my ups and downs again.

By the third year, we went to the Super Bowl again, and I was able to stay on the field because when they called Rocky, I would go on with him, and when they called Franco, I could play next to Franco too. I was on the field with Franco when he broke a number of his records.

Ted Petersen, Steelers Offensive Lineman, 1977-1983, 1987:

My time with Coach Noll, definitely. His stress of the fundamentals and mental toughness. We were always fundamentally better prepared than our opponents. He was a great teacher and expected that his assistant coaches were as well. That allowed us to impose our will on other teams to get it done.

Those lessons resound in my mind still as I look back.

It was the complexity of the offense. Noll was such a cerebral guy. The playbook was thick. We had more short-yardage running plays than others had in their whole offense. When I went to the Colts, we had five running plays – total. We had twenty-five in Pittsburgh – for the goal line alone. It took a couple of years to really get the plays down as an offensive lineman. The number of defenses and blocking schemes change for each play.

It's funny. I could get the guys together right now and walk into the huddle and we'd know what to do. That toughness and fundamentals were drilled into us.

When we won the Super Bowl and went to St. Vincent's the next season to start camp, we'd start blocking by the numbers again – the ABCs, like we were learning it for the first time. And it paid off.

Tom Beasley, Steelers Defensive Lineman, 1978-1983:

Chuck had a knack for blending personnel. You need a Shell and a Lambert and a Ham. Chuck had the intuitive knack for picking out unique individuals that were different but that meshed well and were great leaders.

Rick Moser, Running Back, 1978-1979, 1981-1982:

I really never expected to make the team. In fact after the second or third week in training camp my rookie year I went up to Coach Hoak and said that I think I'm wasting your time as well as mine or something to that effect. He told me that when he was a rookie for the Steelers he actually left camp (AWOL) for a couple of days. He went home but came back to camp and ended up playing for ten years and coaching thirty-plus more. I guess I owe everything to him. So Dick – if you're reading this – thank you!

Sam Washington, Steelers Cornerback, 1982-1985:

Tony Dungy was my position coach and then the defensive coordinator when Woody Widenhofer left. He taught me my basic philosophy – I'm not a yeller and I got that from him. There are other ways of getting a point across while still being firm and consistent.

He also pushed the basic fundamentals – he did a great job of teaching. No matter how far you go, you need fundamentals. High hat, flat back…I still use that terminology today and the techniques he taught us.

When I went to Cincinnati I played under Dick LeBeau. I remember him for his ability to break down film down to the player – to see their strengths and weaknesses, what they can and can't do.

I learned a lot about preparing for an opponent from him. He was just very detail-oriented. He'd point out how a receiver cuts and pushes off, the depth of the quarterback, can he throw for more than sixty yards…I loved this one: If we played eight yards back and the quarterback was in the pocket and could throw fifty yards, we only had to run thirty-two yards. That was always big, that thirty-two yards.

Tony's cover-two became a big-time coverage in football. He taught players how to read the line of scrimmage, to re-route wide receivers and funnel them to the safety. Tony helped me with that one and I'm still teaching those things today.

Edmund Nelson, Steelers Defensive Lineman, 1982-1987:

Oddly enough I owe my development to John Kolb who of course was a standout offensive tackle during his playing years in the '70s, but became our defensive line coach when George Perles went to Michigan State.

Coach Kolb was a technician and very detail oriented. We played really good defense in those years as well but we never won the big one or got to a Super Bowl. We played hard though and we were still respected as a tough team. Despite the departure of some future Hall of Famers, guys like Ham, Stallworth, Webster, Shell and other great players still remained on that team in

Jed Hughes, Steelers Linebacker Coach, 1984-1988:

First of all, Chuck is a friend. We established a level of trust and admiration that lasts today. When my dad died, he was very empathetic.

Chuck has a level of intellect and knowledge of the game that is unequaled. He can coach any position better than the position coach.

There are several aspects about Chuck that make him unique. He is an active learner who would dedicate every off season to learning a new hobby, some of which included wine, cooking, scuba, and flying an airplane. He's intellectually curious and much like Coach John Wooden, his wife is his best friend.

Chuck was never interested in being in the media. Being around his family and an intimate group of people was important to him.

Mark Behning, Steelers Offensive Lineman, 1985-1987:

I read that Coach Noll's first year, he didn't hire a linebacker coach. He wanted to coach the linebackers himself. He brought in Andy Russell to his office – he was the seasoned vet at that position. Russell thought he was being brought in to be praised and told how he was valued, but instead Noll told him he was a sloppy player. I think about teaching moments like that – about technique. And instead of Russell telling Noll to shove it, he just did what Chuck told him to do. About positioning his feet differently. That's what Noll was all about. Tom Osborne was that way, too.

Lupe Sanchez, Steelers Safety, 1986-1988:

Tony Dungy was great. He was extremely professional. I never once heard him raise his voice in the three seasons I was there.

I remember him saying something along the lines of, "Guys we aren't here to teach fundamentals. At this level either you can do the job or you can't. And if you can't, you won't be here." And it wasn't that he was being mean or negative, he was being very honest with us and we all appreciated it. You always knew where you stood and that was very important.

He was a great teacher not only about football, but about life. He would always walk through the training room as we were getting treatment for nicks and injuries and he would say, "Remember Wally Pip!" We would look at each other and say, who's Wally Pip? He finally told us that Pip was the starting center fielder ahead of Lou Gehrig until he decided to take a day off because he just wasn't feeling so well, and then no one ever heard of Pip again. Tony was a great motivator in many ways.

Buddy Aydelette, Steelers Offensive Lineman, 1987:

Noll was a reclusive coach to some – people didn't know much about him. But when I was the long-snapper, he used to love catching the balls from the punter and handing them to the long-snapper. So I had great conversations with him then and got to know him a little.

He liked to fly airplanes – I didn't know that. One day I asked if he was a veteran and he said no, he just enjoyed flying. He kept to himself, but he was just a regular guy.

Merril Hoge, Steelers Running Back, 1987-1994:

He said I was exactly what they needed. Now, that could be what he told every player, but I found him to be sincere and true.

With Noll – the more you could do, the better chance you had to make the team. You can't be one-dimensional. I could play running back, fullback and could catch the ball. Also, the prior year, the team started six or seven guys due to injuries. So, while I was last on the depth chart at first, I played on special teams and could do more than most of the other backs. That's how I stayed confident – there wasn't one guy on the team who could do more than me.

I knew after the first preseason game too that I had a good chance of making the team. I was put in positions in the first preseason game that you would only be put in if you were expected to produce. I was the first third-down back in and on special teams.

I didn't get overwhelmed. But my first practice, they handed me the ball. It was a basic gut play – not difficult. Just J-Step and hit the four-hole. So, I hit my J-step and saw the hole open up then close before I even got the ball, then open and close again. I said to myself – "Holy Mother!" The game was so fast and quick. Wicked fast. I thought to myself then that I'd have to adjust to that if I was going to make it. I needed to go to a different gear and mentality.

These guys were playing for their jobs – their livelihoods. There was a level of ferociousness I had never seen before. I'd never been in that environment before. I knew I had to take that same approach or I wouldn't make it. And it took me just one play to realize that. I'm glad it didn't take a month to do so or I would have never made the team.

Brian Blankenship, Steelers offensive Lineman, 1987-1991:

My best memory of Chuck was his ability to have a comment on all subjects. We were in the weight room at old Three Rivers and a janitor was mopping up some water that had leaked from the stadium above. Chuck could not resist going over and showing the clean-up man that having the mop a certain angle was the best way to remove the water. Always coaching!

Tim Worley, Steelers Running Back, 1989-1993:

Playing for Chuck Noll was just awesome. It was a dream because he saw the potential in me. I went through a period of time where I was very disappointed in myself because I felt I had disappointed him.

He taught me a lot. Playing for Bill Cowher was cool too, even though I only spent less than half a season with him. Bill Cowher was great because he could just relate. I could go to him and talk to him man-to-man.

Jerrol Williams, Steelers Linebacker, 1989-1992:

I liked both Cowher and Noll. Sometimes I needed a kick in the ass to get me going. You can't give me slack. Cowher was like that. He was an energy dude and liked to get fired up. He was new school – put the fastest guys in and let them make plays.

He gave me an opportunity to play full-time. He flew me in after he got there and said it was my job to lose. I wasn't starting then but was making plays as a third down pass rusher.

In the old school system under Coach Noll if you didn't know all the plays, chapter, and verse you didn't start. So I couldn't move up with Bryan Hinkle there. Cowher said the main thing for me was to show the intensity every down that I did as a third down pass rusher.

Barry Foster, Steelers Running Back, 1990-1994:

Chuck [Noll] was a great coach and did so many great things for the organization. But we felt like we needed to be more competitive. We finished third in the division behind Cincinnati and Houston. We had the talent, but no one liked the tight-end focused offense, except maybe [tight end] Eric Green. No one liked the plays. We'd get in the huddle and when a play was called we knew it wouldn't work. It was too complicated.

When Bill came in, the first thing he did was unify the team. From the outside, you don't see or understand it. We were a divided team. The practices were divided. It was always the offense versus the defense. When the offense messed up, the defense yelled at us, and we did the same when they messed up. Even the coaches. The defense had free reign to hit us in practice under Noll – even late. It was Noll's way of trying to instill toughness in everyone. After Cowher came in, I remember one day in practice a receiver, I think it was Calloway, got crushed by Lloyd. Cowher blew the whistle and yelled at Lloyd. He brought all of us in then – had us all take a knee and told us we can't do this. It brought the whole team together. From there we started getting it – that this was going to be different from what we were used to.

Gary Jones, Steelers Safety, 1990-1994:

We respected Cowher. He was from the area. Pittsburgh had hard-working people and that's the way Cowher was. Chuck never said a whole lot. Bill never over-spoke, but he got his message out.

He played linebacker, so he wasn't a rah-rah guy. Just get the job done – that's how linebackers are. It didn't matter who you were – if you didn't do well he'd let you know. He was one of those guys that could push the right button to make you run through walls for him. He was fair and up and up. He was in control – he was no puppet – he ran the show.

Chuck Noll wasn't a real nice or endearing man at that time, but winning and success breeds respect, and he certainly did achieve that.

LeRoy Thompson, Steelers Running Back, 1991-1993:

Chuck Noll and Bill Cowher were totally different. Coach Noll was hard-nosed, old school, and kind of let the assistants coach at this point and just being the overseer. Practices were long and brutal featuring a lot of hitting and wear-and-tear on your body. Coach Cowher, as evident by him only being thirty-four, still wanted to play so he was enthusiastic, high energy, and fun. A true players' coach desiring to win the respect and confidence of his squad. He did not take too long to do so. I enjoyed playing for him more than any coach outside of my high school coach that I played for. That's saying a lot because I played for Joe Paterno, Bill Parcels, Marty Schottenheimer, Chuck Noll, and Tony Dungy.

The adjustment for me from Noll to Cowher was a smooth and welcomed one for me because Coach Cowher brought in Ron Erhardt from the Giants as the offensive coordinator. He used me with a lot of creativity – runs, screens, one on one pass plays, and in the slot like he had used David Meggett with the Giants. I was assured to play because I was the only back outside of maybe Merril Hoge that could catch, run, and block well.

Coach Hoak never over-coached players and trusted that each of us players had made it to a professional level for a reason. Having played the game, both coaches had a great deal of insight, just as lieutenants leading soldiers. It was my sincerest pleasure to play for them both.

Sammy Walker, Steelers Cornerback, 1991-1992:

Cowher took a long time to be the coach he is today, let me just say it that way. When he was young he especially loved special teams. He loved to pick his people. I used to call him Coach Rah Rah. When the media was around he'd get in your face. I'm not sure if it was for show or something. But normally he was always in deep thought. He was more cerebral – like Billichick.

We didn't get along well. I didn't need a drill sergeant. Noll didn't yell – he just wanted it done. He didn't care how you did it. If we had a goal line drill, he'd say the only way to do it is to do it. To get a real feel for the goal line you had to do it. With Cowher, he wanted you to think about it more. Cowher trusted his coaches to do it for the players, and Noll trusted the reactions of his players more. Noll trusted you if he drafted you. He never lied to you.

Levon Kirkland, Steelers Linebacker, 1992-2000:

Me and Bill [Cowher] had a good relationship. When I was drafted in the second round I wasn't too surprised – they were the team I thought really liked me during the scouting process. I could joke with Bill. Capers and LeBeau – they really helped me develop as a player and I got along with them well too.

Haslett – now he and I had a real love-hate relationship. It was heated at times.

We argued about calls. I was more vocal then as a player. We argued on why we did things. Sometimes as a player you don't see the whole picture – you see more of your own role and you understand what the other guys are doing, but the bigger picture can get lost. That's when things got harder – things can get difficult.

Mike Archer helped me a lot – he told me I was better than I thought I was. I needed confidence. It was hard to get noticed with so many great players. I thought I wasn't getting recognition and was being overshadowed. I wasn't used to that. Archer was the guy that gave me the confidence I needed. He told me to trust myself more. I wasn't always sure of myself – it was a new position for me. When he came on the team after the Super Bowl his advice helped me to believe in myself more.

Tim Jorden, Steelers Tight End, 1992-1993:

Coach Cowher was the best head coach I've ever been around. He had a bit of a wild streak, so the players were a little scared of him. However, at the same time he was a player's coach and could relate well with what the players were going through. He had an amazing ability to recognize potential problems and make decisions that helped avoid the problems. He also instilled confidence in his players.

He would tell us before a big game, "You are completely prepared because you worked hard all week. I don't care if you make mistakes as long as you're flying around on the field and giving great effort." I tell the kids that I coach the same thing, so I hope he doesn't care that I have stolen his line!

Kent Stephenson, Steelers Offensive Line Coach, 1992-2000:

Coach Cowher talked about the philosophy of the game a lot. He relied a lot on Ron Earhardt – Ron had a major role in me coming there and on the team in general.

I admired Coach Cowher. He wasn't vain – he wanted older guys as assistant coaches – he wasn't intimidated by them. A lot of younger coaches wouldn't do that but Bill wanted us there. He knew that there were things he still didn't know yet.

I also have a soft spot for Bill Cowher. My daughter lost her baby during training camp. I was devastated. He told me to go and be with her – during training camp. That was unheard of. Family was most important to me – and it was to him too.

Brentson Buckner, Steelers Defensive Lineman, 1994-1996:

The guys I work with are college guys looking to live their dreams like I got to do. I look back to Coach LeBeau and how he stressed the mental aspect of the game. Getting them prepared every day to work on the fundamentals. Coach LeBeau was like a father figure for life in general - he was more than just a coach and I try to work the same way with the kids I work with.

John Mitchell taught me about stressing the truth. He didn't sugar-coat anything. It was a working relationship – you're there to work. When I interned twice with the Steelers Coach Tomlin stressed that there was a time to work and a time to play.

Cowher and Tomlin were similar. Both were serious about their job. They had a spirit about how they attacked their job. Cowher's attitude was that we needed to work harder than any other team. Tomlin was the same way – you have to outwork the thirty-one other teams.

Mike treated players more like grown men – he was not going to be a babysitter. You knew the rules and if you didn't follow them you wouldn't last long. Cowher liked to have more control – it's not a bad thing. He worried about everything though.

With Tomlin, if you didn't work the right way in the situation he'd just move away from you.

Myron Bell, Steelers Safety, 1994-1997, 2000-2001:

It was an honor and a privilege to have been coached by such great men and legends during my career. Being a professional and being held accountable for your actions on and off the field. Coach LeBeau's teaching has had the most influence on my approach to mentoring/coaching young people. His ability to show compassion for people and appreciate the unique talents of each individual are what I strive to convey to the youth.

Brenden Stai, Steelers Offensive Lineman, 1995-1999:

Kent Stephenson was my line coach, he scouted me, worked me out and drafted me along with Tom Donahoe and his staff of scouts. I started as a rookie which led to starting in Super Bowl XXX. As we were warming up for the game the coaches normally would all walk around and give each player their blessing. When Kent approached me I thanked him for allowing me this once in a lifetime opportunity...he looked me in the eye and said "thank YOU for being a winner." It is amazing what simple words can do to somebody but those words have inspired me for a long time.

Oliver Gibson, Steelers Defensive Lineman, 1995-1998:

Cowher was fiercely intense and stoic. Tomlin's style is unlike any other – he's the most real guy I've ever seen as a coach.

When you checked in to Latrobe, there's a v-shaped concrete seat in front of the door. Tomlin was sitting there when I checked in calling out to the players as they went in, telling them they needed to produce, that they couldn't make the team from the hot tub… No one expected him to be there.

That's who he is. He's blatantly honest – you know where you stand with him. Every meeting he has examples of players who did something interesting and guys who didn't. You know exactly where you stand with him. Cowher was more of the old way…

Coach Mitchell is arguably the best defensive line coach in the NFL. The proof is in his tenure – what, nineteen years? I learned how to play defensive line in the 3-4 due to John Mitchell. I'd ultimately like to be a defensive coordinator in the NFL.

No one outworks John Mitchell. The perseverance in his career, he was one of the first Black players at Alabama. His work ethic and attention to detail are amazing.

Mike Archer, Steelers Linebacker Coach, 1996-2002:

It was not that different coaching 3-4 linebackers because I have coached that defense most of my life. The hard part in the NFL is finding those kind of players, who can play the run yet also drop into coverage. It is very challenging to identify those players and project them to play at the NFL level.

When you project a defensive lineman to become a linebacker you first look at athletic and football ability and the ability to run and drop into coverage. We tried to interview as many of the projected linebackers as possible to gain an understanding of football schemes and how they best were able to learn and their football knowledge and understanding.

Carlos Emmons and Mike Vrabel were two guys who both came in as defensive ends and were able tobe come great NFL linebackers. Both had a great desire to work to be great and were outstanding pros.

Success to me comes from taking a game plan each week and coaching it, seeing your players have success as they execute it to win an NFL game.

Tom Myslinski, Steelers Offensive Lineman, 1996-1997, 2000:

We were in Japan for a preseason game in 1996 and my roommate and I took a mid-afternoon nap before our team meeting at 7 p.m. Needless to say, the next thing I know, Chet Furman, our strength and conditioning coach at the time, was banging on our door because we overslept and didn't hear every alarm going off in the room.

The first thing I saw when I sprinted downstairs was Coach Cowher snarling at me. I don't think I slept another wink until I got on the plane after the game

Steve Conley, Steelers Linebacker, 1996-1998:

Coach Archer was a good coach. The one thing he would always tell me was he could not promise how many snaps I would get in a game, so make the best of the opportunity when it comes.

Coach Cowher was perfection for us. The one thing I learned was to always be prepared. The Friday before each game, he would randomly call a player's name to see if they knew their assignment in the game. You did not want him to call your name and not know the answer. That's one reason why his teams have been so successful…we were always prepared.

Courtney Hawkins, Steelers Wide Receiver, 1997-2000:

Cowher's deal was that he was good with the players. He was a player's coach – he listened to the pulse of the team. If the team was tired, he cut practice back. He was accommodating. The "my way or the highway" approach doesn't work. I played for coaches like that. Cowher was loose, but he didn't allow us to cross the line.

Perles was more stand-offish, but he had to be as he was dealing with college kids. Cowher's was the formula I wanted to use here.

John Jackson, Steelers Offensive Lineman, 1988-1997:

I appreciated Cowher's candidness. He told us he wasn't a good football player but was a pretty good coach, and if we listened to him he'd take us where we wanted to go. That was important to see him take that leadership role.

He put alarms in the exit doors of our dorm rooms so no one could go out at night – we thought it was funny. Someone would go through those doors every night and every once in a while he'd come up and do a bed check. You never knew when he'd come in.

The team had the same mindset – it was Coach Cowher who had to adjust to us at first.

Practice was treated like a game for us – we went all out and beat ourselves up. We beat the crap out of each other – we were old school playing under Coach Noll. We learned to practice under Cowher – he had to tone us down. He said we're not playing the Steelers this week – we can't hit each other like that. We'd have nothing left for the game!

John Fiala, Steelers Linebacker, 1998-2002:

I loved the role I played on special teams. It was full speed, high impact, and there were always opportunities for big plays.

I believe that my success on specials was due to how serious I took my role. There were many players that were concerned with just being a starter on offense or defense and I knew that I could excel in that role with special teams. This was the reason I was able to play with the Steelers for six years. I was a leader of the men on the special teams, studied, and watched film just like I did as a linebacker.

You can learn a lot by film study and tendencies by becoming a student of the game. Leading by example and playing every snap I was on the field at full throttle also helped. My role was a special teams player but every opportunity I received to play at linebacker, I made the most of. The defense never skipped a beat when I was in. I had a chance to learn and backup some great linebackers when I was there.

Shar Pourdanesh, Steelers Offensive Lineman, 1999-2000:

I loved playing for the Steelers. I felt free and I remember feeling like I could let loose on the field. I remember coach Cowher talking to me prior to my first start as a Steeler as he said "Shar, I want you to let loose! I know that during the course of a game you will probably get one or two personal penalties. That's ok. That's why you are here. Let loose and have fun. The collar is off of you!" I loved it. I played great!

Chris Combs, Steelers Defensive Lineman, 2000-2001:

Our Defensive Coordinator in Pittsburgh, Tim Lewis, had played the game at the Pro Bowl level but he was also very articulate and well-studied and you could tell it was important to him to know the answer to any question you might have. When I was a coach I worked with intelligent kids at Duke who had tough questions and wanted to know the 'whys' of a lot of things so I tried to make sure I was on the ball. I enjoyed coaches who had the gift to motivate.

Coach Cowher used to meet with each of us individually after the season to assess what we needed to improve on during the off-season. Even though we had just completed a six month season I left those meetings highly motivated and with a clear sense of where I stood. When I was coaching I tried to meet individually with my athletes both to keep them motivated and to give them individual feedback – I just think that's good management.

Kimo Von Oelhoffen, Steelers Defensive Lineman, 2000-2005:

The first great lesson I learned came from Coach Dick LeBeau: the Team. "We win as a team. We lose as a team." And for a team to truly be strong, you need every member of that team to be the most productive they can be. It takes a selfless approach.

Rodney Bailey, Steelers Defensive Lineman, 2001-2003, 2006:

Coach Mitchell. He was a big inspiration for me – still is. He worked me very hard because he was potential. He told me I needed to grow up fast – that this wasn't college. And he was right.

He was more than a coach. He kept it light. He was a friend. You talk to any other lineman – any other player – and they'd say the same thing.

Chris Hoke, Steelers Defensive Lineman, 2001-2012:

That's the Steeler way of doing things. They have a very technical way of playing – it's very technique oriented. If you heard [Steelers Defensive Line Coach] Mitchell in his press conference after drafting Ta'amu, he said he didn't care what he's done – he was going to teach him the Steeler way.

He takes young guys with or without a pedigree and starts from scratch. He teaches them technique – leverage, using your hands well and to hustle. In college you may rush upfield and that's it. That's not the way in Pittsburgh – there's a specific way of doing things.

We usually came off on third downs. Teams now though may run three or four times against us to see if they can do anything and then just start passing all the time. That's what New England did – lots of quick outs to Welker. It was the run alternative. We had the number one defense over the last decade probably if you add up the numbers. But the pass-focus now takes the nose tackle off the field when teams go to their three and four wide receiver sets and sub-packages. Then they run the ball in those sets and have more success doing so against us.

Guys just have to know where they fit in on those packages and know where to support. It's harder to know where to line up and add support in those sets.

Jeff Reed, Steelers Kicker, 2002-2010:

Cowher took special teams seriously, but Tomlin made them more of a focus...fifteen minutes a day were dedicated to special teams, but it was "balls to the wall"...this was no rest period – overall, Cowher was very easy to play for despite his sideline antics and "chin" at times...he is a great man...I'm blessed that he and Mr. Rooney gave me an initial opportunity... that's where it all started.

Charlie Batch, Steelers Quarterback, 2002-2012:

Coach Tomlin knew the internal rumblings he had to deal with – many wanted and expected either Grimm or Wisenhunt to be the coach. All weren't on board at first, but they all got it together quickly. Mike took it head on, talked about that with the players and the veterans understood it. It was the Rooneys' decision, and the players accepted whatever their decisions were. The veterans understood it

Chidi Iwuoma, Steelers Cornerback, 2002-2006, 2006:

I was fortunate to have played for coaches who expected me to be disciplined and tough both physically and mentally. In high school Coach Tip Saunders taught me that the hard work always pays off. In college, Dewayne Walker, taught me that size does not matter, heart does. In the NFL Coach Cowher taught me that a true team is made up of individuals who take pride, accept, and execute the role.

I have carried each of these lessons both on and off the field and they have made me the man I am.

Verron Haynes, Steelers Running Back, 2002-2007:

Man, there are not enough good things I can say about Bill Cowher. He is a class act and stand up kind of guy on and off the field. As far as football and Bill Cowher, "People lie and numbers don't." The records of his career speak for itself. Off the field Bill Cowher was a humble, intuitive, and charismatic man. He may have yelled and cursed us on the field, but having a house of women with all daughters made him a teddy bear deep down.

I learned early on from Cowher to never become so tied up in my career, because family is precious priority.

Tyrone Carter, Steelers Safety, 2004-2009:

Ray Horton, Darren Perry, and Dick LaBeau all did. LeBeau was a Hall of Fame player and coach – he keyed in on the details. The mindset of Cowher was huge. In 2004, when I got there he asked me what I thought my opponents were going to do – what routes they were going to run and what to expect. No one ever asked me that before. He showed me that I needed to know how to see what opponents were doing. Alignment, assignment, and adjustment was what he preached. That was the essence of being a pro – to learn about your opponent as well as your own work. It made me better and faster as a player.

Shaun Nua, Steelers Defensive Lineman, 2005-2007:

Dick LeBeau, John Mitchell, and Bill Cowher are the coaches I have learned the most from.

Coach LeBeau's humility and wisdom is what stood out to me. I will never forget the peaceful feeling I had after a loss when LeBeau conducts our meetings; it was calm, simple and very insightful on why the defense didn't play well. He would never over react or show any signs of panic. His humility, calmness, and wisdom are characteristics I will always hope to attain in any profession I strive for.

I will always remember Coach Mitchell's emphasis on intelligence. You have to be a smart football player to play for Coach Mitchell. I always believe that Mitchell would prefer smart players over just athletic ones. He always told us that there are a lot of athletic guys on the street because they weren't smart enough to play this game. I believe this and I always go back to this philosophy while coaching our defensive line or our scout teams.

Coach Cowher's energy and enthusiastic leadership style was second to none. His mentality sets the tone every day. He did a great job of instilling the tough mentality but at the same time did it with class. I loved his passion for the game and his competitive spirit, and that I will always remember.

Max Starks, Steelers Offensive Lineman, 2004-2012:

Tomlin was never a head coach before. We knew he was a Dungy guy. And we knew he was a defensive-minded guy. But he was young and really unknown to us. He had his own style. I remember seeing him pull up in a Dodge Magnum with Louis Vitton seats, all speakered-out! Really, a Magnum? He had an urban feel to him.

He took his lumps the first year. He had a veteran team. Faneca, Farrior...heck, he played against Farrior in college! Now, he's leading the ship...he proved himself by being consistent – tough and no-nonsense. He understood the monotony of the game. As a player-coach, he understood how we felt.

He was too tough the first year. He had us in pads through week thirteen – proving himself too much maybe. We were wound down – maybe that's why we lost in the playoffs to Jacksonville that season despite being well-positioned in the playoffs. It was just too rough – we had nothing left.

But, he made the change the next season. He took care of us during the week and told us he'd take the chains off us dogs on game day. We won the Super Bowl that season. He also set up an advisory board of veteran players so we could express our grievances to him. It wasn't a dictatorship. He was willing to bend. That led to our success.

Carey Davis, Steelers Fullback, 2007-2009:

I think the thing that set Coach Cowher apart from most people is that he held everyone to the same standard. It didn't matter if you were the first man on the roster or the last man on the practice squad. He expected everyone to play at a high level.

Jeremy Parquet, Steelers Offensive Lineman, 2007-2008:

The day after St. Louis released me my agent called and said that the Steelers were going to sign me with no workout. I found that to be odd. Mike Tomlin was on the Buccaneers coaching staff when I played in the 2005 Senior Bowl. Upon my arrival to Pittsburgh, Mike T pulled me into his office and we had a real candid meeting about my career and what goals I had for myself. I needed and appreciated that because that was exactly what I needed to get going again!

Dezmond Sherrod, Steelers Tight End, 2008:

Playing for Coach Tomlin was an awesome experience. He's a natural leader who caters to the situation to produce the best outcome. He knew when to make practices tough to prepare for a big game but also he knew when to cut the team a break or "throw us a bone" as we said, to lift the spirits of our tired or worn out team.

"Don't be the guy" is a popular phrase of his. Don't be the guy to be late to meetings. Don't be the guy who missed his block that would've made a big running play. Don't be the guy who ends up in the newspaper for doing something crazy. Those words meant a lot to us and it paid off. No one "was the guy" that cost us to win the Super Bowl but everyone had a part in us winning it.

Leadership:

There are times when it takes more than team culture and even good coaching to keep things on an even keel. When things go awry, fractures occur in the bond between players, and between players and coaches. Losing teams suffer through these fractures the most as players become frustrated and start finger-pointing. That's when it takes special players who can step up and show true leadership. Who other players both fear and respect enough to listen to and follow. Who can remind the team what it takes to win.

These are the players who have the respect of their peers and the assumed authority to keep players in line when they don't give their full effort or refuse to respect other players and coaches. They also have the trust and ear of their coaches and often serve as the liaison between the team and the coaching staff.

Every successful team has these types of leaders. And the Steelers certainly have had their fair share who have stepped up. Some of these names are obvious – Joe Greene, Andy Russell, Hines Ward, and Terry Bradshaw, but others were more surprising like Bubby Brister and Dwight White. They all helped create those winning teams over the past fifty years.

Darrell Dess, Steelers Offensive Lineman, 1958:

I do remember – the veteran players in Pittsburgh always tried to have parties for the rookies – tried to get them drunk. A lot of them – like my roommate – didn't drink. But I remember they threw a big party and Bobby Layne came. They had a band and Bobby didn't like the band – didn't like the music they were playing. So, he fired them right there and got his own band to play for the rest of the night. That showed how much pull he had.

Joe Gordon, Former Steelers Director of Communications:

In '75 it was Noll's policy to hold special teams practices on Saturday mornings – home or away games. One Saturday morning I saw Chuck walk by my office and I sensed something was wrong. He came back in again with Dan Rooney and let me know that the players felt that the media had too much access to the dressing room. I told them I'd go in and talk to them.

I went into the dressing room and told them I understood their concerns. I let them know the media wasn't eavesdropping on their personal lives. They wanted the players to be successful, I told them, because it made their job easier. I told them I'd meet with their captains next Tuesday – that now was not the appropriate time to talk.

Well, next Tuesday I went to the dressing room and asked Joe Greene when he wanted to get together for the meeting. He just looked at me and said "What meeting?" That was typical Joe Greene.

L.C. Greenwood, Steelers Defensive Lineman, 1969-1981:

As Ernie Holmes said "We had a bunch of individuals." I don't think we had leaders, per se. Joe used to go around angry because we lost all the time and some players looked up to him. But others didn't pay attention to him because he was always so angry.

We were always so loose. It was pretty interesting. I don't think people knew that. I don't think Chuck knew on any given Sunday if we'd win or lose. Chuck would get so pissed in practice because no one was listening and practicing well. Then we'd play great on Sunday.

Bob Adams, Steelers Tight End, 1969-1971

Anyone who resisted the changes left on the next plan or bus very soon thereafter. As I recall fourteen rookies made the active squad in 1969, and the unquestionable leader was Joe Greene.

Andy Russell was a leader by example and one of the really mature men on the team who was a student of the game, highly respected by Chuck Noll and Art Rooney. He was in his late twenties and had some visible grey hair, which added to his sage persona. He also held an MBA from Missouri, which was quite a feat in its own right. I think everyone respected Andy for his intelligent play, character, and integrity.

A few times during my rookie year and again when I became the starter, he would acknowledge me for my play. He asked me one time how I was able to get through the "wedge" on kickoffs and make the tackle so often. That meant a lot to me because he was All Pro and asking a rookie this type of question. I don't remember my answer but it probably had something to do with the fact that I had no liking for head on collisions with 275 pound linemen and did what I had to do to avoid it.

Rocky Bleier's comeback, miraculous as it seemed, was achieved by the love and compassion of the Rooney's for the players, giving Rocky time to heal and look at the outcome. When Rocky ran his forty yard dash in seventy it was over five seconds, limping while he ran in pain from shrapnel logged in his toes and scar tissue rock hard in his instep.

I know the pain he was in. I roomed with Rocky in '71. I massaged his foot. In order to take the pain, he would put a rolled towel in his mouth lay flat on his stomach, put a pillow over his head to cover sound, and as I kneaded out the bundled up scar tissue in his tendons, he screamed into the towel his body so tense it shook. He would have me repeat it until his foot relaxed and his toes could extend fully. Rocky took it just like he took his Army tour in Vietnam. He had so much in the way of courage it rubbed off on everyone. When he ran the forty in '73 he ran a 4.5 and Chuck made him run it over again to prove the watches wrong. Rocky did it again and rumor has it Chuck said that was the first "miracle" he has personally witnessed.

John Rowser, Steelers Cornerback, 1970-1973:

Pittsburgh was in last place but they were rebuilding. They just got Joe Greene, Preston Pearson, Henry Davis...I was able to take a leadership role on defense there. Not total leadership – players take on their own roles. But people asked me a lot of questions due to my experience in Green Bay and dedication to the game – the way I played. Guys like Mel Blount tended to listen and follow my example.

Woody Widenhofer, Steelers Linebacker Coach & Defensive Coordinator, 1973-1983:

I think it was in 1977 – we were talking three peat that season. Well we had lost two in a row and lost to Cleveland at home. They hadn't beaten us in a long time before that. After the game, there is a lobby in the stadium where the players and coaches were able to sit while they waited for the crowds and traffic to clear. I came out of the locker room into that area and Jack Hart (Steelers Equipment Manager) came up to me and said that Jack Lambert hadn't turned in his uniform yet. Well, it was forty-five minutes after the game. I looked at him and said "Really?"

I went looking for him and went into the Pirates' locker room, which was further down the hall from ours. I looked inside and saw Jack sitting in the sauna, in tears, with his uniform still on. He was upset about the team maybe not making the playoffs. I talked to him – told him we needed to get his uniform off, but that's how hard he and the rest of those guys took it. Here he was forty-five minutes after the game – he didn't take a shower – didn't even take his uniform off.

After that, the team went seventeen straight quarters without giving up a point. I think Jack and Joe Greene held a team meeting after the loss. That's the thing with those guys. They were great leaders. You never had any problem with loafers on those teams.

Marv Kellum, Steelers Linebacker, 1974-1976

I remember Preston Pearson on the opening kickoff of the Super Bowl – it was so loud. We were all huddled up and Preston said to us that he'd give anyone two hundred dollars if they made the tackle inside the twenty yard line. It wasn't that it was a lot of money, but here's a veteran speaking up and being a leader.

L.C. yelled at me as a rookie when I made a mistake that I was playing with his money. It was a bit of humor but helped show that he expected better.

Tom Beasley, Steelers Defensive Lineman, 1978-1983:

Joe Greene. I learned more about the game through Joe Greene than I did through all of the coaches I had. He knew I was there to replace him, but he didn't get angry and didn't hesitate to help me and teach me about playing the game.

One of the things I remember that sticks out in my mind – was my first opportunity to start. It was for L.C. Greenwood who injured his knee that Wednesday. I started in the middle of a triangle between Greene, Lambert and Ham. Joe was such a student of the game – as was Ham. I saw a level of the game I never knew existed before.

That challenged me to spend the time it took to get to that level.

Another example was in camp. It was the first week the veterans were back. One of the offensive lineman took a cheap shot at my legs. I came out after that play. Joe pulled me aside and said to me "Do you want to stay in this game a while Tom?" He told me the next time that happens, no matter if it's a teammate or opposing player, I needed to let them know I wouldn't take that. If it meant kicking them in their teeth or nads, you do what it takes.

Through extensive study of film, Joe had a knack for reading plays and personnel.

Against Buffalo early in my second year, Dunn was out with an injury. In warm ups someone stepped on Furness' ankle so he couldn't play. So I ended up playing left end.

In that game, Joe called out the blocking schemes before the ball was snapped by reading the linemen…it totally changed the dynamic of the game. Learning those things – they add up. Those details make all the difference.

Ron Johnson, Steelers Cornerback, 1978-1984:

When we talk about characters or personalities on the team, Dwight "Mad Dog" White has to be mentioned. Dwight would curse out opponents and his own teammates during the heat of the battle. However, during a game in my rookie season, I had yelled at Dwight and the defensive line because we were getting manhandled. Dwight came to my locker after the game and said "Johnson, I started to jump on your ass out there today." My response to Mad Dog was "How many Super Bowl rings do you have?" He said he had two rings. I told him that I didn't have any Super Bowl rings and that I was trying to get one, so if we get manhandled up front again, I would do the same thing.

Jack Lambert was truly a character and a team leader. Lambert would come to my locker and say things like "…Johnson don't get scared now because Earl Campbell is going to run your ass over…" or "…Kenny Burroughs is going to run past you." That was Jack Lambert's way of testing your heart and to get you motivated. I always told Lambert to just do his damn job and we won't have any problems.

Craig Wolfley, Steelers offensive Lineman, 1980-1989:

The one I look back on is Joe Greene – he was such a legendary character – remarkable in so many aspects and the foundation of the team

I remember when we lost to Oakland my rookie year in 1980 – it was a Monday night game and we played terrible. We're all talking and taking off our pads in the locker room and we hear a loud BOOM and see a helmet banging on the floor.

The name on the helmet was Greene's. He gets up and says "It's a little too much damn noise in this place!"

I'll never forget that – it got as quiet as a church in there.

Calvin Sweeney, Steelers Wide Receiver, 1980-1987:

Bradshaw was a professional and very competitive. He'd jump on you if you made mistakes – I remember him telling Steve Courson to get his head out of his you-know-what once – to step it up. He may not have been the leader of the team, but he was the leader of that huddle.

Sam Washington, Steelers Cornerback, 1982-1985:

I definitely remember the playoffs – it was a totally different atmosphere. It was spearheaded by Lambert. The bullshit was set aside – I was really impressed with the whole approach. The way players walked into the locker room, the way they sat down and paid attention, the older guys – most like Franco, Ham, L.C. – they were still there. And the air – you could cut it with a knife. It was...rich. I can't describe it but it was present.

Rich Erenberg, Steelers Running Back, 1984-1986:

I would have to say Mark Malone and Jack Lambert were the two leaders of the teams of the 80s. They were both hard working guys that lead mostly by example rather than what they said. Although Lambert was certainly the more vocal of the two.

If Lambert said something to the team or an individual player, you listened because Jack was tough and didn't mess around. He knew what it took to win and wanted to make sure the rest of us knew it too.

Kendall Gammon, Steelers Long Snapper, 1992-1995:

You have to give Coach Cowher credit. He weeded out the guys that didn't fit and brought in real leaders, like Kevin Greene. We worked hard and efficiently. We didn't work too long or too short. Coach Cowher was upfront with us that different players got treated differently. I didn't expect to be treated the same as Rod Woodson. He was tougher on me and I appreciate that – it made me a better player and extended my career.

Reggie Barnes, Steelers Linebacker, 1993:

Rod Woodson, you could tell he was a pro's pro. The way he approached it. He and Carnell Lake, they all ran extra sprints after practice. The rookies would look over and realized they needed to do it too. Those were leadership qualities we all saw. Kevin Greene also ran sprints after practice, he did the same thing. Looking at the other veteran players, they were leading by example, and as a rookie, we learned that everyone goes to practice and they go home to family after. It wasn't like college where you went to the dorms, so you had to make the most of what was happening then and make the most of every practice.

Kordell Stewart, Steelers Quarterback, 1995-2002:

Being a starter...that's when it all changed. It was a new role – I had to be strong and understand everything and have the answers for the guys – to lead by example. It was every man for himself before, and now it was more of a team concept. And success early meant that I didn't have all of the answers. I figured that if I was good all else would take care of itself. With my abilities, I felt like I should just go out and make plays. The idea of a mobile quarterback was still very new – especially in Pittsburgh. It was all new – the field was my world. I loved it. I grew up in a neighborhood where we all played football – and I played with my older brother's friends – he was five years older. We competed all the time. I thought that if I could do well against those guys at my age I could do even better against guys my age.

Lee Flowers, Steelers Safety, 1995-2003:

Sometimes I got carried away – especially after games. I felt I had the pulse of the locker room – and Cowher usually embraced it. Dan Rooney definitely embraced it – he told me I spoke for him too.

They never really had a problem with it. It put a bullseye on our back but we were Pittsburgh, we had a bullseye regardless. I thought that if that made us play better, then great. There are eighteen games in a season and it's hard to stay focused. I was just trying to keep the passion to win.

All I said and did – those guys I knew would still fight for me though if I took them into a dark alley with me.

Cowher pulled me aside a couple of times, but he never yelled at me. He just told me I may have gone too far.

One game I remember was when we were about to play Cleveland. We were on a two game losing streak and I promised we would not go 0-3. That meant I partly promised we would win – I said I'd bet my house we wouldn't go 0-3.

Cowher was upset about that one. He said I didn't show Cleveland any respect. Well, I'm not going to lie – I didn't have any for Cleveland – that was the year they came back into the league. Cowher just pulled me aside and told me I need to be careful because the media can twist my words. But they didn't have to – that's just what I said.

Chad Scott got hurt that summer. They were looking to move Carnell Lake to corner but Cowher didn't believe in me at first. He heard stories about me going out late at night and thought I was a wild guy. He didn't have confidence in me yet.

Donohoe was the GM then and I guess they were looking for another corner in free agency but couldn't find one. Cowher called me the summer before camp and told me I'd get the opportunity to win the starting job. The first preseason game was the Hall of Fame game and I had the best game of my career. After that Cowher said I did it. He had respect for me then and after that I began to study more. I wouldn't repeat mistakes.

Steve Conley, Steelers Linebacker, 1996-1998:

The leader of the team my first year was Greg Lloyd. He was a great defensive player in his prime. His plays were contagious and were a big reason why the team was so good.

The next leader of the locker room, keeping everybody entertained was Fred McAfee. He was our special team's captain and made the pro-bowl one year because of how good he was on special teams. It was nothing for Fred to get up in the middle of the locker room and tell a joke or imitate someone. He would also use his personality to get the players motivated before the games. Great player, great guy.

Kimo Von Oelhoffen, Steelers Defensive Lineman, 2000-2005:

The first person that comes to mind is Dermantti Dawson. His personality, his smile, his willingness to say "Good morning!" and "Hello!" to every single person in that locker room from the oldest to the youngest. It was unfortunate that I only got to spend a couple of years with Dawson – but that lightness, that openness in that first year helped to spread that team attitude. When you have one of the best players to ever play the game smile and treat a rookie like a veteran – rookies never forget that. And as they grow, they tend to portray those same characteristics and it spreads like wildfire.

Jerome Bettis is another one of those guys. His ability to make everyone feel comfortable yet competitive I believe was a huge part of our team. Again, he was a Hall-of-Fame player who took the time to treat everyone as he would want to be treated; to compete in a manner of which you couldn't wait for the next competition. Those attributes are great to see as a young player and a veteran and it also spreads like fire.

Michael Jones, Steelers Linebacker, 2001-2002:

The best example was a Monday Night Game. At the time, Eric Dickerson was doing Monday Night Football as a sideline reporter. I played with Eric one year with the Raiders. As I was talking to Eric, I see a couple of young players (DeShea and Jason). I see both of them laughing, so I know they are talking about the "old folks" I tell Eric what they are doing. When DeShea and Jason get around to where we are, Eric says to both of them, "Mike when he was young like yourselves, use to laugh at myself, Ronnie Lott, and Marcus Allen. He used to say we were old like you are doing, I am telling you what I told him, "Stick around long enough and someone will be making fun of you being the old guy."

Anthony Trucks, Steelers Linebacker, 2007:

The difference between the Steelers and other teams I played for was that we really were a family. As a core group they looked out for one another. My first week in Pittsburgh was

Thanksgiving and I had nowhere to go and James Farrior invited me over to his house where I was welcome with open arms by other teammates and his family.

Larry Zierlein, Steelers Offensive Line Coach, 2007-2009:

My memories of the Steeler teams I was with will always begin with what high character guys those players were. The leadership in the locker room was outstanding. The players controlled that environment and kept everyone headed in the same direction.

Their expectations were high and more often than not they met those expectations. Those were probably the most tight-knit of any teams I've been around. They cared for each other.

Tyler Grisham, Steelers Wide Receiver, 2009-2011:

I was encouraged a great deal by Aaron Smith my rookie year. He had been there and done that, so he didn't shy away from giving praise where praise was due. Aaron would tell you when you performed well and would also be honest when you needed to pick your game up. Not only was he a force on the defensive line and a leader and mentor for every other defensive lineman, he also led in the locker room and many people benefited from his experience and willingness to teach others.

Troy's presence was felt both on and off the field. He is a genuinely a kind person who cared for his teammates. He was protected all throughout training camp and during the regular season practices so he could perform on game-day, and to watch him on the field at full-speed was something else. I am thankful I got to spend three years with him. A cool story I like to tell about him is that I commented one day on the shoes he was wearing-they were a pair of New Balance tennis shoes. I had been looking at getting a pair and I guess he could tell I was interested in them, so he took them off and told me to try them on. I did not in any way ask him to give me his shoes (after all, even I could have afforded them on a practice squad salary!), but he would have given them to me had they fit.

A Funny Thing Happened
on the Way to the Riverfront

This was easily one of the favorite subjects for players to talk about. The infusion of humor into the day-to-day of the team helped break up the monotony of practices and to lessen the stress players felt as they vied to make the team and retain starting positions. Some used it for their own relief, others understood the role it played in helping reduce the stress of others. It was, simply, an essential tool to keeping the team loose and allowing conflict to be put aside in lieu of laughter.

Some humor occurred spontaneously, on the field – the byproduct of plays that went wrong, players that made mistakes. In the locker room, many of the antics were planned. Some ingenious. Most the perfect mix of childish jokes that brothers often play on one another. Perhaps the best jokes were those planned outside the locker room – not on the field. Those played on peers as they spent time together away from the typical venues of the sport.

Each team had its share of pranksters. Terry Hanratty, Gary Dunn, Fred McAfee, even Troy Polamalu and Greg Lloyd got into the act. Did they take it too far sometimes? Sure. But more often than not, they lightened the mood, relieved stress and helped players bond with one another.

From the infamous Thanksgiving turkey giveaway, the "mongoose" and "the snakebox" to Merril Hoge's midget speech and "the crab", there are numerous stories captured here, from the 60s on through to to-day's teams. Many of these were given reluctantly, as there is always the Las Vegas mindset …that what happens in the locker room stays in the locker room. But that concern lessens over time, as players worry less about their affects and their desire to have those memories last take precedence.

Dale Dodrill, Steelers Defensive Tackle, 1951-1959:

Ernie Stautner never knew what it was like to go around some-body. Once we played the Browns. Paul Brown had just in-vented the fullback trap fake, where they pull the off-guard and the fullback fills the hole. They gave the fullback the ball the first play against us and it went for a big gain. I asked Ernie who blocked him and he said two guys were on him. They ran the play again later and it went for another big play. This time Ernie said three guys blocked him. Well, when we looked at the film later, we saw no one touched him!

I remember the buckets of water they used in practices and in games. There was a dipper in it. But the coaches didn't think that drinking water during the games and practices was good for you, so they put oatmeal in it. You ended up with oatmeal on your face whenever you tried to drink water or cool yourself off.

Don Sutherin, Steelers Defensive Back and Kicker, 1959-1960:

Bobby Layne was a character – I'm, sure you heard a lot of good stories about him. I remember when we were playing the Bears – Doug Atkins kept knocking Layne on his butt – blood-ied him. So Layne tells us to let Atkins come free next time, and he throws the ball at Atkins, right in the mouth! Well, Doug killed Layne after that.

When we flew back to Pittsburgh after the game, Parker put the whole team on waivers, except for a few of the better players. I think that was the first time that ever happened. He pulled them back shortly after, but I think five guys got cut because of that game. We should have won that game.

"Red" Mack, Steelers Wide Receiver, 1961-1963, 1965:

I hit it off with Bobby Layne. I was running pass patterns in practice with shoulder pads and shorts. Fred Williamson, who used to be a receiver, was moved to defense and he cold-cocked me and knocked my helmet off. I got up and swear to God hit him so hard with my helmet I knocked him out cold.

Later that night I was watching Layne and some other guys play cards. Layne said that we need to keep this crazy bastard – you never know what will happen. That's when I knew I made the team.

Lou Cordileone, Steelers Defensive Lineman, 1962-1964:

I remember one game. I was playing next to Big Daddy Lipscomb. We're lining up, getting into position and there's a worm on the field – there in the dirt next to him. He hated anything like that – we used to put fake worms and bugs in his locker to scare him. Well, he sees it and jumps back five feet and starts yelling that there's a worm on the field! The officials blew the whistle – they couldn't believe it. We were all laughing so hard – the offensive lineman busted his balls all game.

Clendon Thomas, Steelers Safety, 1962-1968:

Occasionally I was asked to line up as a receiver. Someone was hurt and this was one of those occasions. We were playing Detroit and our left guard Mike Sandusky is matched up with Detroit's tackle Alex Karras. Mike was giving way an advantage of thirty-to-forty pounds of muscle to Alex. Alex's game plan when he took his glasses off was to beat the snot out of Mike. He was probably the only player he could see clearly. Mike's game plan was to keep Alex off of Bobby Lane – whatever it took. Mike had padded the back of his legs in the locker room in case Alex got away from him and he had to heel whip him at the last moment. Mike had help at Center – Buzz Nutter and right guard – Ray Lemek.

Well, sometime during the first quarter Mike began begging for help. Alex had gotten by and Mike had cut him down a few times. Mike is telling Buzz and Ray he had to have help. Alex was yelling at the referee but he isn't doing anything about it. The referee is grinning and knew Alex would take care of the problem. In the meantime, Alex is head butting Mike with a bull rush and a little blood is running off the front of his nose.

Bobby Lane was all business. There wasn't a lot of unnecessary chatter in his huddle. Bobby got fed up with the chatter from Mike, Buzz and Ray and finally told them to just shut up. Ray said he would take care of Alex. We ran another play and came back to the huddle. Mike is bent over with both hands under his armpits groaning. Ray looked over and said - Mike don't worry about Alex. His hand was sticking out of the pile and I stomped it off. Mike pulled his hand out and you could see the skin peeled back. Now I know it's not right to laugh at someone's misery but Bobby had to call a timeout while we laughed and taped up Mike.

Lou Cordileone, Steelers Defensive Lineman, 1962-1964:

Our first exhibition game that year was in Canton, Ohio versus Cleveland. I had a good game but we got the shit beat out of us. But it was an exhibition game. Well, we all got beers after and were sitting around talking, and we were told not to say anything to Buddy – he got crazy after the loss. Later, Myron Pottios, and me are sitting together on the plane back and Pottios tells a joke and I laughed so hard. Well, LaVerne Thompson walks back to tell me that Buddy wanted to talk to me when we landed. When we did, he cut me. He wouldn't tell me why at first, but I was laughing too hard after we got the shit beat out of us and that upset him.

Well, I was waiting to see if I'd get picked up by another team so I stayed around a couple of days. I was in the back of the film room the next day with everyone watching the film of the game. Buddy would ask – who made that play – and it was me. He'd ask again – and it was me again. The players kept telling him that that was the guy you just cut coach! I was just sitting there.

A reporter shortly after asked me when we were at Dante's together why I didn't just call him and see if he'd take me back. I did, but he was too upset. I took a shot.

Jim Bradshaw, Steelers Safety, 1963-1967:

Buddy Parker was a great coach. He just had trouble controlling his emotions. He was a real master when it came to offenses and defenses, he just couldn't stand to lose.

I remember playing in Yankee Stadium the final game of the season versus the Giants. We win, we go to the championship game. Well, of course we lost. Buddy went crazy. I remember he cut off his necktie on the airplane he was so mad at losing.

The team was just hysterical. The locker room was always loose. I remember Preston Carpenter ran out of the tunnel one time as the offense was being introduced. He was wearing Charlie Bradshaw's size seventeen shoes – and his helmet – backwards. Well, he ran right into the goalpost and knocked it down. It fell backwards right on to the cameraman who was filming the game!

In Atlanta, Carpenter came running out of the dugout of Ponce de Leon field and did a perfect hook slide into second base!

Even Buddy got into the act. I remember him standing on the wooden benches we had in he locker room at the time, talking to the players. He was smoking those huge cigars he smoked, with a can of foot powder on the bench next to him. Well, every time he stamped his foot, the powder would puff up -he kept doing it to make it look like the smoke was pouring out of him – the room was hysterical.

Jim Bradshaw, Steelers Safety, 1963-1967:

I also remember when Mike Ditka was traded to Dallas near the end of his career. Mike was a very tough, mean competitor. I had received a permanent indentation to my skull from Mike's forearm, so I gave every effort to give out as good as I received. Mike knew me pretty well because of a mutual friend, Bill Wade, formerly with the Rams and a member of the Fellowship of Christian Athletes.

We played Dallas in Pittsburgh. Sometime during the game, Mike ran a strong post pattern to the end zone. That's when the one post holding the uprights was close to the goal line. I hit him when he and the ball got to the goal line. The hit knocked him offline into the pole. He was down on his hands and knees swearing at me. As he finished swearing at me, he finished with "You Fellowship of Christian Athlete SOB. He was stunned enough he didn't know he hit the pole. He thought I had given him a tremendous cheap shot.

I admit, when I figured out he thought I had hurt him –I took credit for it! I also told him if he ran another post pattern I would really hit him next time!

Two weeks later we played in Dallas. During warm up, Mike yelled at me, laughing – that wasn't you it was that "blank" pole!

Tommy Wade, Steelers Quarterback, 1964-1965:

Bobby Layne was quite a character! Wow!

Something I will never forget is riding all night over New England during training camp in a car with Bobby Layne and a driver singing songs to him. We got back just in time for morning practice. I was totally wiped out. He never missed a beat! What a night!

Frank Lambert, Steelers Punter, 1965-1966:

John Henry Johnson was the most colorful character. Not only was he a future Hall of Famer, he was a larger-than-life personality. He talked fast and laughed a lot. He excelled at the give-and-take that makes life in locker rooms so memorable.

When I first joined the Steelers, Buddy Parker was the coach. I remember walking into the first team meeting and being taken aback by the lack of banter prior to the meeting. In New York, the Giants were a lively bunch and people like Roosevelt Brown initiated all sorts of horseplay until Coach Allie Sherman called the meeting to order. But, here there was silence.

The players talked little and only in subdued tones. The assistant coaches sat on one side with their arms folded. And Buddy Parker sat at the front glaring out at the team. And then John Henry arrived. He entered talking a blue streak laced with colorful language. He paid no attention to the dirge-like setting and bounded in full of himself. Instantly the place was transformed with laughter, catcalls, etc. Even Buddy laughed. John Henry missed much of the season because of a knee injury. We missed him as much for his off-the-field presence as for his on-the-field performance

John Hilton, Steelers Tight End, 1965-1969:

One of my first experiences was with J.R. Wilburn and Gene Breen. J.R. had this terrific Corvette and this kid came around and made some bad remarks about it. Gene came up to him and hit him so hard he knocked him out of his shoes.

I went once to a bar with Mike Magac – he was a former Steeler and the biggest guy in town. He was huge, and for some reason I decided to go one on one with him there in the bar. I got in my stance and knocked him into the partition – everything in the place went flying. We went outside after that and I jumped on his back and he flipped me over. I still have the cinders above my eye from that night – it cut me open. The next day coach Nixon threatened me with a $160 fine if I didn't get my helmet on and play. I had blood everywhere but still played.

I remember – I was with Chuck Sanders there in Detroit and he got hurt. I was getting ready to step in and play for him and suit up. But Chuck painted my seat with black shoe polish- just lathered it in. I sat on it and my entire backside was black! He told me after that now we had two Black-ass tight ends.

Roy Jefferson, Steelers Wide Receiver, 1965-1969:

My second year, Coach Austin tried Paul Martha and another guy at wide receiver and tried to move me to defensive back. Remember, a lot of guys were still two-way players then. I knocked out a few wide receivers in practice. Austin just said, "Go home after practice, we're keeping you at wide receiver."

Larry Gagner, Steelers Offensive Lineman, 1966-1969:

I'd say Mean Joe Green had more presence than anyone on that '69 team. Even though it was his rookie year, you knew he was destined for greatness. He also displayed a keen sense of humor exhibited when he nearly laughed me out of training camp in 1970 upon my arrival with two huge, wooden-turned fern stands atop my Porsche secured with rope tied through both windows. I know it had the look of a couple missiles atop a silver bullet.

Roger Pillath, Steelers Offensive Lineman, 1966-1967:

I remember in Pittsburgh, after a game, Bill Saul – the middle linebacker there then – he was a good wrestler too. We were bragging over who the best wrestler was, so I had to show him I could put him down. I pinned him – he couldn't believe it. He was a good guy.

J.R. Wilburn, Steelers Wide Receiver, 1966-1970:

Hanratty was the guy who played the jokes. Before Thanksgiving, he told the defensive players that the Rooneys bought a truck full of turkeys for the players, but there were only twenty so they better hurry before they were gone. Guys were running to the truck in their jock straps, but there was no truck. Or turkeys! He tried it again a couple years later but only the rookies fell for it that time.

Lloyd Voss was another guy. He was from Nebraska but hated cold weather, if you can imagine. His fingers and toes were really sensitive – he hated it when people stepped on his toes. It would drive him nuts. People used to step on his toes on purpose to get him fired up.

Larry Gagner, Steelers Offensive Lineman, 1966-1969:

Especially as an athlete, it seems most important to be able to claim at least your fifteen minutes of fame. One would think, however, that this would be almost a given at the pro-level of competition. Think again. As an offensive lineman, more often than not, your name gets announced because of some rule infraction instead of a spectacular thrown block. So, sometimes you have to innovate with name recognition!

I was at a car rental concern located out by the Greater Pittsburgh Airport seeking some rental information, when the salesperson discovered that I was a former Steeler ballplayer (but certainly not by my name recognition). She then reached underneath the counter and presented a pair of blue snow boots that apparently Terry Bradshaw had left behind after returning his rental car. She asked if I would be able to return them to their rightful owner, Terry. I said I could. She then gave me them to do so with.

But, they just happened to fit me to a "T", and since I permanently returned to Florida shortly after, these "keepers" I wore for years and bragged to untold numbers of people of how I, only, happened to be wearing the exclusive line of Terry Bradshaw Winter Footwear. Thanks Terry for your unknowing act of kindness. Paybacks (for offering a personal showing of game films to my girlfriend in your apartment no less) come in all sorts of forgettable common objects made famous by a previous owner's wearing of them.

Dick Shiner, Steelers Quarterback, 1968-1969:

Frank Parker was a defensive tackle that was traded with me to the Steelers. Well, Chuck had a new play he designed called the twenty-four Wham Trap. It was a lead play by the fullback, where the offensive guard and fullback both pulled to hit the defensive tackle.

Poor Frank – I felt for him – the guy had bad knees too. He was a buddy of mine, so after the meeting I went to his room to tell him about the play. I wanted to warn him to watch out for it in the next day's scrimmage. I went in to tell him, and he said "Shine Man [that's what he called me], who gets hit on that one?" When I told him, he said "What are they going to do to me? Gee bleepity bleep. They are trying to send me to the house!"

Well, the next day Chuck comes in and calls the play during the scrimmage. I told Ray Mansfield that I let Parker know about the play. So, we get up there to the line and we wink at him to let him now we're running the play. "Geezus!" he yells. "They are going to send me to the house!" All of the offensive linemen fell on the ground laughing! Chuck asked what was so funny, and I had to tell him I told Parker about the play.

Ralph Berlin, Steelers Trainer, 1968-1993:

We had a lot of fun – we kid around. I remember there was that stuff Mint Glow – it was like Ben Gay. They used to put the rolls of t-shirts, jock straps and slacks in everyone's locker. Once, they put some in Bradshaw's jock and he went out to practice with it. He had to run back in and change – Chuck was not happy about that.

Rocky Bleier was taped to a shopping cart and left in Chuck's office.

We used to put a list up every year before Thanksgiving for rookies to sign up to get free turkeys. There were no turkeys of course. Once, Mel Blount told Tony Dungy that he wanted to have Tony bring his turkey to his house where Mel's wife would cook it and a ham for Thanksgiving dinner.

I told Tony to talk to Jim Boston, the business manager, to pick up his turkey. Jim said he saw it but didn't know whose it was so he gave it to Dan Rooney. Tony went to Dan's office and let him know Jim said he gave Dan his turkey, so Dan told him he didn't know who it belonged to so he gave it to Chuck Noll.

Well, Tony wasn't going to go to Chuck's office and ask for the turkey. So he went to Mel and told him he didn't know what to do now, and everyone in the locker room started laughing.

We did the same thing for Christmas trees right before Christmas. Believe it or not, some signed up again.

Word got out in the following years about the joke. We did the turkey sign up a few years later and some rookies still signed up, including Terry Long. That year though, Franco and Lynn Swann bought cooked turkeys and put them in the rookies' lockers. Terry ate his right at his locker!

Things like that made it fun.

Mike Taylor, Steelers Offensive Lineman, 1968-1969:

Bill Saul is the one I remember most as the biggest character on the team. We had these rookie parties where Bill would always challenge the rookies to beer chugging contests. When it came to chugging glasses of beer, Bill could place the whole glass in his mouth and just tilt his head back and it was gone! Needless to say, he was always the champ. The next day we all paid our dues on the practice field from those rookie beer chugging sessions.

Terry Hanratty, Steelers Quarterback, 1969-1976:

My last career start was "lovely", if you thought you heard booing for a 1-13 season.

Chuck released me and I went on to play for Tampa Bay. I was having steak with [head coach] John McKay and he said "Terry, I have a great idea. We're going to start you against your old teammates!" Great…

So that week we have a phone call for the radio - me, Myron Cope, and Lambert. Myron asked what we had in store for the Steelers – I told Jack we had a special plan – ten special quarterback sneaks so I could run right at Jack. Jack laughed at that one.

In the game, we never passed the fifty in the first half. They were on me in two steps. L.C., Joe, and Jack just sort of laid me down. McKay told the backup quarterback Steve Spurrier to go in the second half. They kicked the shit out of him. Steve came to the sidelines and yelled at me – "You SOB – your boys took care of *you*!"

Dick Shiner, Steelers Quarterback, 1968-1969:

I went to a reunion in 1986 of former Steelers quarterbacks. There were about twelve of us and each one of us gave a two to three minute speech. I said to them, there's good and bad in everything. The bad thing about the 1969 season was that we were 1-13. The good thing, was that we were 1-13. Because we were 1-13, we were able to draft Terry Bradshaw. There'd have been no Super Bowls if we weren't 1-13.

I got a standing ovation! Now, did it hurt to say that? Sure it did. But I have great memories of Art Rooney, Dan Rooney, and played for people that in tough times still rooted like crazy for you.

Warren Bankston, Steelers Fullback, 1969-1972:

I actually laugh when I think about my rookie year. Here I was a second round draft choice from a hot and humid area in Louisiana. I was approached by a sportswriter who asked how I would use the unusual hot muggy weather in Latrobe to my advantage. I responded, "Well, I feel sorry for those guys from cold weather states. I played in New Orleans and it is oppressive down there. This will give me a decided advantage, and I intend to take full advantage of it." Of course I was the first one out – for three days no less – with heat prostration.

Terry Hanratty, Steelers Quarterback, 1969-1976:

Every day Lambert would walk into the locker room and glare at me as I smoked my cigarette and had my coffee, then go to his locker. Well, one day he put his shoulder pads on and out dumped two cups of water on his head. I put the two cups in his shoulder pads.

This went on for three days in a row – every day he'd do the same thing and the water would dump on his head. On the fourth day, I went up to Jack and said "You dumb SOB, you're getting boring! Check your shoulder pads next time!" The fifth day he checks his pads – no water. He looks at me with this big grin like he just won something. The next day, he puts on his pads, and dumps another two cups of water on his head!

Another time with Lambert. In practice we're lining up across from one another and I blow a kiss at him. So he yells across the field to Chuck "Chuck – Hanratty just blew a kiss at me!" Well, he realized as soon as he did it what he said, and everyone started laughing – even Chuck!

I got Noll too. When we first went to Three Rivers Stadium, there were no places to eat around there. We had to get there really early to watch film. So Preston Pearson, who was our player rep at the time, went to the Rooneys and asked for them to provide the players food. They got us burgers, soups and stuff. Chuck hated the idea – he hated anything extra for the players. He told us that we better not get sleepy and tired eating all this food.

So in practice, during stretches, as we're all on our backs, Chuck walks by. I started snoring and pretending to be asleep. I don't think Chuck liked that.

Terry Hanratty, Steelers Quarterback, 1969-1976:

Terry and I roomed together. We did a lot better than people thought we did. Terry used to come to my house for Thanksgiving – I was in his second wedding with JoJo.

I remember one of the Pittsburgh papers had a contest – name your starting quarterback. They were having fun with this thing. So I was going to take out an ad – it cost $240. Rooney heard about it and said "Run the ad – I'll cut the check."

The ad was my own contest – name your favorite sportswriter – with all the writers from that paper listed. I included a write-in on the ballot – porn-star Linda Lovelace. She won!

Bob Adams, Steelers Tight End, 1969-1971:

In '72, Andy Russell's wife held a party for Andy in their home. Most of the players were there, some brought presents. When it was time to open the gifts, we went into the family room. There was one larger than the usual presents sitting on the floor. Andy did not choose that right away, he opened several gifts and then said, "Well I have to see what's in there," and proceeded to take the bow and wrapping paper off. He unfolded the top of the box and to everyone's surprise, particularly Andy's, none other than Myron Cope jumps up out of the box yelling, "Happy birthday Andy!" The room went wild with laughter and Andy was all smiles and very pleased with the caper. Myron and Andy were very close. It made the party and I'm sure tickled Andy to no end.

Bob Adams, Steelers Tight End, 1969-1971:

After a series of losses, tempers were getting short and there was some blame going around. We came in from a practice and were stripping down, cutting off the tape and moving to the showers when yelling started. It was a war of words between Roy Jefferson, our star receiver, and John Brown, our offensive tackle. Name calling each other in choice four letter words was an understatement. The most common two-syllable word was "mother" adjective modifying a second two-syllable word made a noun from a verb starting with an "f".

All eyes turned on to these naked gladiators. Each picked up a galvanized steel garbage can filled with tape and paper, and from their positions ran at each other like two knights charging on their steeds, and collided throwing ankle wraps, tape, paper cups in the air. Then they raised their weapons above their heads, and crashed the cans against each other. This was so improbable a battle the entire team began to laugh. They proceeded to clash the cans together once more and perceived the effect they were creating and themselves began to chuckle. The laughter continued for at least five minutes and the war ended in a handshake.

John "Frenchy" Fuqua, Steelers Running Back, 1970-1976:

I met Noll in '67 with Baltimore. He always gave advice. Noll was not very loquacious. He was a guy that, when he told you something, you paid attention. He demanded it. He was like a CEO. He delegated through his staff. In meetings, he talked a lot about his family and told tales that never added up. We could never figure out what he meant. He was a student of the game even as a coach.

To be successful in Pittsburgh, you couldn't make mistakes. I learned early, after practice and dinner, you got into the playbook. If you made an error, he didn't jump on you. He asked you what you were thinking on the play. If you could make sense, he would tell you that he'd consider it, but you do it the way he says. That we play as a team. If you didn't make sense, he would just ignore you and walk away from you. He always said, "Whatever it takes, but no mistakes." I studied there more than I did in college. It worked out well. I knew the halfback and fullback plays. He asked me who the tailback was supposed to block when I was to run the ball – he'd quiz me. Me, Preston, Dick Hoak, we all used to get together at 7:10 a.m. before 7:30 a.m. meetings to go over what we weren't sure about – to go over those things.

Noll was a man of few words. I remember when we played the Vikings. All week he was telling me that I had to block Carl Eller – I needed to get a stalemate on him. It was a close game, and the play we needed to run was out of the thirty-four special alignment. I needed to get my shoulder into his stomach and head on his outside hip – not let him get to the outside. We were on the two yard line and I took a run at him – and he ran straight at me. I saw his forearm and he ran right over me, but it was a textbook block, just enough for Preston to get to the outside and score the winning touchdown. As we ran off to the sideline, Noll looked at me. He just nodded. That made my career. All week I heard that I had to make that block. It just shows you how much goes into making a play. He just took my arm and looked at me. Didn't say anything, but I knew.

Tom Sorensen, Steelers Kicker, 1970:

The equipment manager was always playing tricks. He tried to get me to take this helmet that was way too big. It had a large dent in it – it had been Greene's! Everyone got a laugh out of that.

There was also the saga of Bradshaw driving his pink Cadillac to meals, and complaining that he wanted his name painted on it – the linemen didn't much care for that – but all that settled down quickly.

I'll also never forget being on the sidelines during practice and watching Bradshaw throw a 50-60 yard pass on a straight line and hit the receivers' hands so hard you could hear the bang. I had never seen anyone throw like that – soon the NFL would find out!

Dennis Hughes, Steelers Tight End, 1970-1971:

Joe Greene and L.C. [Greenwood] played a lot of jokes. Once they put a rubber snake in John Brown's locker. I always got blamed because I sat next to them – my locker was next to theirs. I didn't know they did that to John and John was deathly afraid of snakes.

Well, John picked up a stool and beat the hell out of that snake – he was scared. They tried to tell him I did it but I got to him quick and told him it wasn't me!

Lou Riecke, Steelers Strength and Conditioning Coach, 1970-1980:

The first time I met Bradshaw was after he was drafted as the team's number one pick. There were a bunch of teenage girls that used to come and watch him in practice – to see the new young star. They would yell out to him and he'd yell back "Come over here – that's too far to walk for me!" So they'd all come running!

Once when I was lifting Webster and Brown rigged the weights so they wouldn't go up. They nearly killed themselves they were laughing so hard.

Dennis Hughes, Steelers Tight End, 1970-1971:

My funniest memory was when a bunch of us rookies went to Three Rivers Stadium before it was done being built. All of us rookies were running on to the field and the workers all stopped working. Then they stood up and started booing us! It's the God's honest truth.

I told Terry that we gotta change those boos to cheers!

I also remember the preseason game we had in Shreveport, Louisiana. They had one there Terry's rookie season because he was the number one pick and from there. All of Terry's friends and family were there – we were all hyped up for the game.

Well, we're in the huddle for our first series and I asked Terry if he as ok, and he said "Yeah!" I said "Ok, let's have a good one then!" Then right after that, Terry threw up, right there in the huddle. It was the funniest thing I'd ever seen!

Well, we just all moved the huddle over as a group and went on from there!

John "Frenchy" Fuqua, Steelers Running Back, 1970-1976:

He [Beatty] never had the body to wear outfits like I could. Every time we'd go to a new city, we'd both go shopping for the oddest outfit that you could find, that you could never find in Pittsburgh. We were like Ali and Frazier – we would talk trash to each other. We hid outfits from each other before each game so that we couldn't see each other's outfits, and we'd have the ballboys get them from our cars after the game.

Beatty never had anything original! I told him once that we killed a cow from Texas – it was all white – just to make my belt, and got my spurs from Roy Rogers' pistols. I got a glass cane in Cincinnati that went with my cape outfit, and when we went to the airport we always entered the planes from the rear, which is good because they never would have let me take that glass cane if they saw it.

The goldfish shoes came to me. I remember after we broke camp, on the news a newscaster said that Frenchy did it this time! I was in the shower so my wife ran to me and told me they were talking about me on TV, so I dried off and ran in to watch the news. What happened was I had gone to a Dapper Dan event a little while before and ran into a shoemaker there who told me I needed goldfish shoes and he said he could make them for me and send them to me. I gave him a "business card" with the Pittsburgh Steelers address on it. He figured out that it was a Steelers address somehow so instead sent them to Channel 4. So I went down to the station and got them. You could see the flap where you'd put the water into the bottom of the shoes, but boy did they hurt my baby toe when I put them on. I got fish, but every time I put them in there they'd die and float to the top. I started to get hate mail, people said I was just killing fish for pleasure, so I went to Joe Gordon (head of PR at the time for the Steelers) and asked him what to do. He just turned to me and said, "Just keep killing 'em, Frenchy." After that, it was too much for Chuck Beatty, it just blew him away. Our last dress-off I wore a cape, a cane and had a contest with fans to see who could get me the best hat. Someone made a hat for me with three plumes and I gave the guy one hundred dollars and wore that.

Babe Parilli, Steelers Quarterback Coach, 1970-1973:

The Rooneys were the best. I remember the old man – he used to bring cigars into my office and we'd smoke them together. Chuck couldn't stand the smoke. I got Bradshaw to smoke the cigars too and we'd all sit in the quarterback meetings smoking them. I asked Chuck if the smoke was bothering him. His eyes would be watering but he said no – he knew Rooney brought us the cigars. But he went out and got a big fan and put it in the room to blow away the smoke!

Larry Brown, Steelers Offensive Lineman/Tight End, 1971-1984:

Hanratty played a number of practical jokes. I also remember Dennis Hughes who was a tight end from Georgia. He and Hanratty used to go back and forth, taking things out of each other's' lockers, putting that hot gel stuff in people's shorts… they were always doing something, hiding clothes.

Well, one day, Dennis just got done getting someone with a practical joke. He was so excited that he got someone – he was laughing and walking to his locker. But he didn't see his clothes. He just said "Dog gone – someone stole my clothes!" The whole locker room started howling. It finally occurred to him that he was wearing them the whole time!

Ed Bradley, Steelers Linebacker, 1972-1975:

Regarding Coach Noll I had little or no knowledge about him. To illustrate that, when I went up for rookie orientation he came up and introduced himself and I said "Hey Chuck nice to meet ya!" I wasn't really sure who he was. Well, later on when we had our first group meeting and he took the podium…I slid down in my seat and said to myself "Damn, way to go Ed. He's the head coach. Chuck Noll!"

I can't say they tried to take advantage of me [when replacing an injured Lambert in Steelers-Vikings Super Bowl]. In fact, I'm not sure they even knew I was in there at first. I know Curt Gowdy with NBC didn't. With Jack's number fifty-eight and mine thirty-eight, and the level of the defense being the same, every play I made at the beginning he called Lambert instead of Brady.

How do I know that? My grandmother watching the game back in Connecticut told me. Boy, was she mad at Gowdy for the longest time after that.

Anyway, being a part of the two weeks of preparation for the Vikings, I knew what I had to do. Of course, playing within the system we had and the caliber of players in front of me and to the left and right and behind me, how couldn't I look good?

Gordon Gravelle, Steelers Offensive Lineman, 1972-1976:

About eight years ago I met Bill Walsh at a charity golf tournament in Northern California. As I introduced myself, I mentioned I played for the Steelers when he was an assistant coach under Paul Brown at Cincinnati. He looked at me as he pondered for a minute, then pointed at me and said "best team ever." I was surprised and I asked him "how about your 49er teams of the "80s?" He thought again for a minute and then said, "We would have given you a run for your money, but, no (as he pointed his finger at me again) best team ever!"

J.T. Thomas, Steelers Cornerback, 1973-1982:

I had no idea I was going to Pittsburgh. Ironically, I was watching the Immaculate Reception game in Palo Alto at the East West Shrine game. We were watching the game at a restaurant and just to be different and controversial I bet the guys around me thirty dollars each that the Steelers would win. Keep in mind I had less than one hundred dollars in my pocket and it was a nine hundred dollar bet! When they were losing I tried to sneak out, but the sous chefs there were as big as linemen and they saw me and told everyone not to let me leave. They put a chair to the door!

All of the sudden, there goes Franco. I was never so excited about a football game! I got two cooking swords and pots from the kitchen and stood on the chair banging the pots, telling them no one can leave until I got my money!

John Banaszak, Steelers Defensive Lineman, 1974-1981:

The show and the singing in the cafeteria were the only forms of hazing that the rookies were faced with.

After the show and the cardinal puff beer drinking game I headed back to my room. Ernie Holmes grabbed me and said we were going to go get something to eat. I told him I was broke and couldn't buy a burger and he told me it was on him. When we got to Super Burger I went in and Ernie told me he left his wallet in the car. As I was standing in the restaurant I watched Ernie pull out of the parking lot.

As I was walking back to campus I noticed the veteran cars in the parking lot of the old 19th Hole. Ernie by that time had told everyone what he had done and as I walked in to get a ride back Ernie pointed at me and they all had a big laugh. The joke was on me but in retrospect it did feel good to have the vets buy me a couple of beers.

Paul Uram, Steelers Conditioning and Special Teams Coach, 1973-1981:

I remember coming off the field with Terry Bradshaw. Chuck was in the training room with Lou Riecke and we walked by them. Chuck yelled to Terry that he should "Go in and pump some iron!" Terry just told him that "The ball only weighs a couple of ounces!" He just walked on by!

Terry never lifted. He didn't think it as necessary. You can't question somebody that has accomplished so much.

One guy came in back then and talked Chuck into seeing how guys ran. He had them run laps after practice, four laps. Greene just asked "When do you think that I as a defensive tackle will ever have to run four hundred yards?" He never even ran the quarter mile. He'd walk half the way. Who was going to tell Joe Greene to run at a certain speed?

J.T. Thomas, Steelers Cornerback, 1973-1982:

Dwight White was our Richard Pryor. He was funny, smart and talked for sixty minutes. He'd drive the referees crazy. Dwight didn't trust Ernie. Ernie ran his own game. At the snap Ernie would change his mind and not do what he was supposed to – but he was always right. Dwight called the plays and Ernie just did what he wanted. Ernie would philosophize about it later but it never made any sense – his head was in the ozone layer!

Marv Kellum, Steelers Linebacker, 1974-1976:

I knew the Steelers were looking at me. Lionel Taylor came down to interview me. Dallas was interested to. When Lionel talked to me after the draft I jumped at the chance to sign with the Steelers. I thought I had made the team! I didn't realize about all the camp stuff.

I remember after that going to the barber to get my hair cut. He started telling me about all the great linebackers on those Steelers teams and told me he'd see me back next week! I got mad at him and almost walked out!

Gary Dunn, Steelers Defensive Lineman, 1976-1987:

Well they moved me to nose tackle when they moved the team to a three man front. I asked Webster to take it easy on me in practice. I had just come off a season where I led the team in sacks and thought I'd be the sack guy, but oh well.

Well, Mike said "Sure Dunny, I'll take it easy on you." The first play he knocked me back so far I almost took Lambert's legs out. Jack asked me if I was going to make it. He abused me the whole practice. I was so dejected, riding home that day in my GTO because we had the next day off. Well, Webster drives by me on the freeway in his Lincoln, and beeps at me and says hi. I just gave him the finger.

Well, we're talking and he tells me to pull over on the freeway and I do. He asked me why I was angry and I told him he made me look bad. He said no, I did well. The next thing you know we're doing drills on the side of the Turnpike. I drove him into his Lincoln and he said, "See, you're getting it." Then he threw me over the railing, started laughing and walked to his car and drove away still laughing!

Gary Dunn, Steelers Defensive Lineman, 1976-1987:

Steve Courson was just huge – he was a great friend of mine. I remember driving to Coral Gables in my van and a cop pulls me over. I asked him why he pulled me over – I wasn't speeding. And he said he knew, but the van was bouncing up and down. Well, that was Steve in the back, practicing the crab.

I asked the cop if he wanted to see "the crab" and the cop said sure. So he and his partner go to the back of the van and open it up and there's Steve. Steve pointed to the first cop, who had his hand on his gun and the flashlight on Steve, and asked him if he wanted to see the crab, and the cop said "Sure!" He asked the other cop and he said yeah too.

So, Steve tears off his shirt and does the crab – his muscle pose, with his immense veins sticking out of his shoulders and biceps! The cop looked at me and said "You and It, keep going and get out of town." I just said "Yes sir."

Steve used to go places and tear off his shirt and scare people. When we went to play Houston once he tore off his shirt, put on his camouflage blazer and blared that Apocalypse Now music and stood on the hood of his truck doing the crab – the fans went bananas. He even camouflaged his face and body!

Mike Kruczek, Steelers Quarterback, 1976-1979:

To me the biggest character was Terry Bradshaw. He played practical jokes on me all the time. It almost always dealt with my locker. He would put baby powder in my helmet and I wouldn't know it until I put it on and he'd be lurking around busting a gut laughing. He'd put a cup of water on the top of my locker where my shoulder pads were, and when I reached up and pulled them off I would get a very unexpected shower; this usually happened just before practice.

Gary Dunn, Steelers Defensive Lineman, 1976-1987:

On my first day, Coach Perles told the rookies we were practicing headbutts – where defensive linemen take on the offensive linemen. He asked who wanted to start. I said I did – and he said great! He said I was going to break the record for the most headbutts in one day.

Then I realized I was the dummy. He had me be the offensive lineman! Joe went first and he had a bad shoulder so he went at half-speed and took it easy on me. Then it was L.C.'s turn. He was tall and lanky – I thought I could get underneath him and could take him. The vets were yelling at me – "Watch the cape!" So I fired off and L.C. jumped to the side and I went headfirst into the turf. L.C. just looked at me and said "Welcome to the NFL rookie."

Gary Dunn, Steelers Defensive Lineman, 1976-1987:

There was always the Atomic Bomb in the underwear. They tried to put it in my underwear once, I remember. I was getting in my suit for a speaking engagement and I could smell it. I said screw it, I just won't wear underwear. I was driving and then I'll be damned, but they put it in my pants too. I think it was Beasley...

I remember once Chuck read something about the benefits of pasta – how it helped your eyesight or something like that. He gave us a big lecture on pasta one day. The next day Swanny filled Bradshaw's locker up with pasta – he said it would help Bradshaw with his eyesight!

There was also the turkey sign up for rookies. They'd always tell the rookie class that they had free turkeys for Thanksgiving and that they had to go ask Dan Rooney for the turkeys. Of course there weren't any turkeys.

One time though Swanny bought turkeys for all the rookies and the vets were asking where theirs were!

Ted Petersen, Steelers Offensive Lineman, 1977-1983, 1987:

Mike Webster was a practical jokester – he was forever doing stuff to other people. He and Furness were good buddies. One time, I think it was on Furness, he lifted the hood of his car and cross-wired the spark plugs so the timing was off and it backfired. Furness never made it out of the Fort Pitt Tunnels.

I remember we got him back once and put black pepper in his Skoal chewing tobacco.

Bleier was one of the biggest. And Greene did so at times as well. I remember one time he took kicker Matt Bahr, while Matt was still in his boxers, and put him in shopping cart and pushed him into the lobby for the world to see. I'm not sure what the cart was doing there!

Craig Colquitt, Steelers Punter, 1978-1984:

Bleier, Stoudt, and I handled most of those duties. Menthol atom in the jock. Spilled Skoal in socks. Vaseline placed in places that took time to remove.

Mike Webster, John Kolb and I used ankle tape to bind Bleier at his last practice before retirement. It was about twenty-seven degrees and raining. I tackled Bleier, which he did not fight, and Webster and Kolb did the taping. They even carried Bleier to the goal post and tied him upside down to the base pole. The whole team looked, laughed and left the field with Bleier still hanging.

About thirty minutes later Coach Noll brought a freezing blue Bleier back into the locker room in a shopping cart. Bleier of course had his constant smile. Noll pushed Bleier into the locker room saying, 'Here, I don't want him either.' It was a good retirement memory.

Tom Beasley, Steelers Defensive Lineman, 1978-1983:

Well, one of my better pranks was on Lambert. Lambert enjoyed hunting. I had a friend who hunted rattlesnakes – name was Gary.

So, to go back a year, Jack came into the bar that me, Dunn, and Stoudt were at. Said to me "Thanks for buying me a drink!" He was being sarcastic. So when the waitress came over, I told her to bring him a Shirley Temple, with a pink umbrella, and tell him who bought it for him.

Jack came over and "accidentally" spilled the drink on me. I told him I'd get him back for that.

So, a year or so later. My friend Gary comes in and says he's going rattlesnake hunting again. I tell him to bring his snake box, and a spare one too. He asked why but I just told him he'll see.

So, we all meet in town for dinner. We all go to Gary's truck and Gary opens up the snakebox and there are six rattlesnakes in there. Jack hates snakes. He's petrified of them. So he runs to his car which was right near the truck and pulls out his 9mm gun and says he's going to shoot the snakes. He flipped out – Gary put them away and I told Jack to watch out for those snakes tonight.

So when Jack left the dorm later that night I snuck into his room with the spare snake box and left it in there opened up.

When we all met with Chuck the next morning, Jack told him he was going to have me arrested for attempted murder! Chuck told us all he needed to keep us busier as we all obviously had too much spare time. I told Dunn I was getting out of there!

Greg Hawthorne, Steelers Running Back/Receiver, 1979-1983

Bradshaw was always a fun-loving guy. Everybody had their moments, really. I remember once in Cleveland – it was snowing so much we couldn't see out of the windows. The bus driver was backing up but couldn't see, so we all helped him and told him how far to back up, when "Wham", we had him back up into a pole on purpose! We were all cracking up. He was so pissed but we were all laughing, because it was Cleveland, so we didn't care.

Thom Dornbrook, Steelers Offensive Lineman, 1979-1980:

On the first day, when the vets came in, I remember all of the people on the hill – the press watching. We ran the Oklahoma drills and got to see Lambert on top of me, swinging at me. I knocked him on his ass during the drill, and Franco ran around him and taunted him with the football. Lambert hit me and I hit him. It became a big fight – Rollie Dotsch, George Perles and other coaches jumped in to stop us and it became a big pile.

Lambert – say sorry? Come on! I was pissed off. Webby took my hand later, put me in a car and drove me to the 19th Hole for a beer. Lambert came in, so I ordered him a Shirley Temple. He laughed, and we had a beer together then.

Later, when we played Buffalo in a preseason game, I ran downfield on special teams and knocked one of their player into the goalpost. I was on the ground – and you know when you get that feeling that everyone is looking at you. Well, I looked up and there were Buffalo players all around me. I thought I'd have to fight my way out of there...they were pushing on me when, all of the sudden, they all just went away. Disappeared. Behind them was Jack, with Joe Greene and Dwight White. They grabbed me and walked me back to the bench.

Steelers offensive lineman Dornbrook lines up versus Buffalo.
Photo courtesy of Thom Dornbrook

Dornbrook celebrates touchdown with teammates.
Photo courtesy of Thom Dornbrook

Craig Wolfley, Steelers Offensive Lineman, 1980-1989:

A good example. Tunch was the backup center – and remember, in practices there were no names on the back of the jerseys. Well we're in film study and coach Rollie Dotsch is going on and on about how horrible Ilkin looked playing center – hand was too slow, etc. He's just tearing in to him and Webster's giggling as Ilkin's sweating bullets.

It's because it wasn't Tunch – it was Webster on film. But Dotsch couldn't tell. Ilkin creeps up to Webster and asks him to tell the coach it was him. Webster finally does and Dotsch just stops and moves on to the next player. Doesn't say anything further about Webster.

That's the kind of respect the coaches had and have for the great players.

Tunch Ilkin, Steelers Offensive Lineman, 1980-1992:

Gary Dunn and Beasley. Once they took John Goodman's bed, clock, fan, everything and put it all in the bathroom stall. They left clues behind to make it look like I did it. Kohrs jumped on the bandwagon and he and Goodman accused me of doing it and later got back at me by doing something to my room.

There was also this box with a spring-loaded top that would snap open if you released the latch – it was Dunn's. He would tell the rookies he had this wild Mongoose in there. I was the keeper of the box after he left. We'd tell the rookies about this nasty mongoose in there – how it would tear up snakes and that we'd let them go feed it someday.

If you looked at the box you'd see this furry tail sticking out. We'd throw chicken bones in there for noise and tell the guys to take this straightened out coat hanger and poke at the mongoose in the box – really playing it up. Then we'd hit the latch and the tail would go flying out. Keith Willis knocked over three guys running out of the door and down the stairs yelling "The mongoose is loose!"

Michael Fabus, Steelers Photographer, 1980-2011:

For the *Steelers Digest* in 1981, we had a great cover of Rod Woodson. Bob Labriola had the idea to dress Woodson up in a Superman costume. He said I had to sell it to Rod though. So I went to his locker and told him I wanted a picture of him in a Superman costume, and he asked why I wanted to do that. That year, he wanted to return punts and play wide receiver in addition to playing cornerback. I told him I thought this would be fitting. He said sure but that he would only do it on the practice field.

He didn't want his teammates to see him. Changed in the equipment room then took the picture.

I actually had wanted him to wear a suit over the costume and come out of the locker ripping the shirt off. We fitted him with the costume at a costume shop on the South Side. They gave it to us for free if we promised to mention him – and we did.

Greg Lloyd – people said he was mean but he was very kind to me. I wanted him to hold a Darth Vader helmet for a picture, with him wearing his cross and bones tee shirt in the weight room, like he usually did. Well, he asked me if it was a racial thing! I said no – you're like the dark force – no one wants to go near you. He said he'd have to ask his wife and did. The next day he came in and said yes – so I had Rodgers Freyvogel – the equipment manager – put a gold stripe down the helmet, the Steelers logo on the correct side and the number 95 on the back and took the picture of him in the weight room. It was great stuff.

Rick Woods, Steelers Safety, 1982-1986:

One of my favorite ones, you had to be careful shampooing your hair. The guy next to you would pee on your leg when you did if you weren't watching. One time tight end Frankie Wilson peed on Gary Dunn. Gary opened his eyes and chased Frankie into the bathroom stall and Frankie locked himself in the stall. Well, and this is the truth – Gary could pee twenty feet. So he peed over the top of the partition and drenched Frankie!

Rick Woods, Steelers Safety, 1982-1986:

I remember playing Chicago in '85. Malone was the quarterback – which didn't help a lot either. We were down by 14 points, and with Mark in there that was really the game. They were running Walter (Payton) the rest of the game. I'd meet him about three yards downfield and took a beating each time! It happened about seven or eight times in a row – he was picking me up. It was really rotten.

Gregg Garrity, Steelers Wide Receiver, 1983-1984:

My biggest memory was as a rookie having my locker next to Jack Lambert. He was a mean guy, on and off the field. Some players are mean on the field but nice off of it, but Jack Lambert was mean on and off the field. So as a rookie, I remember sitting on my stool in the locker room during my first training camp and Jack Lambert said to me: "Hey Rook, you're from Penn State, right?" I said yes. He said, "Well, you need to clean out my ashtray twice a day. The last Penn State guy to do that was terrible." Well, that guy was Jack Ham. And Lambert smoked a lot of cigarettes, even at halftime. Even the coaches smoked at halftime.

It was a family type of locker room, you didn't feel it was a big business even though it was. You could be yourself and all was good. I remember my first wide receivers' meeting. We were all the meeting room with wide receiver coach Tom Moore. The lights were out, we were all watching film and going over the playbook. All of a sudden the door flies open and slams into the wall and the lights go on. I look over and in comes Mel Blount. He walked around and announced that he just wanted to see the fresh meat. He walked around and looked at each of us one at a time and then walked out. He wasn't one of the nicest guys. All the players were very cool, but a couple of them you just didn't speak to until they spoke to you first.

Ray Snell, Steelers Offensive Lineman, 1984-1985:

I have to tell you this story! I remember playing Cleveland in Cleveland. I truly did not realize then the level of rivalry that existed between the two teams until I hit the tunnel. I thought Chicago and Tampa Bay had a rivalry. But as I went through the tunnel, the Dawg Pound and other fans....our uniforms were dirty before we started playing because of the eggs and other stuff they threw at us.

Webster said to me when we were in the tunnel – "Start running immediately and as fast as you can!" I just thought, sure. After the game, I thought, we were truly hated here! I asked him if our fans did the same thing at Three Rivers, but he just said he didn't know.

That was the most memorable time I've had. In every city, the Steelers were truly hated. And I liked that! We'd come in with nonchalant game plans and beat the heck out of other teams. Of course they hated us. We won because of our attitude and workman-like approach – Noll was the reason for it.

Rich Erenberg, Steelers Running Back, 1984-1986:

Being a Colgate guy I got a little extra grief if I made a mental mistake. When I did, I'd get a comment like, is that what an Ivy League education got you?

The interesting thing about having graduated from a good school is that the coaches and many of the players assume you are smart so the expectations are a little higher in regards to the mental aspect of the game.

Scott Campbell, Steelers Quarterback, 1984-1986:

One of the funniest things I can remember about my time in Pittsburgh was at my expense. We were playing a preseason game in Minnesota and I threw a swing pass that was tipped and then intercepted by a very tall defensive end at about mid-field. He had a head start, but I caught him at about the five or ten yard line. Instead of going for his legs I dove and tried to jump on his back. He proceeded to stiff arm my chest and I totally whiffed on the tackle to the fans delight. As I was walking off the field they were replaying the play on the JumboTron and the fans were laughing like crazy. As I got to the sideline I saw Chuck Noll watching the replay and laughing his head off as well.

The other funny moment for me was against the Redskins at home my second year in the league in 1985. Woodley was starting at the time because Malone got hurt the week before and was not dressed for the game. They gave Woodley one hundred percent of the practice plays that week (I got none) to get him ready to play. When we went out for warm-ups I noticed that Woodley wasn't out there and I was the only quarterback on the field. He was in the locker room sick as a dog. Chuck Noll comes up to me and very matter-of-factly states, "I guess you're starting." This was my first NFL start. I hadn't practiced one offensive play all week. Such is life in the NFL.

Merril Hoge, Steelers Running Back, 1987-1994:

I remember Mike Tomczak and I used to do a fake broadcast on Fridays during practice when we were on the sidelines watching the other guys. We'd switch off doing play-by-play and color, commenting on what just happened and joking about how unprepared our teammates were. It was fun to joke with the guys and poke fun at them.

I also remember on Fridays, Neil O'Donnell and I used to race home in the HOV lane to see who could get home first. Probably not the smartest thing!

I also remember Rick McMaster – he used to own the Grand Concourse and now owns the Capital Grille. They had the best cheesecake. On Fridays, everyone would race out after practice and I didn't know what was going on. It turned out McMaster had brought in trays of cheesecake for the team. It took me eight weeks to figure out what it was – I thought it was just some cake laid out for everyone.

Rodney Carter, Steelers Running Back, 1987-1989:

I remember our running back meetings. Tom Modrak was the personnel guy then. His office was right next to the meeting office when we were in Latrobe and that's where they released guys. He used to type with one finger and you could hear that old typewriter tapping when he typed. Well, when Hoak was running the meetings he would call on you to see if you knew what you were seeing on film, while the lights were out in the room. He'd call you out, and sometimes a guy didn't know something and there'd be this silence. Then all of the sudden you'd hear Abercrombie or someone else making the banging keys sound, copying the old typewriter, like Modrak was typing up the paperwork because he was letting someone go. We'd all start cracking up. Hoak never knew what we were snickering about!

Hardy Nickerson, Steelers Linebacker, 1987-1992:

I remember when we played Cleveland. Delton Hall was covering Webster Slaughter on a deep ball and had great pass defense on him. He goes up and knocks the ball away and falls on his backside. He played one more play then went to the sidelines. When we all came out we asked Delton what happened. He told us, "When I hit the ground, it felt like my bottom split in half!" I just remember that explanation – it still makes me laugh today. Funny stuff like that happens on the sidelines all the time.

Merril Hoge, Steelers Running Back, 1987-1994:

When I was drafted, I was so naive coming to Pittsburgh. Coming in from the West to the East – it was all so different. I had only flown three times in my life when I came to Pittsburgh, and never to the East. When I was flying in to Pittsburgh, I looked down. Now, the West is all mountains and desert. But looking down, I saw all of those hills and trees and thought, this is where they must have filmed all of those Tarzan movies!

The language was different too. As a rookie, I was asked to go speak at a midget football banquet. Wolfley was supposed to do it but they said he got hurt in practice. I said sure, though I didn't remember Wolfley getting hurt. I just thought maybe it was one of those things veterans promise to do months before and change their minds.

Well, I hurry and go home and get changed and get directions. There was no GPS then. And I was thinking to myself, I never saw a midget football game before. They must have at least thirty-three midgets to form a league – to have enough of them to have enough teams for a league. I said to myself, "Good for them! They have their own league." It was really inspirational and I thought it would be really cool to see them play.

I started forming my speech in my head...it was the little league, not midget football!

Well, when I got there a lady was sitting there when I walked in. All I see is the welcome Craig Wolfley banner and a bunch of parents and kids. I was late, so she hurried up and announced me and gave me the microphone. I'm sitting there saying to myself, "Oh my God!"

I had only prepared the midget football speech. So, I gave them the speech anyway – I explained to them what I had thought and they were rolling on the ground they were laughing so hard.

I was so green and naive then...to this day, I still have people who come up to me reminding me of that speech!

Danzell Lee, Steelers Tight End, 1987:

One night during a card game in our room (I roomed with Walter Abercrombie) some of the fellows notice my arrangement, I guess. I can't remember who it was, but someone asked me "Say man, what kind of deodorant do you use?" I wasn't thinking, but I did notice some snickering going on and some weird eye movements and whispering! I responded as I turned and looked at my arrangement of my stuff and immediately remembered and realized that I had picked up my mother's deodorant. I started talking and stopped when I looked at the deodorant stick that was named Secret! I just dropped my head and the entire room burst into laughter that last about fifteen to twenty minutes, so it seemed. There was no way to explain what actually happened before my trip, so I just took it.

Several times during camp practices, I would hear some of the guys say, "Man, I need to tell you something, but it's a Secret" with laughter to follow.

Rick Strom, Steelers Quarterback, 1989-1993:

One of my funniest memories occurred during an afternoon practice in the training camp when we were installing Joe Walton's offense. Late in practice, Bubby fumbled the snap and offensive guard Brian Blankenship picked up the ball and continued back to pass as if he was the quarterback. He quickly looked down field then threw the ball incomplete to the tight end. Let's just say, tension was running very high. In the evening film review meeting, Chuck Noll was sitting in the back of the room. As soon as the play ran on film, Chuck spoke up, "Hey Blankenship," there was a brief pause, "Your first read is out in the flat!" Laughter erupted and tension was diffused.

Tim Tyrell, Steelers Running Back, 1989:

The funniest thing I remember was Merrill and the ice tub. He was sitting in the tub and I bet him fifty dollars he couldn't stay in the tub of ice up to his neck for a minute. He told me I was on – so we starting throwing ice in the tub. He was up to his waist like it normally would be to ice your legs. But if it gets up past your heart for that long it's like suicide. Well he calls over three ball boys to cheer him on. He goes up to his waist and he just has this calm expression as he kept telling the ball boys to keep cheering. Well, he lasted the minute – he ended up doing it. He came out looking like a tomato. I gave him his fifty dollars and told him that was the greatest fifty dollars ever. It was crazy – he could have had a heart attack!

I also remember Bubby. He was just nasty. Always had a big chew and spitting in a cup. One day he came to the tub totally naked. He stands where all the powders and lotions were and, balls hanging out as he was talking to the guys in the tub, just takes a whole thing of powder and puts it on all over his chest and starts patting himself with it into this big cloud of smoke. "That's just about do it," he said, then just walked away. That was Bubby…he should have been a defensive lineman – he had that kind of mentality.

Rick Strom, Steelers Quarterback, 1989-1993:

Somewhere towards the end of the twelfth round of the 1988 draft, I called my parents in Pittsburgh to tell them how much I hated football and was adamant that I was not going to a training camp to be some team's "extra arm" in camp. While I was talking to them, the Steelers called my parents' home looking for me. In the middle of my self-pity party, my parents asked me to hold on so they could answer the other line. When they came back on the phone they told me, "Hang up, the Steelers are going to call you!"

After a few minutes discussing the Steelers quarterback situation, I was asked if I would be interested in working out for the Steelers in Three Rivers Stadium with the intent of signing as free agent quarterback. Suddenly, I loved football again.

My first appearance in a regular season game was in 1989 at the end of the first half against the Houston Oilers on a cold and snowy day. Bubby Brister threw a screen pass and ran off the field after the completion to get to the restroom. He did not know we were called for a holding penalty and had to run another play. Merrill Hoge ran over to the sideline to tell me to get in the game because Brister was in the bathroom. I had to take off several layers of clothing and put on a frozen helmet to take my first snap–and take a knee.

Richard Shelton, Steelers Cornerback, 1990-1993:

I remember playing in Buffalo in '93. Rod Woodson got a concussion in I think the second quarter. He was on the sidelines and it was cold, so he was standing by the heater. After a while, his pants caught on fire!

I also remember a certain Steelers linebacker was hit so hard he actually had an accident in his pants. He had to go to the locker room and change!

There's some crazy stuff that happens that you see on the sidelines.

Gary Jones, Steelers Safety, 1990-1994:

I can't remember who did it, but someone played a joke on Carnell Lake. Carnell always dressed real preppy – khaki pants, loafers, button down shirt. Well, we were coming out of a meeting and we saw that someone hung his shirt on a hanger from the ceiling, with his khakis tied to the bottom and his shoes on the floor beneath them. It looked like an invisible mannequin!

Kent Stephenson, Steelers Offensive Line Coach, 1992-2000:

Earhardt was always feeble with the phones. I remember we were all on the sidelines once and he was talking to Dick Hoak. He was talking to Hoak asking if he could hear him and Hoak said "Yes." Then we hear Ron answer back – "You can? Well, I can't hear you!"

Another moment was a preseason game in Arizona. It was hot but rain was predicted. We were standing on the sidelines next to the fans and Ron turned to Dick and asked him if anyone told Coach Cowher about the terrible winds. Dick just laughed and told Ron he was standing in front of the fans!

Justin Strelczyk was a guy who had his own drummer. He was an exceptional player – could play offensive guard and tackle. Someone was always dinged and he came in and played as well as the starters did.

He was hilarious too. I remember a Monday night game – they started at 9:00 p.m. then. It was midnight and we were playing the Bills. We were well ahead near the end of the game and Mike Tomczak was in and called a time out. We asked him what he was thinking calling a time out and he said Jugs (Strelczyk) wouldn't let me call the play! We asked him what he was talking about and he told us Jugs didn't want to throw the ball – he was telling him to run the ball because he didn't want an incomplete pass to stop the clock - the bars closed at 2:00 a.m.!

With Justin, you always had a full-time player. You never worried about him on the field.

Elnardo Webster, Steelers Linebacker, 1992-1993:

I remember a funny story with Rod Woodson. We played at the old Three Rivers and were there in the summer. We'd go to the foul line in the stadium and run "striders" – running from foul line to foul line. We'd go at about seventy percent and would do about ten of them a day. Well, when Rod went, his seventy percent was like my ninety percent. I used to joke with him that I could keep up with him – now, he was a world-class track guy. Well one day he asked me how much of a head start I'd need before he could catch up with me and still beat me. So I said, for a 220 yard run, I'd need about a fifteen-twenty yards head start. I think I understated that by about half. He beat me by fifteen yards! And he told me the next time he'd really run fast…

Leon Searcy, Steelers Offensive Lineman, 1992-1995:

The guys would give me directions on where to go – they wanted Krispy Cremes – and I said ok, cool. I'm sitting at my locker and Woodson comes up to me and says "Hey Rookie – you better get my order right!" I wasn't sure if he was joking or for real. I thought he was being a hard-ass – was he punking me out?

So, I bought the donuts ten-dozen, powdered white sugar donuts. Now, no one likes powdered donuts – those are the worst ones. I thought it was funny – but everyone was pissed at me. I remember in the locker room (rung backs coach) Dick Hoak came up to me and told me that if Joe Green were here, he'd snatch me up and make me go out and get more donuts. I just told him Green wasn't here, now was he? Well, we got into it, so Cowher called me into his office. He told me it was tradition and that I was stepping on too many toes and to go get the right donuts. From then on I bought the right ones!

Woodson laughed when I reminded him of that story. I laughed when I did it then, but I probably was just being a jerk at the time.

Mike Tomczak, Steelers Quarterback, 1993-1999:

In Pittsburgh, McAfee was a comedian - like Eddie Murphy and Matthew Lawrence. He was a happy guy - the kind every locker room needs. You need that levity. It's not always perfect – you try to be, but once you all see that game video on Monday, there's a lot of humility.

Kirkland was the judge of the Sunday best wardrobe contest. He was the fashion police – gosh, I remember once he wore this salmon colored suit like he just fished it out of the water. Once he came in with a lavender suit and top hat – he must have had a date…it all helps to break up the monotony.

Reggie Barnes, Steelers Linebacker, 1993:

Guys would mess with us as rookies. We had a rookie night where the veterans would take the rookies out. Chad and I were the only rookie linebackers that year. Greg Lloyd said that they would take care of the limos for us. We walked outside and saw three limos pull up, but there were only seven linebackers. I told him we didn't need three – and he said he and Kevin would take one, and we'd take our own as well. I asked him who was going to pay for all this, and he said you are. So I sent one home! The vets were trying to take advantage of us. When we got to the restaurant, Greg Lloyd ordered five entrees. They were gouging us!

Ray Seals, Steelers Defensive Lineman, 1994-1996:

Funny thing was, Greg Lloyd and I became good friends. I was in the training room and the trainer introduced me to Greg as "Big Play Ray". Lloyd just turned to me and said he never saw me make no big plays! Two weeks later though, Greg was calling me "Big Play Ray!"

Greg was a great guy – played so hard he knocked me out a couple of times in practice!

Oliver Gibson, Steelers Defensive Lineman, 1995-1998:

Lloyd was the biggest character. He was the first grown man I met that would intimidate other grown men.

As a rookie, he had me come to his Tae Kwon Do practice with Carnell Lake to work on my pass rush. He was insane. He was kicking his students against the wall. Carnell would ask him if that was okay and he'd tell Carnell they liked it!

I was the demonstration demo somehow. I don't know how that happened. I only went for six lessons – it was torture. He had me in all kinds of moves, bending my wrists back…

He was a darn fool. He broke Kirkland's wrist showing him a wrist lock one day…

Greene was also a character. My rookie year, I was lined up next to Greene. We were playing Tennessee and LeBeau calls for a straight rush. Well, I look over and Greene winks at me. Tells me we're running a stunt. I'm trying to say no to him but he rushes inside, so I'm hurrying trying to get outside, but there's no way I can catch Steve McNair and he runs for a first down.

Well, LeBeau is furious. He asked Greene what that was and Greene told him I called the stunt. What was I going to do – I was a rookie. Tell him Greene was lying?

Earl Holmes, Steelers Linebacker, 1996-2001:

I told Coach Cowher when he drafted me that he got the best linebacker in the draft…Kirkland used to tease me about that – he pretended he was me on the phone telling that to Cowher, imitating me!

Mike Quinn, Steelers Quarterback, 1997, 2004:

The first time I saw regular season action was against the Ravens at Three Rivers – I remember that well. It was 37-0 – we were blowing them out. Cowher was about to put Tomczak in and Mike asked Cowher "Why don't you put the kid in?" Cowher thought about it and said, "Ok, go tell him" – Tomczak came over to me and said he got Cowher to put me in the game, "but it was going to cost me fifty bucks," so I came in in the fourth quarter and finished the game. The next day Tomczak asked me if I had fun – then asked me for the fifty dollars. I laughed and he said "No, where is it?" So I gave him the fifty dollars! It was pretty funny.

Lance Brown, Steelers Safety, 1998-1999:

My rookie year, we were about to have a practice at Three Rivers Stadium. I had a brand new pair of Nike turf shoes on. Greg

Lloyd comes up to me chewing his tobacco and says, "Hey rook! I like those shoes. They new?" I said, "Yeah, I have a Nike contract. They just sent them to me." Then, he spit on them and walked off! I was like, "What just happened?"

Shar Pourdanesh, Steelers Offensive Lineman, 1999-2000:

I truly enjoyed my time in Pittsburgh. I was free to express myself. I remember having fun with guys like Jerome Bettis and Mike Tomczak.

Mike got me real good once. During my first start before a game, as I went to my locker to get ready, I saw a note from the offensive line coach asking me to see him before I get ready. Now let's just say that Kent (OL Coach) and I didn't see eye to eye. He thought I was a loud mouth jerk, and I thought he was a stiff suffering from perpetual diarrhea of the mouth.

So, needless to say I wasn't happy to have my pre-game routine interrupted by one of my detractors. As I slammed the coaches' locker room door open, I catch Kent naked by his locker. I give him a big scowl and I say "What!!" to which he replies with a simple "WHAT!" I then eloquently reply with an extremely loud "WHAT!" To which he replies with "what the fuck do you want?" Me: "Goddamit Kent, what the fuck do you want? You are the one leaving notes telling me to see you immediately!" He then breaks into a laugh (and I'm pretty sure it was the only time he ever smiled at me) "Oh boy, someone knows about how you and I feel about each other and they are probably laughing their heads off right now."

I leave and as I make my way back to my locker, I see Tomzack rolling on the floor laughing. As I sat next to him by my locker I said: "Mike, I don't have time for this crap. This is my first start and it's week thirteen! Come on! Seriously, grow up. I don't have time for this now." To which he said "You are right, I'm sorry. Just get your stuff on and get your head into the game."

To my relief I started to get dressed. Almost finished. As I went to put my cleats on, I noticed that they were unusually heavy.

To my horror I saw that they were filled with pistachios. Mike: "Come on my friend. How better to welcome a Persian to the Steelers than with some delicious pistachios?" Mike was great. Couple of days later I decided to soak his jockstrap in some icy hot. He really loved that!

Mike Schneck, Steelers Offensive Lineman/Long-Snapper, 1999-2004:

Bettis didn't like to get tricked. He had his TV show then and they'd go and ask players questions for the show. They asked me what would surprise people most about Jerome and I told the crew he had a hairpiece. When they ran it during the middle of the show Jerome was not happy!

Chris Combs, Steelers Defensive Lineman, 2000-2001:

I got a kick out of our fullback Jon Witman and this pickup truck he used to drive – we called it "The Steeler Mobile" because it was all decked out. John Fiala was always upbeat and had a great sense of humor – he used to shout out random things during team stretch periods before practice that kept us laughing.

Kevin Henry's wardrobe on game day was memorable – Earl Holmes used to call him "Dr. King."

Chris Hoke, Steelers Defensive Lineman, 2001-2012:

Troy Polamalu was always doing pranks on the field. He'd roll up tape into a ball and stuff it into the trainer's horn so when he blew it during practice no sound came out. Ward would throw grass into people's mouths when they talked. Ward was a good locker room guy.

Kendall Simmons, Steelers Offensive Lineman, 2002-2008:

One night, Troy Polomalu and a couple of the guys were hanging out. They decided to play a prank on my wife and me at three a.m. They rang our doorbell and ran away after leaving old food at our door. They came back again and this time, I let my Great Dane out on them. A year or so passed by until I found that Troy was behind it all.

Antwaan Randle El, Steelers Wide Receiver, 2002-2005, 2010:

Harrison was always a character – his style. The way he is now is the way he was as a rookie. When he came in, he was just running into stuff and yelling, telling everyone how crazy he was. We'd be talking to him and in the middle of the conversation he'd just say "Forget it – let's just knock those guys out!" I was like, what? He kept that angry look on his face all the time too. You could never tell if he was serious or not.

Barrett Brooks, Steelers Offensive Lineman, 2003-2006:

I remember when we played New England when they had that winning streak going. Right before half time Reed kicks a forty-six yard field goal, but I clutched my fist and they called me for offsides. Reed missed the field goal afterwards. When I saw there were only a couple of seconds left before the half I ran to the locker room before Cowher saw me. But he saw me running and chased after me. Hampton, Hines, Porter were all in his way as he was running up the steps after me – he almost knocked those guys down chasing me. He was yelling at me when he caught up to me "You're wrong," he was yelling and cussing me out. Hines and Casey were laughing as he cussed me out. It didn't seem funny then – I still remember days later Casey and those guys laughing at me, telling me that Cowher almost knocked them down the steps chasing me!

Russell Stuvaints, Steelers Safety, 2003-2006:

Troy Polamalu always wore these reggae shirts. We didn't know who those guys on his shirts were. One day he wore one with Peter Tosh on it – we didn't know who he was but it was a picture of a small guy with dreadlocks. We called Troy Peter Tush because of that one.

Max Starks, Steelers Offensive Lineman, 2004-2012:

I also remember Randle El – how small his feet were. One day I'm taping up my ankles and looking for my cleats. No one else has size nineteen cleats. Well I look over and Randle El is running with my cleats on – with his inside of them – to the football field laughing. I was getting mad – he was messing up my orthotic inserts! That was the year we won the Super Bowl. It was an elite fraternity of brothers.

Rian Wallace, Steelers Linebacker, 2005-2006:

Butler let his meeting rooms go with constant humor. We'd tell Laffy Taffy jokes before each meeting. Our linebacker corps was the funniest part of the team.

We also used to invite other teammates into the meeting room and have our disco club – we'd flick the lights on and off and dance. If I were a coach, I do what Coach Butler did. It's great to help the players relax and enjoy their job too.

Trai Essex, Steelers Offensive Lineman, 2005-2011:

Max will kill me about this one. Every year we did a Christmas gag gift. We'd pick each other's names from a hat – like Secret Santa – but with funny gifts. Kendall Simmons got me once and the thing he got me…it was a life-sized yellow peanut M&M cut-out, but with my picture on it. He told me I was shaped like a big peanut M&M and I needed to work on my body!

Well – it was an annual tradition. And getting back to Max. You know that in close groups there's that one guy that isn't good at telling jokes. They were just corny. Well, Max was that guy. So every year – without his knowledge – I'd make a list of all the bad jokes he told. I'd bargain with others who wanted the list and they'd use it every year like the David Letterman top ten bad joke list and show it on the screen!

Jovon Johnson, Steelers Cornerback, 2006:

In the first game of the season we played Baltimore. We were playing Cover Two – I was pressing the receiver. Troy Polamalu was supposed to be the safety covering my side but I looked over and he was in the box. I was waving to him – I didn't know if he knew what the play was – I was yelling at him asking what he was doing. Well, they threw the ball, and I looked and saw

Troy had intercepted the ball twenty yards downfield! When we got to the sidelines I told him he had me clueless.

Dallas Baker, Steelers Wide Receiver, 2007-2009:

I remember when me, Hines, and Limas Sweed, would all roll up paper balls and shoot them in the trash for fifty dollars a shot. Hines had endless money and it was just a way to help us relax. There was a lot of pressure. With Ben we'd shoot pool. For me, it was twenty dollars a shot but for him it was $150. I couldn't decide whether to play pool or study, for the $150!

Derek Moye, Steelers Wide Receiver, 2012-2014:

Also, when I caught the touchdown from Ben. That was a great experience. It was a funny story. Before the game we had practiced that play during the week. The game was the second or third game of the season – a Monday Night game versus Cincinnati. I was one of the last guys on the roster, really. As I was getting dressed to leave to the game, Ben told me to be ready for the play. Well, Emmanuel Sanders catches a long pass during the game – to about the one or two yard line. As I was running on to the field Ben told me to be ready – he was throwing the pass to me regardless so I better be ready. I knew I better catch it – if not I wouldn't be there the next day!

Leslie Bonci, Steelers Dietitian:

The first year I went to training camp, there was a thunderstorm, so I got there late. It was rib night and as soon as I walked in, I hear a voice saying "Oh no, here's the nutritionist!" And everyone was clearing plates. However the sauce around mouths and on fingers was a giveaway! You can run, but you can't hide when Lil Mama is around!

The Times They are Changing

When you discuss any organization's existence across an expanse of over seven decades, ultimately the success of that organization depends on its ability to manage and lead change and to instill that mindset into its players and staff.

Perhaps what most enabled the Steelers to become so successful was its ability to not just deal with change, but to *embrace* it. Instead of waiting to be affected by changes in society, or to allow itself to be limited by the way players were scouted, drafted and utilized, the Steelers instead pushed forward with its own agendas. The courage and foresight to draft players other teams were inclined to ignore, to change the way the game was played in order to improve chances for success –the way the team navigated these changes became incorporated into its culture. For all of the stodginess one imagines of the Rooneys and a blue-collar football team and city, the team was on the cutting edge of strategy, physical development of players, and race relations. It wasn't a forced process – it was simply an honest approach to doing all they could do discover new ways to improve and succeed. Old ways be damned, the team built into its culture a desire to win, mentor others, and to treat players fairly - everything else simply mattered much less.

Race:

Humor came to the team easily, a natural reaction and defense mechanism to the daily stress and grind. However, the team had a number of more serious approaches to team bonding as well, and issues to address that couldn't be resolved by locker room pranks.

While the 60s and 70s Steelers teams were, by the admission of many African American players, more progressive when it came to racial equality than most teams, they still had issues that related to the times they lived in. And those issues were compounded by the fact that when Chuck Noll was hired, he and the team made a highly concentrated effort to scout and draft players from the previously neglected, but often highly talented, small Southern Black schools. That allowed the team to amass a great deal of talent. But that talent had a great deal to prove – to itself and others. That they belonged in the NFL, and more than that, that they should be respected and paid accordingly.

It didn't usually manifest itself as a source of tension between players. But there were realities of the times. Players at first tended to "stay with their own." If the team was ever going to succeed and fully embrace itself as one complete family, it needed to bridge those gaps. Football, as a team game that requires continuity, requires that all be on the same page. It took players willing to reach across those lines – *in both directions* – to allow for that to occur.

There were a number of incidences of players doing so. And some, frankly, of situations that got in the way of that progress. Overall though, the organization treated it as a non-issue. It just didn't matter. The coaches – especially Chuck Noll – just wanted the better players to play. And the players just wanted to win. While racial issues on occasion brought themselves to the forefront, race was more an issue of an existing barrier to be broken down, than it was a divisive issue.

Brady Keys, Steelers Cornerback, 1961-1967:

After my first exhibition game in New York, on the off day afterwards, I met with the bank there and didn't travel back with the team. Then when we were in San Francisco I advertised for franchises and met with some possible franchisees.

When I got back I got a tip from a buddy – he said I was done. He said the NFL was not happy – I was creating the image the NFL didn't want – that a Black person could play and run a business.

He said I was blackballed – I'd see when I showed up on Tuesday.

I called the bank and told them what happened – that I was blackballed. They said we can't make the NFL keep you but we can make it worth your while to leave. They told me not to talk to anyone – even Pete Rozelle – that they would get lawyers and file a fifty million dollar lawsuit against the NFL.

They'd have it all ready when they blackballed me, they said.

So when I get back I was called into the owner's office. He said I had a call from Pete Rozelle. I called the bank first and went in. Pete Rozelle was on the phone and told the owner the bank called him. That they'd have to negotiate with me. I had to stay on the team, but I couldn't play or talk to anyone.

After that season I went home. I couldn't play anywhere after that. They are making a movie on my life as we speak – a documentary.

Ken Kortas, Steelers Defensive Lineman, 1965-1968:

In those days, there were clubs for White guys and for Black guys. That's just the way it was. Well one time Chuck Hinton, Ben McGee, and another guy dared me to come with them to their club. I said fine – I took them up on it. Well, when I walked in the whole place stopped. I walked up to the bartender and bought a bottle and told him to give shots to everyone in the place. It all worked out ok. We all got along fine.

Frank Lambert, Steelers Punter, 1965-1966:

I will give you my most poignant memory: 1965 was a year of great racial tension in the United States. Coming from Mississippi, a state characterized at the time by race segregation and white supremacy, I had a great deal of apprehension. My apprehension focused on meeting Marv Woodson, a defensive back for the Steelers and a resident of my hometown, Hattiesburg, Mississippi.

We did not know each other. I attended the all-White high school, he the all-Black school. I received all kinds of local attention, he none. I attended the University of Mississippi, which at the time denied admission to African-Americans. He went to Indiana University where he was an All-America performer. So I could only imagine the resentment he must have felt toward me. But, before I could seek him out, he found me, extended his hand, and said, "It is great to have someone here from my hometown." That remains the classiest act I have witnessed.

John Hilton, Steelers Tight End, 1965-1969:

I also remember playing in New Orleans. Willie Asbury [Steelers running back] was attacked by a fan who hit him with a bottle. Roy Jefferson and I stopped the guy – Roy kicked him down. It was some crazy fan who tried to take Willie out – it was a Black-White thing. Those things never should have happened.

Jack Leftridge, on Father and Former Steelers Fullback Dick Leftridge (1966):

As near as I can tell my father's problems in Pittsburgh first started when he was cheated out of his signing money. This had a very negative effect on his attitude and performance.

Also, there was the issue of him dating Caucasian women. The head coach at the time would meet with my father in private and tell him he could not date Caucasian women and that he would not play him as long as he did. My father continued to not give full effort as a player and dated as he pleased. The Steelers cut him and put in the media that it was due to him weighing nearly three hundred pounds.

My father had only informed me of having a real problem with one of the coaches…and that was the head coach. He attempted to try and tell my father who he could and could not bring to his own apartment (Caucasian women). My father's roommate (Jerry Simons) would get out of my father's car on the way to the stadium on game days and walk the last block or so.

There would usually be some Caucasian girls waiting on my father there and Jerry would say that he didn't want the head coach coming down on him too.

I really have not seen much that the Steelers have ever said to the issues. The weight issue is just not true…I have old news articles where the head coach actually does state my father's true weight for both of my father's years there and it ain't three hundred pounds, 235 pounds his first year and 242 pounds his second.

These weights are over the 230 pounds the Steelers wanted but definitely not three hundred. This non-truth has lasted about my father all of this time.

Ocie Austin, Steelers Safety, 1970-1971:

Pittsburgh was different. Berkeley and Oakland, California were the sites of a lot of political activism and protest movements (University of California at Berkeley San Francisco State and the Black Panther Party just to name a few). Unlike Baltimore, the Pittsburgh Steelers had a large roster of African-American players A poll of NFL teams in an *Ebony Magazine* article in 1970-71 had the Steelers as the poorest paid NFL team. This troubled me and eventually I think management thought I could become a disruptive presence on the team.

Not signing the contract offered me by the Steelers in 1971 doomed my career in the NFL. The other African-American players on the team were aware of this situation I'm sure but never at any time did we discuss salaries or work conditions while I was a member of the Steeler organization. It was an unwritten rule that management frowned on players discussing their salaries with each other, especially with white players.

Gene Mingo, Steelers Kicker, 1969-1970:

I just wanted to play the game, but being the first Black field goal kicker was wonderful. It was a joy having people come up to me and say that they had never seen anyone like me – I didn't look at me being difference from any other player though. I was a PRO and that was all that mattered – even today people come up to me and say how they enjoyed seeing me kick and play football.

When the owner of the Kansas City Chiefs – before he passed away – Lamar Hunt, looked me in my eyes and told me he told his sons that "Gene helped save the AFL." Coming from him that let me know that I had accomplished a lot and contributed.

Jon Kolb, Steelers Offensive Lineman, 1969-1981:

J.T. Thomas taught me something a month ago. He told me about his grandmother Mariah. He grew up in Macon, Georgia in the 50s. When he was a kid he drank out of a water fountain but couldn't read the sign that said "For White's only," a white man hit him and cut his cheek open.

If it were me, that guy would have been in pieces. I would have grown up in a rage. But he's a loving person. He said he asked his grandmother a question as a boy. He asked her if she ever asked God for anything, and she said "No." He asked her why, and she said "I'm too busy thanking him for my blessings."

This is in a time when they had so little. I want to develop Mariah's heart.

Those were the kinds of guys we had on the team. There are tons of stories like that about Donnie Shell, Mel Blount, Stallworth...they were all like that. And Cunningham and Tunch, with all the agony he's gone through the past few years.

The racial issues were just never an issue for me. In Oklahoma, we had Blacks, Indians, Mexicans...we were all together and we didn't know anything about Native Americans and Latinos. We were just all together.

Jon Staggers, Steelers Wide Receiver, 1970-1971:

As you mentioned, I was around those colleges growing up. I felt accepted and at home in Pittsburgh. It was a very tumultuous time then – there was so much going on then. You got there and wondered where and how you fit in. But the team was warm to me. Sam Davis was also from those smaller Black schools for instance and I could talk to him about those things.

I remember Ben McGee and John Hinton would drive me to the airport. They would sit in the front seat and say the same things to one another and nod to one another. I could see they were in sync and understood them. It was a good mix of young and old that all understood each other.

Mel Holmes, Steelers Offensive Lineman, 1971-1973:

I've always had confidence in my ability to be a good football player. However, coming from a small NAIA small historically Black college, I realized that my chances of playing in the league would be slim. Remember, this was a time during segregation. I came out of high school in 1967, in the South, toward the ending of segregation. Large, predominately major White colleges just weren't recruiting Black athletes at that time, especially southern major colleges in Division I. If I may recall, I cannot think of one major Southern white college with a single Black athlete on their roster at that time.

Funny thing, when USC came to play Alabama, USC had a plethora of black players. They completely ran over Alabama and ended up beating them bad.

After the game Bear Bryant, the coach at Alabama made the comment that if they are to win football games they must get some black players like USC. That sort of set the trend for southern white colleges getting black football players.

A perfect example being our fine offensive guard who I played with. Sam Davis attended Allen University, a small all-Black college located in South Carolina. Sam went on to play, I believe fifteen or more years in the league. One of the best offensive lineman I ever met, bar none. I believe he was a product of segregation

Larry Brown, Steelers Offensive Lineman/Tight End, 1971-1984:

I think it goes back to the draft. Pittsburgh recruited the best players available no matter what – and when you say that, it expands where you look. Color doesn't matter if that's the priority.

It turns out there was a tremendous amount of talent in the smaller schools. They set up their staff to scout the entire field of available players – they went after all of the field actively and discovered gems that others didn't look at. We had good talent because of that and were able to field those championship teams.

That instills a confidence in players. That the criteria is how you play – your talent, effort and intelligence. So if you trust the system, you all have an equal chance to make the team. There was no need to worry about the political or social elements – the team was going to keep the best players, no matter what.

J.T. Thomas, Steelers Cornerback, 1973-1982:

People talk about those teams of the 70s – but few talk about the chasm that first existed on the team. What brought it together? Chuck Noll? Some – but there are two people who were responsible that no one knows of now or talks about.

The first was Hollis Haff. He was the local Chaplain and had a church in Pittsburgh. He got a couple of us together for Bible study and soon all the players came. It started with him and his wife in his apartment. Eighty percent of the guys came every Sunday before the game. Those guys got to know each other – the White and the Black guys all started to break down the segregation borders through Bible study.

The second guy was Vaughn Nixon Nixon. He was a doctor who lived in Mt. Lebanon, PA. After every home game he invited all the players and their families to his home and threw a huge party. His place was incredible – no place we could have gone to would have been nicer than that place. Almost everyone showed up and the players and families got to know each other at those parties.

The barriers – fear and anxiety – were resolved through those guys. Those guys are never mentioned, but they were the catalyst for bringing us together.

J.T. Thomas, Steelers Cornerback, 1973-1982:

I knew the team was in transition. Our income matriculated because of tenure not because teams were paying a lot.

I was traded to Denver in 1982, Elway's rookie year, retirement was two-three years away and there were cheaper players. The game is a business and is all about bottom line.

Also, it goes back to the racial issues in '72-73. We were most of us from the South – we had that back of the bus mindset. That was our baseline of commonality. We played for dignity. The attitude then was about our manhood.

We were a segregated team in many ways then. The Black players and White players went their separate ways – it was just the way of the time – not a Steelers thing. The walls were slowly being broken down, but you don't change your attitude in three-to-four years. Access does not equal acceptance.

The Steelers were a great organization – they were one of the most liberal and cutting edge – that's how they got to that Steel Curtain defense. But it was just the times. People didn't wear the jerseys of Black players then, you know? No white kid was going to put on a Joe Gilliam shirt and say he wants to be Joe Gilliam!

It wasn't a chip but personal pride and dignity that came out of the struggle to be recognized as men, a human being with intrinsic values. No one talks about it, but our success had a lot to do with our mindset having all gone through that together and needing to prove ourselves.

Take Joe Gilliam – he attended Tennessee State University, an all-Black university and Joe came from middle income Black family. Joe's athletic character and background was primarily within a Black environment where he wasn't familiar with the institutional racism and had not develop a true understanding or skill set to deal with it. No one talks about this stuff. We saw Joe step away from all of us. We saw it happen as he struggled.

Chuck had liberal ideas – he had no hang-ups. The system was bigger than him so he worked the system as best he could. He could communicate with any guy on the team.

With me, he'd just give me a nod or shake his head. With Greene, he'd hold longer conversations and with Bradshaw he'd give him a hug to help his confidence.

What he gave most was value beyond football. Some guys got it. He talked about your life and purpose – your life's work. Football was a stepping stone – he always had you look beyond the game.

Innovation and Changes to the Game:

One thing the Steelers organization gets too little credit for is its innovative approach to the game and the way it adjusted to change. For all the stereotypical, blue-collar mindset the team epitomized over the years, it was often on the cutting edge of game in terms of strategy, technology, medical advancements, and scouting strategy. Much of that was due to the innovative approach of Chuck Noll, who, as discussed earlier, seemed fearless in his willingness to test new strategies and processes.

To be fair, he had both the support of the organization and the luxury of taking over a team that had a great deal of room for improvement: strategically, talent-wise, and wit the conditions they played and practiced in. The team had little to lose by trying new strategies.

From a revamped scouting approach and department, the introduction of concussion testing, unique weight-lifting strategies, and new offensive and defensive schemes, few if any teams benefited from innovation and adapted to change like the Pittsburgh Steelers.

There have also been recent changes to the game implemented by the NFL itself. Ones to protect players. Speaking to players and getting their take on those changes was an interesting undertaking – and surprising. For all of the issues many of these players face today due to the physicality of the game, their take on those changes has been, at best, conflicted. Many are less than supportive, tough most seem to appreciate the changes and are happy to see them being enforced.

Dick Haley, Steelers Cornerback, 1961-1964, Steelers Director of Player Personnel, 1971-1990:

Art Rooney Jr. was the leader in their scouting advancements. He pushed it further with Dan – they pushed hard on spending time and money to develop their scouting organization. That was the main reason we were able to develop those 70s teams.

People didn't have scouting departments and player information then. The Rooneys started by having a guy go to every college in the country and have their own territory. All the scouts went to schools in their area. We started seeing all the players and got accurate measurements for the first time of their height, weight, and speed. None of that was available before – it was a big factor in the early years.

Bill Nunn was a major factor. He had the All American team he picked with the Pittsburgh newspapers and had good connections in the Southern Black schools. He was a major factor in spotting talent. He and Art Rooney Jr. expanded the scouting in those areas and that gave us a big jump.

Bill had inroads into those schools. I had the smaller Southeastern schools – forty or so schools – some smaller and some bigger. I knew a lot of those coaches. If I could have taken you to Tennessee State, you would have had the greatest time. The coaches loved seeing the NFL scouts. Bill knew them for years – laid the groundwork there. Tennessee State practiced like Ohio State – you couldn't tell the difference.

Jim Bradshaw, Steelers Safety, 1963-1967:

Bill Nelsen was my roommate. He was drafted as a defensive back. Parker told Coach Mike Nixon he could draft anyone he wanted in the later rounds so long as it wasn't a quarterback. Well, Nelsen was quarterback, but Nixon drafted him as a defensive player. Of course he ended up at quarterback anyway!

In camp, your first day they left a yellow and black jersey in each of our lockers. They let us decide whether we wanted to play offense or defense. I took yellow – for defense. I was a running quarterback in college – I know what it was like to be hit! Bill took black for offense.

In those days, Pittsburgh was one of the first teams to draft athletes rather than positions. I remember listening to Jack Butler and Art Rooney Jr. going through the draft, talking about drafting athletes, not position players.

Gene Breen, Steelers Defensive Lineman, 1965-1966:

We wrote to Mr. Martin – the new head there at the NFLPA. He has responded to me and we're putting together a new NFL alumni program in Florida. The big guys making the money don't get it. They don't think they'll get hurt. They don't see themselves and peers hurt – they don't realize it can take a long time to see the effects of these injuries. Look at me – I retired in 1970 and just saw the effects in 2004.

We have to get these players to protect themselves better. To wear the right helmets – like the ones that connect to the shoulder pads. And to wear the right pads and get more frequent MRIs.

Look at James Harrison. When he got fined he said I get paid to hurt people.

And the bounties – they aren't anything new either!

I got one hundred dollars to tackle someone inside the twenty yard line, and a television to tackle someone inside the ten yard line. I got five TVs!

The Rams gave us one hundred dollars to knock someone out in the 60s. Lombardi didn't do that – but the bounties were nothing new.

You see, I was a good example of spearing players with my helmet to hurt the opposition. That's the way it was then. Even at Virginia Tech they'd line up eleven offensive players against me and I had to beat through them all to get to the quarterback and spear him with my helmet.

Frank Lambert, Steelers Punter, 1965-1966:

The mid-1960s represented a turning point for the NFL. Pete Rozelle negotiated a huge television contract with CBS that did two things: one, it helped make professional football the entertainment and media event that it has become, and two, it brought an infusion of funds into the league and to the teams. Joe Namath signed a $400,000 contract in 1965, dwarfing previous player contracts.

And, Rozelle, along with owners like Sonny Werblin of the Jets, understood that, while professional football was about play on the field, it was about public perceptions of every aspect of the game. Rozelle came to each team's training camp and gave a pre-season talk about the importance of perception, including that of avoiding any negative publicity. He would give us a list of establishments in NFL cities controlled or patronized by organized crime, and he instructed us to stay away from them, even if they were well-known restaurants.

J.R. Wilburn, Steelers Wide Receiver, 1966-1970:

Bill Austin was a Vince Lombardi coach. He tried to instill the same things as Vince – to emulate Lombardi. But no one could do that. If he had just tried to be himself instead of being someone else I think he would have done much better. He had trouble dealing with some of the players. He was a great offensive line and assistant coach – he just wasn't a great head coach – didn't know how to dot the *i's* and all that.

The first thing Chuck did when he came in was to get hold of all the players that wanted to play – not the most talented ones – and got rid of the other guys. That brought the unity back and he built on that.

Mike Taylor, Steelers Offensive Lineman, 1968-1969:

Frankly, I think something has been lost with all the wide open offensive sets and the passing game aerobatics that have changed the game so much. Don't get me wrong in the sense of entertainment value because it works. But I'm an old-schooler who was taught some valuable life lessons on the football field through my exposure to the game. Grinding things out is relative to life as a team working together as one by performing your individual task to help the team effort.

Today it seems like it's more about individual performance first, before anything with the team.

Lee Calland, Steelers Cornerback, 1969-1972:

You can't touch receivers now within five yards and can't touch them – they'd love the rules!

I understand the changes. Concussions and injuries weren't a concern then. It's a horrible thing now, we just didn't know better then. I think the rules protecting players do great things for safety's sake. I think officials take it too far sometimes though it's hard. It's a collision sport – that's why people come to watch.

Guys like Goodell and Rozelle are super guys. I was on an elevator with Rozelle as a player in California. He was talking to me about all kinds of stuff about the league. I never met him before. How did he know me? Of course I knew him but not sure how he knew me. That was the kind of guy you have to have.

I know you can't please everybody. But in the end you have to take care of your players and the league. You can overdo it but it's better to be on the side of safety.

L.C. Greenwood, Steelers Defensive Lineman, 1969-1981:

I don't like it one bit. You can't make it less physical. How in heck can you hit somebody and not be physical – especially when players are faster and stronger? Kids are not taught to make tackles anymore like we used to be. They tackle now with blocking techniques. But running that fast, with that size, you'll hurt people that way.

Now, you don't have to practice with pads. I think that's detrimental to them. They are babying them. Now there are too many injuries – I think it's because they aren't in football condition. You have to hit, block and tackle. Now they aren't used to getting hit when the season starts.

I don't know why it upsets me so much now – it just looks like they don't care about their future. You have to know how to hit and be hit and get used to it. The more you are hit the more you can take it. The new CBA – you can't train bodies to take hits. Probably many injuries could be avoided if they trained better. Just my feelings…who knows, maybe the players are okay with it and being injured and collecting paychecks these days.

Chuck Beatty, Steelers Safety, 1969-1972:

Maybe the biggest thing Chuck and the front office did was to start providing a meal to the players during those long all-day preparations for the next game. Also practicing in Three Rivers instead of on the racetrack, where we had to shovel snow before we practiced.

Terry Hanratty, Steelers Quarterback, 1969-1976:

There were definite issues. But being 1-13 my rookie year didn't bother me. I was Noll's second ever pick – Chuck had a plan.

He doesn't get enough credit.

There were horrible facilities then. Things changed when he got in. He installed a weight room – we never had one. No more horse shit on the field – we used to have receivers catch balls and land in that stuff. It was just really wrong.

The locker room was an old house. We got our ankles taped up on the second floor and took showers in the basement. There were four shower heads and the water would go up to our ankles. I just ended up going home to shower so I didn't catch a disease.

When you go to the pro ranks, when you are that bad, you expect lots of changes. Players just kept their head down and hoped for the best. You share locker rooms and eat together – you form immediate friendships and feel bad for those guys.

Roy Jefferson was the guy that fought him a lot. They had a rule – no cars could park in the circle of the dorm at St. Vincent's. Well, Roy would park there every day just to piss Chuck off. He'd yell at the quarterbacks if they missed passes, asking them "Who are you?" You knew it wasn't going to end well with him – and he was eventually traded to Baltimore.

Joe Gordon, Former Steelers Director of Communications:

All teams – all sports organizations – there's a division between business and the playing end. Dan was involved in both. It was obvious Chuck had a great deal of latitude though to operate on his own philosophy of building through the draft.

The Steelers had been known as loveable losers at the time. Playing in an antiquated stadium and losing so many games, there was lots of negativity. The move the Three Rivers uplifted the entire organization. Sam Davis, Andy Russell, Ray Mansfield – the holdovers from the old regime – it was positive for them. The move was one of the biggest things that led to the success of the team in the 70s.

Noll knew we couldn't be successful at Pitt Stadium. One of the main reasons he accepted the job was because he knew we were moving in '70.

From the standpoint of football operations, his direction of building on a long-term basis through the draft was very important. Before Noll, Buddy Parker traded draft choices for players looking for the get-good quick approach. But that didn't work. The operative word with Coach Noll was patience and all bought into that.

Lou Riecke, Steelers Strength and Conditioning Coach, 1970-1980:

I had to sell the weightlifting program to the players first. I had them come in – first Joe Green and the stronger guys. I lifted some weights and asked them if they could do this too. And they couldn't. I was only 158 pounds, so they were ready after that! I told them this couldn't make you anything but stronger and faster. That impressed them.

Some of them were worried and asked me if it would make them too muscle-bound. So I did a standing back flip and asked them if this looked too muscle-bound to them?

All-Pro Mike Webster told me after starting the program that he really wanted to thank me. He said he was going to quit, but because of the program he felt like I added three more years to his professional life.

Webster, Larry Brown and the rest of the offensive line were the guys that took to it most, I think. Bradshaw was exceptionally good too.

And sure, some were skeptical. But I had great backup – the head coach told them to do it! And he'd come in and watch them, so they did it.

One of the things I did too was to run with them. I ran track in high school and college – the one hundred meters. After practice, the coach would have them run sprints, so I ran with them. As fast as they would run, I would keep up with them and that impressed them too. They were concerned about getting too big and too slow and stiff – this showed them they wouldn't.

Bob Leahy, Steelers Quarterback, 1970-1971:

It gave you a new appreciation for the equipment guys, trainers, assistants…all those people were an integral part of the team. Chuck was the first coach to hire a strength-training coach. And a stretching coach. No one was doing that at the time. I was fortunate to be around that. Those were the beginning phases of the Steelers network. I never realized how much – until I read Tony Dungy's book – how important Bill Nunn was to all of that. As the story goes, he was a reporter and wrote a scathing article about the team. Instead of Mr. Rooney getting hostile, he called Bill Nunn in. Bill talked to him about the small Southern Black schools and brought him on the staff. That's where the Steelers were way ahead of everyone else. Look at the roster then and you can see.

Dr. Joseph Maroon, Steelers Neurosurgeon:

I became involved with the Steelers at the request of Coach Chuck Noll over twenty-five years ago.

Several of the players had concussions at the time and because of my interest in the management of head injuries, particularly those related to sports, I was asked to become the team consultant in neurosurgery.

In 1990 I told Coach Noll that his starting quarterback could not play against the Dallas Cowboys the following week. He asked, "Why?" I stated because he had a concussion and the guidelines specifically state a minimum of 2-3 weeks without contact – regardless of symptoms.

He questioned this and said that he wanted "objective evidence" for keeping a player out of sports rather than just arbitrary guidelines. He was correct!

I then called my friend and neuropsychologist colleague, Mark Lovell, and we put together the first pen and pencil ImPACT test which subsequently has evolved to a computerized version.

The ImPACT system has now been used to baseline over 1.8 million athletes in all sports.

Dan Radakovich, Steelers DL & OL Coach, 1971, 1974-1977:

Noll was worse than me! He loved new ideas. Problem was, he wanted to take the new ideas and make a whole new offense out of them every time. I just wanted to make adjustments – he wanted to make everything a big deal.

I have to say, he and Paterno were some of the most open coaches so far as new ideas go – they were the best coaches to work for.

We won the Super Bowl with the tackle trap – no one ever trapped the nose tackle before. That play took us to the Super Bowl when we used it against Oakland. We scored two touchdowns using it – the Brown 92-93.

Larry Brown, Steelers Offensive Lineman/Tight End, 1971-1984:

I played tight end according to their offensive design. Tight ends were essential in the running game. They wanted a tight end who could block but also catch passes, so my versatility was helpful.

In hindsight it worked out well – it extended my career. The year I switched I had a knee injury I was still recovering from. I wasn't able to due to the running and cutting you needed to do to play tight end. That was anticipated by Chuck.

We met in his office and he told me that because I couldn't run due to the injury he was going to have me learn the tackle position. That once I got healthy he'd move me back to tight end. In the meantime, before that, they drafted Bennie Cunningham and signed Randy Grossman. They saw themselves as being in a good position at tight end and had great need at tackle at the same time, so they never moved me back.

Then they traded away tackle Gordon Gravelle, so I stayed at the position for eight years and won two more Super Bowls!

I envisioned myself as a tight end before the move to tackle. At some point you have to decide that you have moved on though. I was used to playing with the ball – catching and running. So I guessed I missed it, yeah. But not to the point where it was difficult to overcome, and with my knee issues, it made things more manageable for me at tackle.

Dan Radakovich, Steelers DL & OL Coach, 1971, 1974-1977:

I changed it all year one. That was the year we became the Steel Curtain – those were my guys.

First, L.C. was just a backup – he spent two years on the bench. He could run like a deer – he lapped the entire team in practice. I started him at left end and moved Dwight to right end. I kept Joe Greene where he was – I wasn't crazy!

We traded Hinton to the Jets. We kept Holmes but he wasn't eligible to play – he was a great prospect but he was a taxi-squad player then. And I let McGee and Voss alternate at right tackle.

That was the year the radio announcer before the Miami game had a contest to name the new Steelers defense – that's how the Steel Curtain name came about – it was the winning name.

We had five centers on that team. Peterson, Webster, Clack, Kolb and Mansfield all played center. We'd screw around in practice and have our left tackle line up at center. It would drive Coach Perles crazy – he'd get so upset. We never did that in a game but you could – creating unbalanced lines would be terrific.

And why not? Moving them around and trying different things was something I always believed in. New ideas are usually tougher for the coaches than the players to accept.

They say keep it simple and I agree, but I also believe in doing as much as you can. You can do an infinite amount of stuff without confusing the human mind.

It's like coaches who use the huddle all the time in practice then expect audibles to work in the game. How do they get used to it if they never practice it? Speaking of which, Bradshaw audibled every running play versus Oakland in the playoffs. Dummy quarterback, huh?

I like to do it all. Some call it fraternity ball but it worked.

J.T. Thomas, Steelers Cornerback, 1973-1982:

Many of the great receivers after the rule change would never have made it then. Quarterbacks and receivers and defensive backs had a different psychology because receivers couldn't run across field without thoughts and fear; yet they still had 4.5 seconds to deliver and catch the ball. The five-yard rule took away the head game because before that a receiver never knew when you would hit him. Typically, you only got one shot at a good jam…we were just good at that one shot.

As you are aware that rule change was made using film of the Steel Curtain to justify the change.

Paul Uram, Steelers Conditioning and Special Teams Coach, 1973-1981:

Lots of the stuff I did was gymnastics oriented. I coached gymnastics for 15-20 years before and won three or four state championships. So, I did a lot of gymnastics work. I brought in a side horse and spring board in Pittsburgh and had them work on those. We had no space for a trampoline – I wanted to bring one in but there was no room there at Three Rivers for one. Chuck was all for all of it. I felt that I could have taught them more on the trampoline than anything – if you could control your body on a trampoline that would be the ultimate.

Randy Grossman, Steelers Tight End, 1974-1981:

Everything has changed and nothing is different. To win championships you've got to be the smartest and toughest team and have a little luck thrown in. You don't win championships by tricking teams. It's all about fundamental, tough execution.

The only part of the game that I find pretty ridiculous are the on field player celebrations for runs, catches, sacks, tackles, etc. I suppose we live in an era of self-promotion and inflated self-importance so that is reflected on the field.

Tom Beasley, Steelers Defensive Lineman, 1978-1983:

In the early and mid-70s there were no huge scouting combines like today. Chuck had a ten times more effective scouting department than other teams. Through that department he found guys like Lambert at Kent State that no one else did. How many teams even knew about Lambert?

He found lots of guys from smaller schools. Superior players gotten with lower picks found because of that scouting department. Those no-name players from small schools.

Ray Snell, Steelers Offensive Lineman, 1984-1985:

Last December, I was invited to Jimmy Giles Ring of Honor ceremony. I saw the nuances of today's athletes.

I was in awe of the training table, new meeting rooms, electronic gadgets, the playbooks that were now on iPads. Everything changed so much. The athletes today are a different breed now.

We helped build that. We had a shanty of a weight room and training room in Pittsburgh. Did we need more than that to be successful? I don't know if we would today or not, but today's athletes get the best of it all. We set the table for them, just like players in the past did for us. I'm just disappointed we didn't get more of that ourselves.

Delton Hall, Steelers Cornerback, 1987-1991:

I first thought the rules were the most ridiculous thing I ever heard. I was trained for years to be aggressive. Now they are taking away that aggressiveness from the game. Offensive players can lead with their helmet and do what they want. The defensive players were trained to go helmet to helmet.

Charles Bailey, Steelers Scout and Pro-Personnel Coordinator, 1989-1999:

The Steelers were unique. They had proven Super Bowl success. We were all on the same page with one vision and philosophy. All were set on that.

The draft was more important to us. We developed players through the draft. We were the model teams followed in the 90s. Everyone did a good job evaluating players. We had good battles and discussions on players and once they were drafted they were Steelers and we treated them that way.

We cared if he fit in the locker room more. His character and competitiveness. They had to be the top competitors – not just guys who played hard. Guys like Lloyd, Greene, Woodson, Lake, Chad Brown…they had to be the top competitors.

You watch the tape and see them perform. You don't worry as much about numbers. You see them on tape and see how hard they play. And you look into their backgrounds – talk to the people they know and interact with. It's not always the best player – he has to be the right player for the team.

We really emphasized character more. To me, the Steelers were a privilege and an honor to play for. We needed players who understood the team and wanted to be a Steeler. Character was important – and fans know when the players are not good kids.

Everyone in the personnel department had a lot of input on the selections. On draft day it was me, Tom Modrak, Tom Donohoe and Bill Cowher at the draft table.

The college scouts would come in and stay a couple of weeks before the draft. We aligned our board with the players they liked – from the highest graded to the lowest graded. We all gave opinions on the players. Then we set the board up on draft day. We put up the best two-to-three players we liked at every position and on draft day we tried to choose the best from those.

After those top two-to-three players were gone, we used our bigger list of all the remaining players, ranked from highest to lowest grade. As our picks came up in the mid to lower rounds, we'd call the scouts and ask them if they liked the top guys left at that pick again, just to be sure, and to check for any post-workout injuries or issues.

Some teams have to draft for need. But we were prepared to draft players that were highest graded players. We wouldn't pass up a higher-graded player for lower one at a need position. It's a mistake to bypass a better player.

So, it was always the best player available. Free agency always takes care of the need – that's why we sign players shortly before the draft. Just like when we signed Kevin Greene – that allowed us to draft Jason Gildon later and develop him.

Dan Vitchoff, Hypnotist That Works with Steelers:

Well, to take a step back, I some time ago patented the "Mind Gym" – I'm making one actually for Coach Tomlin. It's to help for the mental preparation for the game. It made its mark in the Olympics. It puts athletes in a zero gravity position so oxygen to the brain is increased. It puts the person in a trance-like state. That, with headphones and a light machine manipulates the brain so that when you are visualizing something – say kicking a field goal, it helps you gain confidence. Repeated visualization enhances that confidence.

What you visualize in that state is like having a dream – but the visualization is also actually physical so it's training your brain patterns.

The subconscious mind remembers. Athletes have to respond without thinking – if you react, your brain is slowing down. For example, when Ben leaves the pocket he's more instinctive – he's more effective. The brain is reacting to what it knows. We have an expression – those who know don't think – those who think don't know.

If an athlete is mentally prepared he's better. How does a player get in the "zone"? The Mind Gym technique shows them how to get in their zone where they perform on instinct.

Mentors:

One byproduct of the team's shift in strategy to improve through the draft was the team's new-found reliance on veteran players to help develop those younger players. Chuck Noll was brought in with an entirely different approach when Dan Rooney took over. He scouted for a new kind of player – adding extra emphasis on scouting only for players that gave their utmost effort – who wanted desperately to win. He did so almost exclusively through the draft - without quick fixes through trades. He felt that was the only to improve the team over the long ruin. That meant the only way the team was going to improve quickly was by getting the young talent ready faster. This required a greater dedication to coaching technique, and a greater emphasis on competiveness. And a greater need for veteran players to help preach – and teach - those principles to the draftees.

But, think about this. These are veteran players, many on the bubble of making the team – developing what were often their own replacements. Yet the desire to win was paramount. The players, almost to a man, bought in to the need. Because winning meant that much to them. Players who didn't buy in to this culture didn't last long. Unlike any other team of its time, a mentoring system informally developed, and the team as a whole took great strides in the 70s because the newly drafted players benefited from the tutelage of the veterans. They were also strongly influenced by the pressure of those veterans to give their best effort back to the team. These veteran players who wanted so desperately to turn the team into a winner were not going to allow anything but one hundred percent effort from the new players.

Furthermore, because of this mentoring culture, the internal level of completion at each position grew exponentially. Players worked harder to keep their jobs, improving the level of play at each position even further.

These mentorships grew into friendships – into relationships that made the players even closer.

In the end, the bonds created on the team between players, and with the organization, were so strong for many that they found leaving the sport was easier than leaving the people they meant while playing it – and the memories of their colleagues more precious than those of their on-field accomplishments.

Lou Michaels, Steelers Kicker and Defensive End, 1961-1963:

Ernie Stautner was a tough, solid player. He could play all day and never gave up. He couldn't stand to be blocked. He padded himself up all the time – he taught me to wear shin pads. He worked way above the other guys and stayed longer than he should have. Remember, there were no rotations then – no specialists to give players a rest.

Ernie was the oldest guy on the team. It took him two hours after a game to get undressed – he just wore himself out so much he could barely move. That's why he was a Hall of Famer. It took two guys to block him. He taught me the head slap too that he used that was so formidable. With him, desire was the word. Once you have that, you have it all.

Andy Russell, Steelers Linebacker, 1963-1976:

I learned how to "play hurt" from Ernie Stautner and how to refuse to be beaten by Joe Greene.

Ham and Lambert also helped me maintain my intensity and concentration as they were both very smart players.

Coach Noll taught us all, "Success is in the details," and he turned the whole program around and went on to win four out of six Super Bowls – just an amazing coach.

Ben McGee, Steelers Defensive Lineman, 1964-1972:

Ernie Stautner – the great defensive end retired the year I got there and was the defensive line coach. He worked with me real hard – on the sidelines I couldn't always hear what he was saying but I saw him yelling towards me when I was playing. When I got to the sidelines he always grabbed me and pushed me to do better.

He taught me a lot of technique – he showed me what he did – he stayed after practice with me and showed me how to use my hands and to come off the ball real quick and read the offense.

Bob Sherman, Steelers Cornerback, 1964-1965:

Dick Haley did more to help me than anybody. We got to know each other well – he was a nice person and genuinely good guy.

He helped show me how to read offenses – to see what's coming. He taught me to read the motion on offense to understand the play.

I also remember Bobby Layne in my second week of training camp, who retired the year before and was the quarterbacks coach. During that second week of training camp, Layne came up to me in scrimmage and shook me and said some things I can't repeat, but told me the "Old Man" (Parker) was giving me a shot with the starting unit. I had played well, and Layne was warning me to be prepared and to do my best.

I did well I think…I made the team!

Chuck Logan, Steelers Tight End, 1964:

I didn't have any mentors while in Pittsburgh. It seemed like nobody wanted to share anything. I had a couple of good friends on the team, Paul Martha, Jim Kelly, Bob Sherman, Ray Mansfield, and Bob Soleau.

Van Dyke: Ray Mansfield. He and I roomed together for seven years.

He taught me how to sneak out at night and drink beer! He showed me how to be a pro. His biggest help was in pass protection. Teams ran a 4-3 then and the tackle always lined up over the guard. Ray would be freed up to help us in pass protection and we'd always call out for help before plays.

Roy Jefferson, Steelers Wide Receiver, 1965-1969:

Bobby Layne was the quarterbacks coach then and he said "Roy, if you work hard, you could be a star in this league." I was impressed with that.

Brady Keys was responsible for me. He made me look at film of Paul Warfield and told me that "This is what you should incorporate into your style of running." He was hard on me – I worked out with him and was instrumental in my becoming a better wide receiver.

Rocky Bleier, Steelers Running Back, 1968-1980:

It's easier to become a mentor when you are a starter and secure in your position. As an older guy starting, you have a certain security. It was easier for me earlier on. But when you struggled to make the team and fought hard to be there, it's tough to give that up. You're still competitive. You got there and worked hard. You help the younger guys and encourage them, but you are still fighting for your job. You help answer questions and try to make the team better. But down deep, it was hard.

Dick Capp, Steelers Linebacker, 1968:

Rocky Bleier and Andy Russell taught me attitude and technique. There were some awesome vets and young players with great attitudes and maybe just not enough talent but plenty of heart. There were many others that impressed me, but there were enough with bad attitudes that needed to go.

L.C. Greenwood, Steelers Defensive Lineman, 1969-1981:

I was pretty much on my own. We all worked individually. Guys like Chuck Hinton and Ben McGee I hung out with – I guess they helped me because when I hung out with those older guys I watched them and learned something. There were a few of us rookie defensive linemen – me, Joe and some others that hung out with the older guys.

There were like twenty defensive linemen on the team at first – the Steelers brought in guys from other teams, from waivers… we all had great stories and learned from each other.

Jon Staggers, Steelers Wide Receiver, 1970-1971:

John Henderson took me under his wing – he had an influence on me. I was attracted to his sister for starters! So we all became friends. Sam Davis helped me as did Lee Calland.

Lee helped teach me to slow down. I was a coach's son – I wanted to do it all perfectly. Then I pulled my quad muscle and couldn't practice. My receivers coach would always joke that there were twelve or thirteen guys trying out for four spots. But I was injured – there was not much I could do.

Gordon Gravelle, Steelers Offensive Lineman, 1972-1976:

Franco and I were two weeks late to camp because we played in the Chicago All-Star game, and when we arrived I thought it would be hard to fit in and get to know my teammates. It was the opposite because both the offensive and defense players helped us get settled in.

There was an attitude of determination to improve as a team and we all knew we had to improve as individual players and help the other players improve their game. The most helpful were the veteran offensive linemen Ray Mansfield and Bruce Van Dyke. They really taught me how to be a professional football player and friend. Coach Noll was the best head coach I ever had the privilege to play under and he helped mentor me, even after practices he would work with me on my techniques.

The best position coach I ever had was Dan Radakovich. He came to the Steelers in my third year and I really improved under his tutelage.

J.T. Thomas, Steelers Cornerback, 1973-1982:

The guy I was replacing mentored me, strangely – John Rowser. He played for Green Bay before but had a bad knee and lost a step by the time the Steelers drafted me. The other guys were too young – Mel Blount, Wagner – they weren't talking to me much – they had their own jobs to secure.

John Rowser knew I was there to replace him but he schooled me about the game – he was so intelligent. Bud Carson once came over and said he heard that John taught me as much about the defense as Bud did! John taught me the things you could only learn from playing. He knew his days were numbered – that it was his last year but still schooled me on the game.

Reggie Harrison, Steelers Running Back, 1974-1977:

As a rookie I was chomping at the bit to play. I thought it was about ability. But Frenchy came back and he and I talked about it a lot. He definitely let me know that this was Franco's job. I needed to learn the halfback slot and wait for my opportunities.

Donnie Shell, Steelers Safety, 1974-1987:

My rookie year Sam Davis and Mel Blount mentored me. In the early seventies, there were no player development programs to assist you in coping with life in the NFL. The veteran Steelers players would take rookies under their wings and mentor them. This mentoring was done quietly behind the scenes, but I believe it was one on the main reasons we were successful as an organization. When the Steelers played a West Coast team, I had the privilege of speaking with Sam Davis for three hours about the nuances of the NFL.

Also as a high school and college athlete, I never had to sit on the bench. When I joined the Steelers, I sat on the bench and only got in the game on special teams, goal line defense and prevent defenses. I was becoming frustrated because I was not a starter. Mel Blount took me to dinner and let me know the team goal was to go to the Super Bowl and everyone had to do their job to accomplish this goal. He encouraged me that I was doing a great job and that my time would come to be a starter at my position. He made me recognize that no one individual was more important than the team and this advice came at a critical time in my career and gave me the right perspective.

Robin Cole, Steelers Linebacker, 1977-1988:

L.C. and Joe Greene helped me out. I picked things up for them. I watched Lambert and Ham and learned from them that way – they didn't say much to you.

L.C. took me under his wing and showed me the area around Pittsburgh. He started his own business and knew how to help me get started on a construction business for myself. He helped me become an entrepreneur. Back then you needed people to help you – you didn't make the money that players do today.

Players need to be exposed to good people so you didn't get taken advantage of. You see that happen with so many players who meet guys who just take their money.

Ted Petersen, Steelers Offensive Lineman, 1977-1983, 1987:

Jon Kolb – he was a veteran offensive tackle. And Larry Brown, Gerry Mullins, Webby, Davis – they were all great guys. They helped me in the teaching process on the field.

Off the field I'd try to keep up with Kolb and Webster and their training regimen. It was the dark ages then for strength and conditioning versus today. Kolb was light years ahead of the league. We'd go and work out at the gym in the Red Bull Inn because our gym was so poorly equipped – that was the status quo of the NFL at the time.

Mel Blount has always been like an older brother to me. Mel and I studied film nightly on the opposing team and their tendencies. I am going to take this opportunity to mention Mike Wagner. When we played teams like the Dallas Cowboys and they were constantly changing formations, Wagner always made the adjustments to our defense and put us on the same page.

Frank Pollard, Steelers Running Back, 1980-1988:

When I first started – my first couple of days – I almost got into a fight with Dennis Winston but I walked away. You weren't supposed to fight your teammates. Well, Lambert pulled me aside. He told me that "This wasn't the Cowboys. That the next time he saw me not fight back, he was going to kick my butt!"

That was a big help to me. Lambert was always one of my favorite players. He always had your back no matter what. I grew up watching him beat my Cowboys. I was in awe the first time I stepped on to campus and saw him and the rest of those guys. It made me want to give my best every day. It really helped me.

Calvin Sweeney, Steelers Wide Receiver, 1980-1987:

Bradshaw and I were really close. I broke my foot and had to have surgery. He lent me his car in camp to get around. My girlfriend was in Arlington, VA. He gave me his new Thunderbird to use to drive out and see her. Terry and I are still close today.

Stallworth was like my big brother – he took care of me. I'll tell you what – they were all the ultimate professionals. All of them were. I played behind Stallworth – on his side. We were always talking – how to get off jams and that sort of thing. He was poetry in motion.

It wasn't frustrating to be a backup. The respect and gentleman-ship of the guys made it ok. They were classy players. Swann, Stall-worth - they were great mentors. I enjoyed being around them.

Tunch Ilkin, Steelers Offensive Lineman, 1980-1992, Steelers Broadcaster:

Kolb, Webster, Brown...they were so quick to share their work ethic with me – how to be a good offensive lineman. Me and Craig Wolfley were like baby ducks – we followed them around everywhere. I saw them work harder and figured that if I do what they do, I could at least be half as good.

They taught us to be good players and good fathers and hus-bands and men – men of God. I grew up Muslim. Through their lives I met Christ and am eternally grateful.

I just wanted to be the best player I could be. I had great men-tors. The organization is a great environment for a young play-er if you are willing to listen and emulate the guys in front of you, and I followed those guys around.

You have good days and bad days but over time you figure it out. I was drafted as a center but I knew with Webster there I'd never play. So I volunteered for everything – every line spot and special teams – to get on the field. Eventually you catch the coaches' eyes and get an opportunity to produce.

Keith Willis, Steelers Defensive Lineman, 1982-1991:

My lockermate Larry Brown schooled me up a lot. Especially in my interview process. I had some good success early as a player and Larry would listen to me do interviews. He said I had to learn to tell them a lot but don't tell them nothing. That was im-portant to hear as I handled the media.

Sam Washington, Steelers Cornerback, 1982-1985:

Greenwood called me "His rookie," No one messed with me because of L.C. I have no idea why he gravitated to me – it just happened and I was thankful for it.

Blount was the guy who taught me the dos and don'ts on corner play. I sat next to him in meetings and he pointed out things on film and on the field for me. He'd ask me why I did the things I did and suggested other ways.

He also helped on man-to-man coverage. When to turn, how to speed turn, transition turns, transition turns, and beating receivers to the reception area was talked about a lot.

Bam Morris, Steelers Running Back, 1984-1985:

John L. Williams was my mentor my rookie year. My rookie year was difficult adjusting and I had a particular game that I kept fumbling which was unusual for me. John took me aside and told me, "Block out the crowd, stop beating yourself up for it, move forward and let's win the game."

Preston Gothard, Steelers Tight End, 1985-1988:

Once I got there it was kind of interesting. I was the last guy signed on the team so Tony Parisi [equipment manager] put me in the last locker – the corner locker. No one wanted the corner locker. It was between Webster, Shell, and Stallworth and all of their Rogaine and vitamins were in there!

I was shoehorned in with those guys and it was great. They were able to explain the rigors of the day-to-day life of pro football. I couldn't get better advice.

I'd watch their rituals – how they went about meetings and learning the playbook. I realized real quick it was a business. I kept my mouth shut and emulated what they did. It was invaluable information to have.

John Rienstra, Steelers Offensive Lineman, 1986-1990:

Mike Webster, Craig Wolfley, and Tunch Ilkin all helped me. I was playing guard – which was Craig's position – but he still helped me.

Being friends as well as co-workers – seeing them talk and share their mistakes made me feel more comfortable – as part of the team. That was real important to me.

As a rookie there are lots of things going on. It's a fast, hard, humbling game. The veterans taught me that.

Merril Hoge, Steelers Running Back, 1987-1994; ESPN Broadcaster:

Bubby Brister – I loved his confidence. He was as confident as any player I've ever seen. He always used to tell me that if they didn't want me, thirty-one other teams would. That's how he talked and played. Now he was in a different position than I was, but he was still a backup – though probably better than the starter and ended up starting the next season.

He didn't shy away from anything and that helped me. You have to trust and believe in what you have.

Tim Johnson, Steelers Defensive Lineman, 1987-1989:

Coach Joe Green and Donnie Shell, were a Godsend to me as mentors by helping me to mentally adjust to the level I needed to be in handling my opportunity as a football player but also understanding the business of the NFL.

Donnie Shell, Mike Webster, Edmond Nelson, Tunch Ilkin, Craig Wolfley, John Stallworth, Mark Malone, and Robin Cole. These guys didn't have to assert their leadership as much as they were examples of leadership and their presence in the locker room made a difference amongst us young players.

Brian Blankenship, Steelers offensive Lineman, 1987-1991:

In my rookie year in my first practice at training camp, the Oklahoma drill was a defining moment. I went up against a guy named Duey Forte, 6'5"and 325 pounds and the strongest guy in camp. The whistle blew and I put him on his back. Mike Webster came over to me and said "I don't know who you are or where you came from, but you keep that up you will play somewhere."

That was all I needed to hear. Those who are truly good at their craft are comfortable enough to help younger guys improve because they appreciate the game that much and want to see perfection no matter where or how it is achieved.

Hardy Nickerson, Steelers Linebacker, 1987-1992:

I had Donnie Shell helping me and my locker was right next to John Stallworth's. Merriweather, Little, and Robin Cole were also a huge help.

It was unusual. Guys all playing for the same position and competing with one another but still helping one another out. Those kinds of relationships don't usually happen. They took me under their wing and that carried me for sixteen years.

Lorenzo Freeman, Steelers Defensive Lineman, 1987-1990:

When I first got there Webster was still there – he was up there in age. I thought as a bigger, young kid, I gotta be able to take him off the ball. He knew all the techniques to be a finesses player though and showed me up in practice and frustrated me. He had that swagger after the play, walking back to the huddle.

John Jackson, Steelers Offensive Lineman, 1988-1997:

Craig Wolfley and Tunch Ilkin. I looked up to those guys. They taught me a lot on and off the field. I was one of the biggest lineman they had. Most of the guys were six foot, three inches and I was six foot, six inches – I stood out like a sore thumb.

They taught me how to watch film and understand the game – what to look for in other players. As a rookie, that's big. Developing players through older players – other teams don't take that as a badge of honor like the Steelers do. Passing on to others what we learned was so important to us – to give back to the players and organization. Other teams simply didn't do that as much.

Dermontti Dawson, Steelers Center, 1988-2000:

Mike Webster was a huge influence on my career by the way he conducted himself on and off the field. He led by example in the classroom, weight room, practice, and games. He taught me how to lead by example, by me emulating his actions during my years with Pittsburgh.

Terry O'Shea, Steelers Tight End, 1989-1990:

Easily, Mularkey helped me the most. He was the perfect guy for me. A young guy making more money than he ever could before – your ego can go out of place. He was always considerate – you could say he was a mentor and a gentleman. He was a veteran with no ego and knew how to practice sand play. There are a lot of things he did off the field that I still carry with me today.

I also had the locker next to Tunch Ilkin. He was a one hundred percent quality individual. You didn't have to go to dinner with him – you could just watch how he lived and learn from it. What do they say – you live the gospel every day and preach it only when necessary. That was Tunch.

Craig Veasey, Steelers Defensive Lineman, 1990-1992:

Joe Greene – you always trusted him. He had done it, so when he told you to do something you didn't question it. You knew it could be done because he did it.

Joe taught you toughness too. There are no whiners around Joe – that's the bottom line. I remember he always had a saying – "Are you hurt or are you injured? You can play hurt, but you can't play injured." He taught you to be tough and pushed you mentally. You needed to be mentally tough as a defensive lineman – it's the hardest position I think in football.

Dan Stryzinski, Steelers Punter, 1990-1991:

Gary Anderson. He had such a great work ethic and showed me how to deal with the mental aspect of the game that many don't understand. He showed me how to deal with the pressure. It's different from college – you're still playing football but you're making a living too now, and that makes it different.

LeRoy Thompson, Steelers Running Back, 1991-1993:

I would say Warren Williams helped me the most. He was actually my host coming out of High School on my recruiting trip to the University of Miami so I knew him. He just help me prepare for the mental part of the game which was much more taxing than the physical part because you had to learn so many plays and formations. He also invited me over to his house often to play cards and eat and just relax after a taxing day at practice.

Ariel Solomon, Steelers Offensive Lineman, 1991-1995:

I was fortunate to join a team with a great group of leaders and an offensive line that immediately took me in. Tunch Ilkin was a fantastic player and a great mentor to me. He worked with me on techniques almost every day, showed me how to study film and evaluate the strengths and weaknesses of each opponent.

As I mentioned so many of the lineman at that time were exceptional players and people and they all helped me in their own way. I learned to play center from Dermontti Dawson, guard from Carlton Haselrig and Duval Love. It was hard not to improve with that group of mentors.

Dermontti Dawson showed me how to be as a person. Maybe they all didn't know it, but I followed their examples.

Levon Kirkland, Steelers Linebacker, 1992-2000:

One of the players who mentored me was Jerry Olsavsky, I was new to the position – I was an outside linebacker in college. I wasn't familiar with the inside linebacker position and it was an adjustment. The speed of the game and how mentally and physically tough NFL players are. Plus, I was thrust into the leadership role, having to call signals. Jerry slowed the game down for me and gave me advice on who to follow and how to read other teams' players.

Jerry and I had a ball on special teams. By my second year I caught on to things more. Kevin Green and Greg Lloyd were also helpful – instrumental on showing me how to play the game. They set the standards for all of us and if we didn't play at that level, they let us know.

Leon Searcy, Steelers Offensive Lineman, 1992-1995:

I learned on the fly. I didn't want anyone to disrupt my game. I came from the University of Miami – we won three championships and lost four game in four years when I was there. I didn't want anyone to take away my edge and tell me how to approach the game – I came from a winning program. I wanted my own swagger.

I would get myself in trouble though sometimes – maybe I was too arrogant. I think the only reason I didn't start was because I held out. My agent said Pittsburgh was notorious for underpaying players. The agent said I needed to hold out to make a statement, so I missed training camp and was behind everyone else. The newspapers said I was a bust that rookie season – it was a tough first year. I thought they intentionally didn't want to play me – to teach me a lesson. It all rubbed me the wrong way.

I remember one day after practice – we'd run gasses for conditioning. I was in tip-top shape and was outrunning the other offensive linemen – except maybe Dermontti Dawson. All the vets were pissed off that I was showing them up. They came into the locker room and told me I needed to stop outshining them. Cowher would get on them…

So, the next day they run gasses, but I just stand there for a good five seconds. Cowher came up to me and asked what I was doing. I told him I was giving them a good five lead but I'd still pass them up, and I did. Cowher just smiled – I think he knew I practiced my ass off and he liked that about me. But that's how I reacted to things – I didn't react to things very well sometimes and that rubbed others the wrong way.

Chad Brown, Steelers Linebacker, 1993-1996, 2006:

I was in the locker room with truly great players. Woodson was two lockers down from me. Lloyd, Greene, Kirkland…I didn't have to look far for leadership.

My wife was friends with a lot of the other wives. Once, Carnell Lake and his wife invited us to dinner. Carnell took me on a quick tour of his house and showed me his twelve thousand dollar treadmill. He had it in his den, so he couldn't miss it. It would call his name every day.

To have that, rain or shine was a huge thing to me – to stay in shape no matter what. If it was that important to Carnell Lake it should be to me too. I said, "Note to self – I'm going to buy that same treadmill."

I used all my incentive money to by myself that treadmill. That little thing was a big lesson to me.

Willie Williams, Steelers Cornerback, 1993-1996, 2004-2005:

Dick LeBeau mentored me my first couple of years as my defensive backs coach before he became the defensive coordinator. Coach LeBeau taught me how to play with confidence, something that I was lacking a little my first two years as a pro.

There were quite a few players that took me under their wing: Rod Woodson, Greg Lloyd, Carnell Lake, and Darren Perry. This group of guys taught me how to approach the game and how to perform as a professional. For example, they taught me how to watch film on our opponents, they mentored me on how to approach the off-season workouts and most importantly, they taught me how to play the game mentally.

Craig Keith, Steelers Tight End, 1993-1994:

One of the things people don't know about Eric Green is how intelligent he was as a football player. He was physically imposing. But he showed me how to read defenses and react to defenses. I couldn't do what he did physically, but I could do so mentally. I give him a lot of credit. He could have not helped me, but he did – a ton. He was just a good guy. He and I built a rapport.

Brentson Buckner, Steelers Defensive Lineman, 1994-1996:

I didn't feel much pressure. I came in with a great group. Levon Kirkland was my college teammate – he was there and had experience I could lean on.

Lloyd would come up to me too and would tell me not to pay attention to some of the early articles about me that said I wasn't playing well. He told me I was a second round pick and had the talent and to just have confidence in the Steelers picking me in the second round.

I was playing next to a future Hall of Famer in Kevin Greene. I just needed to go in and become a piece of the puzzle. There were a great group of guys around me – I just needed to do my part.

Eric Green took me in. He could tell I was getting frustrated as a second-round pick that wasn't playing. He told me to make them play you – to show them by the way I worked. He and I practiced together thirty minutes before every practice every day. He told me to trust in myself – that they'd see my extra work.

Eric told me that you could never rest – that you can't think you have arrived – you have to get better every day. People thought he was cocky and wanted him to fail – but that they didn't see all the hard work he put in.

Tim Lester, Steelers Fullback, 1995-1998:

That first year I was a backup to John L. Williams. I learned a lot from John L. Williams by watching his every move on the field. I got most of my work in practice going against Levon, Greg, Kevin, and Chad. Every practice was like a game. They would always tell me to slow down but after being cut by the Rams I had a lot to prove so I never changed my approach to practice.

They were all millionaires. I was trying to get on the active roster. I was on a mission to seek and destroy and make millions like them.

That year I also learned how to cover kicks and play special teams. I scored my first touchdown that year against Green Bay. I also remember running down on kickoffs knocking people out who were trying to block me in the wedge. I loved the fact that Coach Cowher would make highlights of each game to let the rest of the team know what we were doing on special teams.

Erric Pegram, Steelers Running Back, 1995-1997:

There were so many players who inspired me: Dermontti Dawson because he was so up-beat even when we were struggling; Yancey Thigpen, best hands on the team and for stealing my running shoes and giving me athletes feet' Kordell Stewart and me taking him under my wing; Charles Johnson who was so cool as a person and a hell of a competitor; Ernie Mills' Smile, Fast Freddie McAfee and our endless joking on one another; Gregg Lloyd, one mean SOB and I enjoyed watching him work; Kevin Green's long hair and his relentless off-the-corner-rush, the preacher; Levon Kirkland "the run stopper"; and Big Play Ray Seals, giving his all even with a torn rotator cuff. It's those things that make the trip worthwhile and I love them all.

Oliver Gibson, Steelers Defensive Lineman, 1995-1998:

Brentson Buckner was my biggest influence. Don't get me wrong, he was one year older and we were competitive, but he was probably the smartest player I ever played with. Instead of just learning the front seven, he learned all about the other guys too. He changed the way I learned the game. I learned the secondary coverage and linebacker responsibilities too, because of him.

Steve Conley, Steelers Linebacker, 1996-1998:

I was drafted in addition with two other linebackers…Earl Holmes and Carlos Emmons. Being that it was three of us, we stuck together. The one player that helped me out was Levon Kirkland. At that time, we had one thing in common; we both loved the WWF, now called WWE. We would go to live events at the stadium, order pay-per-view events etc., but on the field, Levon was the General, and he put everybody in order.

I remember the first time I played in a regular season game against Jacksonville. He looked me in my eyes and said, "Ok rookie, let's go make a play." I took that to heart and would have sacked Mark Brunell if he wouldn't have run out of bounds.

My first year at Pittsburgh was great!

Earl Holmes, Steelers Linebacker, 1996-2001:

Greg Lloyd helped me – he was the quiet storm. He was a mean guy but a great guy. He and Kirkland both helped me. They both said things to me to help me. Greg – I actually met him at the All-America banquet before the draft. He said he watched me play – I thought, you have to be kidding. He watched me play? He then told me that he thought I had something and that I shouldn't be surprised if I became a Steeler. I appreciated it but thought he was just being nice. Who knew!

Lloyd told me the easiest part was getting drafted. I thought, you're kidding me, right? He said the hardest thing is staying here. It was time to become a professional.

I watched him, Gildon, Kirkland…no one was lazy. The lazy guys don't last long. I wanted longevity so I watched what they did. I learned the defense and worked hard.

I commend the guys that taught me. I started my rookie year versus Carolina. That whole week of practice, the coaches told me to settle down. Playing alongside Lloyd, Woodson, Kirkland, Lake…those veterans helped me to settle down and play.

Carlos Emmons, Steelers Linebacker, 1996-1999:

Lloyd and Kirkland helped us on the field. They could have said "why did they take all of these linebackers" but they didn't worry about it like they do on some other teams. They had confidence in their ability and helped us instead of worrying about their jobs.

Greg stayed with us after practice to help teach us technique a number of times.

Richard Huntley, Steelers Running Back, 1998-2000:

No one really helped mentor me on the field – we all just worked together and learned from each other. I never liked Jerome – and he didn't like me. He wrote about me and faking his injury because of me in his book which was BS. I threatened Jerome – I could do things that he couldn't and he didn't like that. So he and I, we never got along.

For off the field, when I left Atlanta, I saw the different things people were doing outside of football. What guys were doing in there break time. I looked around. I did the same thing in Pittsburgh – saw what players were doing in their down time. They'd play games, read books and newspapers so I started talking to Dermontti Dawson and Mike Tomczak. They were ready to leave the game and we talked about what they were going to do after football. The young guys don't think about that. I talked to Dermontti a lot about that – I wanted to be in their situation financially and emotionally. I didn't want to fall into it all being just about football.

Jeremy Staat, Steelers Defensive Lineman, 1998-2000:

Nolan Harrison sat down with me and told me to chill out. That it wasn't just a game, it was a business. He said you have to understand it's a business. That never dawned on me. I just wanted to play.

Nolan helped me with my immaturity – the game was something more than I knew.

Jim Sweeney, Steelers Offensive Lineman, 1996-1999:

As an older player, it was my duty, honor and privilege to mentor the younger players. It was and always will be about the team and what is best for the team. If it cost me a position on the roster, so be it. That is the nature of the game. Plus, when I was a rookie, the elder statesman of the offensive line for the New York Jets, Joe Fields, took me under his wing. It was my turn to pay back and pass on the tradition.

Jerame Tuman, Steelers Tight End, 1999-2007:

I don't think you can find a better person to try to emulate on and off the field than Mark Bruener. He is a role model in every sense of the word. Off the field he was the nicest guy you would ever meet. On the field he was a warrior! I cannot say enough good things about Mark and what he has done for me as a person and as a football player.

Chris Combs, Steelers Defensive Lineman, 2000-2001:

I remember Aaron Smith inviting me out to lunch during a mini-camp one afternoon in the spring of 2000. Aaron was very down-to-earth and I really got to see him develop and grow into the truly outstanding pro football player he's become.

I also remember eating Thanksgiving dinner at Kevin Henry's house my rookie year. Kevin treated me very well as long as I had his breakfast delivered to him every Saturday morning during the season. Kimo Von Oelhoffen was very friendly and generous with his football knowledge he used to stay after practice with me and help me with techniques.

Chris Sullivan was very quiet but an intelligent guy who had been successful with New England and he had a knack for pointing out things on film that were helpful. Jeremy Staat took me bird hunting once. Our team chaplain Jay Wilson was instrumental in my spiritual growth and development off-the-field.

Hank Poteat, Steelers Cornerback, 2000-2002:

Dewayne Washington and Chad Scott helped me. I sat next to Dewayne in meetings. He would teach me how to dress – to look professional. He even had his tailor make me a suit for away games. I'd go in boots and khakis and he taught me how to look like a professional.

Chad Scott taught me work ethic. He was more of a student of the game – he showed me you have to outwork the competition. I remembered that as I got older. I wish I had listened more when I was younger.

Jeff Hartings, Steelers Center, 2001-2006:

I just wanted to stay focused on what I was doing and I didn't worry about others on the team. I didn't compare myself to others. I just wanted to do the best job I could and play the best I could. If I wasn't good enough, well my career is over then. That's up to me.

I definitely feel like some players don't help others – especially the younger guys who were insecure about their jobs. Detroit was the same as Pittsburgh in terms of players helping one another. It's an individual thing, not a team or culture thing.

Pittsburgh had the better focus on winning and the overall culture of professionalism – in the community and on the field. In Detroit it was more about personal success and money then about winning.

Michael Jones, Steelers Linebacker, 2001-2002:

It was never difficult playing the role of mentor to the young guys. All of them, Joey, Kendrell Bell, Clark Haggans wanted to win and play at the highest level. We had a great group of linebackers. The group was in transition, Jason and Earl were transitioning to more a leadership roles and the young guys were excited about taking their game to next level. With a group like that, subtle things were all they needed. With Kendrell, he sat next to me his entire rookie season. It was exciting watching him develop.

Antwaan Randle El, Steelers Wide Receiver, 2002-2005, 2010:

Hines helped me on the field. You just watched what he did and followed it. Terrance Mathis too – the way he ran routes – he was so precise.

Hines talked to me – told me to stay focused and showed me how to gain the trust of the quarterback. That if I ran the wrong route the quarterback wouldn't trust me next time, so I had to get that right. He also showed me how to use the chicken wing to get open without the referee seeing it. He showed me that I needed to knock the defender out before they knocked me out. "We block out here," he used to tell me!

Charlie Batch, Steelers Quarterback, 2002-2012:

I sat next to Ben nine out of ten years in the meeting rooms. We had conversations on the struggles we faced and just in getting to the NFL. Remember, I played at Eastern Michigan and he played at Miami of Ohio – we knew how hard it was just to get to the NFL from that conference – we knew how special it was for both of us to be sitting in the same room together in the NFL

He had so much success early on – going to the Super Bowl in his second year. But we ran the ball heavily – over fifty-percent. People talked a lot about that and he wanted to be thought of as an elite quarterback. So he worked extra hard to understand the playbook and be an elite quarterback. He put in a lot of hard work to make it to those three Super Bowls.

It was a commitment that worked back and forth between us. We supported each other. We trusted each other – that unfolds back and forth. Seeing him grow up – from a twenty-two year-old to a thirty year-old…it's amazing to think about it.

My role was as a backup – that's why I was brought on the team and I embraced it. I knew my role ahead of time. I knew what the team was thinking when they made an offer and I decided to accept that role. The team needs to make it clear what your role is as a player. That's how they build that trust. And Pittsburgh did a great job of teaching players their roles on the team

Kendall Simmons, Steelers Offensive Lineman, 2002-2008:

Marvel Smith, Alan Faneca, and Jeff Hartings all contributed to my growth while I was in Pittsburgh. Marvel Smith is like my brother off the field. Alan Faneca's knowledge of the game and his physical approach is something I have always admired. I watched him closely and asked a lot of questions.

I owe Jeff Hartings a special thanks for letting me lean on him when it came to blocking assignments my rookie year. Hartings also taught me how to relax on the field.

Chris Doering, Steelers Wide Receiver, 2003-2004:

I was an older player but not highly sought after in free agency. I didn't expect to be signed – when I did I ended up staying in the Allegheny Center in the offseason to work out. I met the guys and became friends with them gradually. I became friends with Tuman, and Jeff Reed and Gardocki – some of the more established guys.

The cool part was being in the wide receivers room, playing with Ward, Burrress and Randel-El. It was such a good group of receivers. I knew Hines from our SEC days. I gradually got acclimated and earned their respect. It was a cool group of special people. The friends I made – I think of it fondly. Unlike other places, we all spent time together after the games.

Plex kept to himself – he was stand-offish at first. My first year, in 2003, we had a different wide receiver coach. In 2004, Arians came in as the receivers coach. He approached me – he wanted me to be his go-between between him and the other guys because I was a veteran guy. It was funny – I was the only white guy in the room! I really enjoyed going out with those guys to the Black clubs and hanging out. That's why the NFL is so great – it's a chance to meet people and get a different experience.

Plex was misunderstood due to his shyness, I think. He seems to have grown up more and endeared himself more to fans. When you have something taken away from you as he did football, you appreciate it more. I know that feeling myself after being out of football for a year due to injury.

Hines – there was not a guy that knew the game as well as Hines. I was older than those guys but learned so much from them. Hines knew all the positions – he played them all. He loved to play – blocking to catching, he was easy to follow. He was always smiling. That's what fans like about him – he's not one of those spoiled players.

Barrett Brooks, Steelers Offensive Lineman, 2003-2006:

I was still a competitor. I wanted to play. But I also understood my role. I was long in the tooth – that was my ninth year in the league. And they clearly defined my role before they signed me. They understood I wanted to play but wanted me to mentor the younger guys. Colon, Max (Starks), Trai Essex, Kemoeatu...my job was to keep those guys out of trouble. To keep the coaches from having to focus too much on them.

Matt Kranchick, Steelers Tight End, 2004-2006:

I learned a lot from the tight end room. Tuman, Risermsma, Cushing and Rasby. They were all professional athletes who knew how to present themselves on and off the field. They coached me on money investments, business, and networking opportunities as a Steeler. I didn't see eye-to-eye all the time with everyone due to the competitiveness of the business, but I couldn't have asked for better examples of how to be a man and a Pro.

For example, at my first training camp at St. Vincent, I was unsure of the play. I asked Jay Rimersma what my assignment was, and he told me and I executed it. Unfortunately, I was set up and the Sam ran free and blew up the whole play and I got crushed by Cowher. I don't know if Rimersma's actions were intentional, but I learned a valuable lesson: my teammates were also my competition. If you want to take someone's job you have to earn it and you do that by knowing your stuff, not relying on someone else.

Travis Kirschke, Steelers Defensive Lineman, 2004-2009:

That's definitely an interesting dynamic to work through – teaching someone the traits of the game so one day they can take your job. That's definitely one way to view it.

I definitely struggled with those thoughts in my mind but I would always try to focus on the bigger picture, bigger than my own successes and in turn try to focus on the team and tasks at hand. By focusing on the team it made it easy to want to share knowledge because it would benefit everyone.

Unselfishness is one of the key elements that I felt Pittsburgh had that allows them to compete at the level in which they continue to do. I believe it has always been a major factor to the Super Bowl years. Coach Tomlin would always say when the team succeeds then there will be enough for the whole team to eat. Meaning, everyone will benefit.

Shaun Nua, Steelers Defensive Lineman, 2005-2007:

I was very fortunate to get drafted to not only a great team but also a team that had people like Keisel and Hoke whom were both from BYU. The veteran leadership on that team especially on the defensive side was excellent.

Kimo, Aaron Smith, Hoke and Keisel did a great job helping the young guys learn techniques and learn the playbook fast. You would think that veterans would not help younger players because they could lose their job to them but that was not the case at all—these men were true professionals and great mentors. They were always willing to stay after practice to answer any questions the younger players had. Off the field, Troy was always a person I'd go talk to if I needed to talk to someone about life in general.

I'll never forget when Chris Kemoeatu and I first came for rookie camp after the draft and Kimo Von Oelhoffen noticed that we were trying to rent a car and he offered his wife's car for us to use. I will always be grateful to brada Kimo for that. Both Chris and I didn't have money yet so Troy took us grocery shopping and filled up our kitchen with food. We told Troy that we didn't know how to repay him, and I'll never forget his response. He said, we could pay him back by doing the same to a rookie next year when they needed help. These are few examples of how great the culture is in Pittsburgh.

Trai Essex, Steelers Offensive Lineman, 2005-2011

Max [Starks] was a huge help – he took me under his wing. Alan Faneca and Marvel Smith – there were Pro Bowlers – I was nervous talking to them. I was intimidated at first. But they had a standard – there was no such thing as a rookie once you're on the team. You just had a job to do. That resonated with me and was the case for every offensive lineman since. There were no airs on the room – you needed to live up to the greats that were there before you. They helped show me that path and helped me maintain it. And Max was the biggest help – he showed me what he learned the year before.

Noah Herron, Steelers Running Back, 2005:

I would say that Jerome was the one who really took a liking to me. We had some similarities that allowed us to find some common ground and build upon that (both being from Michigan and me being a big and him a bigger back with quick feet). He just told me straight up that he had been in this league a long time and he had the knowledge of how to navigate it, all I had to do was listen. So I listened.

Whether you are mentor or mentee, someone is always trying to take your job. That's part of the realities and parodies of the NFL. Getting fifty-three guys competing for the same jobs and still becoming a selfless team or teammate...it is one of the reasons it makes football such a unique sport. You hope your play is good enough to keep your job while at the same time doing like Jerome did, and investing the knowledge he had into me to help me be successful. And I did appreciate it because I have seen it where nobody will help anybody to try to secure their own jobs.

Scott Paxson, Steelers Defensive Lineman, 2006-2010:

My locker was close to Aaron Smith's. With Aaron I learned more about life. I was a single bachelor while with the Steelers and he kept me grounded. Made sure I didn't over indulge with the social life outside football. He helped me see what is most important in life, family, and faith. He doesn't know it, but I watched hours of practice film and game film on him, on hopes to play more like him. He may be the reason I become a Republican too! Truly someone I looked up to on and off the field.

Then there was a guy out of the locker room. A guy that didn't care if you were the first round pick or an undrafted free agent. A guy that was always there to make you laugh, invite you to a Penguins game, invite you out to eat, invite you over to the house to eat and play video games. A guy that made sure other people enjoyed themselves more than himself. And that guy is Jeff Reed!

Jared Retkofsky, Steelers Long Snapper, 2007-2009:

There were a number of players that really helped me make it through. I was given the ability to snap after Greg Warren tore his ACL. Greg was the first person to call me when he was injured, followed by Bob Ligashesky. Greg was always available to help me with technique when I needed it. I had two veteran kickers Mitch Berger, and Jeff Reed who were patient and good enough to deal with some errant snaps. Greg, Jeff, and Mitch were helpful in my development on the field and treated me as a family member off the field.

Martin Nance, Steelers Wide Receivers, 2008-2009:

Heath Miller. He made me feel welcome from day one. He's such a high character guy and he and his wife were great supports for my wife and I as we adjusted to the city. I can't say enough about the respect I have for Heath.

Keiwan Ratliff, Steelers Cornerback, 2009:

The first person on the team I met was Charlie Batch. He made everything easy for me. He took on a leader role on the team by having gatherings, parties, and different functions so that the older guys and new guys would get to know each other. The player who helped me on the field the most was Deshea Townsend. Shea sat next to me in meetings and being that we had similar roles on the defense he went over the play book and film study with me. Shea no doubt went above and beyond to help me learn the 3-4 defense.

Sometimes it is About the Money, Sometimes it's Not

Player motivation can be a nuanced thing. To say players are driven by the paycheck is certainly accurate. But incomplete. Most of the players in the 50s and 60s needed second jobs just to make due. Clearly the pay was not the only factor. Even today's players aren't guaranteed paychecks, outside of signing bonuses, or long careers. Every player is one injury away from a new career. And for every star, there are dozens struggling just to make a roster.

The comradery – the bonds between players – that often provided a greater motivation than the pay. Those bonds were forged through shared experiences – on the field and off. Religion was a key component of those experiences – an underpinning that kept many grounded. It also gave players a much needed outlet for the negative aspects of the game – the stress, conflict, physicality. One they could count on and relate to as a team, even as individuals, their place on the team and their livelihoods felt at risk.

The Business Side of the Game:

For all of the talk of the Steelers being a family-oriented culture, reality sets in when you are trying to earn as much as you can in an often short NFL career. The average player lasts three and a half years in the NFL. They have a short window to earn as much as possible before their careers end, and they did so through agents and, in the 60s when agents weren't in the picture as much as they are today. Especially in the 60s actually, when players were paid much less and usually had to take second jobs in the offseason to make ends meet.

Not that the team culture didn't factor in. It often helped the team sign players for less than if they'd have signed elsewhere.

But the business issues went both ways. Free agency set in, as did the salary cap. That changed the dynamics between players and teams – drastically. Make no mistake – players ultimately are at the mercy of their employers. Job security, being traded, being benched – these were hazards every player worried about. Even highly-regarded veterans got waived, got traded. And the impact can be devastating emotionally, and to their families.

While we see players as overpaid, sometimes spoiled people who are mercenaries for their sport, in truth they are family men, looking for stability for themselves and their families. And ok, sometimes sure, maybe a bit overpaid.

But for those that left for greener pastures in free agency, and for others that were traded away, one thing remained a constant: The players missed the Steelers, and realized that the additional monies earned often paled to the ability to play with teammates that acted like brothers, and for an organization that cared for them like family.

Dale Dodrill, Steelers Defensive Tackle, 1951-1959:

I wasn't aware that I was drafted. No one contacted me. I didn't know much about the NFL then. My dad used to ask me when I was going to get a real job when I first started playing in the NFL. I found out later I was drafted when I got a letter and contract in the mail. I was never contacted personally.

I wanted to be traded in my last year there. I told Buddy Parker that I knew I didn't fit into his plans. I asked Art first but he said he had no control over those things anymore. Buddy said he'd ask around to see if anyone wanted to trade for me, but he told me that no one had any interest. I knew that wasn't true because I knew one coach at least had told me he wanted me. So, I knew he lied. All coaches want their type of player I guess.

If I had played another year in Pittsburgh that would have been when the expansion draft happened and that was Dallas. I would have probably had to go to Dallas, and I couldn't tolerate that heat and humidity. So it was a good time to hang them up. That's when the Broncos coach called me to coach their defense. At first I said no, but when he called me again I decided to do it.

Dodrill shows his charge off of the line of scrimmage.
Photo courtesy of Dale Dodrill

Lou Tepe, Steelers Linebacker, 1953-1955:

Pittsburgh was not my favorite city. When I left I had a lot of bitterness in my mouth. I thought it was the worst franchise in the NFL. I had a friend who wanted me to play in Canada during my time in Pittsburgh. Pittsburgh signed me to a five thousand dollar bonus when I signed with them. But my friend convinced me I should try my hand in Canada with the Toronto Argonauts. They signed me for $8,500 – which was all the money in the world to me then. But I learned from an article in the New York Times that Toronto terminated the contract. Fran Fogarty of the Steelers called the coach in Toronto – who I didn't realize played in Pittsburgh years before – and told him he didn't like the fact that they were picking up our guys. So he said okay to Fran. Needless to say my return to Pittsburgh wasn't pleasant. My experience there wasn't good.

"Red" Mack, Steelers Wide Receiver, 1961-1963, 1965:

In Notre Dame there were no athletic dorms – we stayed with the other students. And no phones in our rooms. At both ends of each hall were payphones. Well, when I was drafted, a guy came down from the end of the hall and told me I had a phone call. It was Fran Fogerty of the Steelers. He was the one that told me I was drafted and told me I should come in to sign my contract.

Well, I go in and they only offer me ten thousand dollars. I asked for twelve thousand dollars and he said no, so I wouldn't sign. I called my high school coach and asked him what I should do. He said to tell them I wanted to talk to Mr. Rooney.

So I go back and ask to speak to Mr. Rooney. He came in and said "I hear we have a problem." I told him I wanted twelve thousand dollars. He looked at me and said "Give it to him." I asked him then for a one thousan dollars bonus because my grandmother needed a new refrigerator. He gave that to me too.

My high school coach told me not to take crap from anyone. He said that I shouldn't tell myself I'm not good enough – let the coaches do that. So, that's what I did.

Dick Hoak, Steelers Running Back 1961-1970, Steelers Coach 1972-2007:

At Penn State I played quarterback, running back and defensive back. Back then you played both ways in college. Because of that I think I studied the game – I stood on the sidelines and saw it all and took it in.

When I took the job, I had an offer from the University of Pittsburgh as well. The coach there asked if I wanted to get into college coaching and I was interested. They said they'd call in two weeks and Coach Noll called me for an interview as well.

I set up interviews for both teams on the same day, but after the interview with the Steelers I called the University of Pittsburgh and told them I have to take the Steelers job.

I think the next year they fired the entire University of Pittsburgh staff!

Clendon Thomas, Steelers Safety, 1962-1968:

I knew Tom Landry though my association with the Fellowship of Christian Athletes and I called him and asked — if I was available, would he trade me to Dallas. He was an outstanding coach and Dallas was getting better every year. Two days later, I saw on the Los Angeles evening news I had been traded to Pittsburgh. Back then there were two places you didn't want to go – Green Bay, which was like the Foreign Legion of the NFL and Pittsburgh, which had never won a Championship in the history of the franchise.

After being traded to Pittsburgh, I went back to Oklahoma and held out for a month trying to get Pittsburgh to trade me to Dallas. I finally decided to report to Pittsburgh and see what it was like. That trade turned out to be one of the best things that ever happened to me. I was given the opportunity to spend five months a year in Pittsburgh trying to win for the next seven years.

I was an All-Pro in '63, second in the league in interceptions – thanks to an outstanding group of defensive linemen and linebackers. We had a great chance to win our division in our last game at NY in '63. We had previously beaten both NY and Chicago, who played in the Championship. I remember Brady Keys, our starting corner could not play, along with two other starting linebackers. I am grateful to have been part of this group of men with a shot at the Championship.

Lou Cordileone, Steelers Defensive Lineman, 1962-1964:

When Big Daddy Lipscomb died, I took his place on the line. Me and Ernie played next to each other. When they let me go a year later, I laid out of the game for three years. Then I went and played in the Continental League for the Rhode Island Indians. Then I went back to New Orleans – that was the first year the Saints were in the league, in '67.

I called them for a tryout – they trained in San Diego then so it was close. They said to me – "Listen. This is your last shot. Keep your mouth shut and play." And that's what I did. I had a good exhibition season and they put me on the taxi squad. I thought that would at least give me a shot to play. I needed a fifth year to get a pension and you had to be active at least three games in the year for it to count. In the second game, Earl Leggett, their defensive lineman, go hurt and was placed on injured reserve. They active me for the Giants game in New York. I was really looking forward to playing in that game and had a really good game.

So, I stayed there for two years. My knee was screwed up and they let me go. They didn't give you any money then for an injury – and that was the end of it.

Clendon Thomas, Steelers Safety, 1962-1968:

You have to pass a physical to get it to the new CBA. I'm seventy-six years old! It sounded good – but who of us can qualify? I both hit and got hit too many times and accumulated too many lingering injuries to pass the physical. The effort on the NFL's part was well-meaning and I'm sure they had good intentions, but it didn't work out for me. However I'm healthy enough to ride my bicycle ten miles around Lake Hefner five or six days a week.

Let me give you a little background information. I signed a contract my rookie year for twelve thousand dollars. Our season lasted approximately five months – temp work. In 1963 with the Steelers, I was paid $35,000, as much as any safety in the league. Again, five months – temp work. Don't get the wrong idea. The Steelers were being very generous at that time in the NFL.

However as to the new CBA benefits, with eleven years playing time, I have no substantial benefits from the NFL. I also spent more money-getting my body repaired than I earned total, my entire career. Would I do it again for the same salaries? Yes – absolutely! I never played for money. In fact, I was always able to go back to Oklahoma and make more in my off-season construction business than playing.

Jim Bradshaw, Steelers Safety, 1963-1967:

Here's a funny story. My rookie contract was for $9,500. I went in after my rookie year to negotiate with Art Rooney Sr. and the business manager, Fran Fogerty. They were both sitting behind this one desk in the office at the Roosevelt Hotel.

Mr. Rooney said to me, "Jimmy, you had a pretty good rookie year. You said your contract was for $9,500, five hundred dollars as a bonus. But if you read the contract, it was for nine thousand dollars – the five hundred dollars wasn't a bonus – it was an advance on your salary. If you didn't make the team, you would have owed us five hundred dollars!" He and Fran nearly fell off their chairs they were laughing so hard!

Ben McGee, Steelers Defensive Lineman, 1964-1972:

I was shocked when they [the Steelers] drafted me. I didn't know anything about the NFL or AFL. The AFL drafted me first – the Jets drafted me in round five. They had me come up to New York to sign but I wouldn't sign for the money they offered, so they told me to go home and pick cotton for a living.

Then the Steelers drafted me in round four. They called and asked if I would sign and I said yeah. They sent someone down the next day to sign me and the Jets called and told me not to sign with them, that they'd send someone down to sign me. I told them I didn't want to sign with them – I'd rather pick cotton.

Chuck Logan, Steelers Tight End, 1964:

At the end of the 1964 season, the coaches recommended that I should try to add twenty pounds and come back in 1965 as a tight end (I guess they realized that I didn't have great speed to be a real threat as a wide receiver). I reported to training camp in Kingston, Rhode Island twenty-five pounds heavier and ready to be a tight end. After our first exhibition game (against the Minnesota Vikings and a dismal blocking performance against Carl Eller and Jim Marshall), the Steeler's released me and wanted to send me for further seasoning to their minor league team- The Wheeling West Virginia Ironmen (I think this was their name).

They wanted me to report immediately. However, my girlfriend and her family were using my car, visiting relatives on the east coast. Consequently, they had to pick me up and drive back to Chicago so I would have my car and then drive back to Wheeling, West VA. As I was cleaning out my locker after getting cut, Danny LaRose, a veteran who was also cut, mentioned to me that the St. Louis Cardinals had inquired about me. Since the Cardinals trained in Lake Forest, Illinois (twenty miles from home), and just having driven sixteen hours from Rhode Island, I decided to cold call the Cardinals and the rest is history. I was able to be with them for four years.

Bob Sherman, Steelers Cornerback, 1964-1965:

I felt honored to be drafted, but I told the Steelers I was going to play baseball and try and make the major leagues. I had a chance to sign out of high school, but chose to go to Iowa to get my education first. I played outfield at Iowa and was one of the leading hitters in the Big Ten.

When baseball didn't pan out my senior year I ended up signing with the Steelers. They had been trying to sign me all along and I kept insisting I wanted to play baseball. I was very positive going to the Steelers at that time because if they had beaten the Giants in the last game of the season they would have played for the Championship.

Chuck Logan, Steelers Tight End, 1964:

I decided to sign with the Pittsburgh Steelers as a free-agent because it was a dream of mine as a child. The opportunity to play for the team I grew up idolizing was amazing. I also knew that I had a great chance to play for a Super Bowl. I probably "left some money on the table" as they say by coming home to play, but I wouldn't trade the experience (I had better monetary contracts offered).

The teams were similar in that I had been coached defensively by Dom Capers who was an assistant coach for the Steelers. I was familiar with the system when I arrived in Pittsburgh. They were different in the fact that Jacksonville was still considered an expansion team. They had only been in existence for a few years when they drafted me in 1997. The Steelers were rich in tradition and history.

Ken Kortas, Steelers Defensive Lineman, 1965-1968:

Pittsburgh was a joy to come to.

I was traded for quarterback Terry Nofsinger in an even man-for-man trade. He started against us a couple of years later and we beat them. I got the game ball that day. It was payback time.

We actually played in the first ever Monday night game in 1964 in Baltimore. The NFL never really picked up on it – we had to play due to scheduling issues with the baseball team playoffs. There wasn't any coverage of the game except on local radio but the game sold out in three hours. No one ever really talks about that first Monday night game.

We used to play Cleveland on Saturdays too. It was always on Saturday nights. Those games were sold out to. The NFL never really picked up on it then.

Lee Folkins, Steelers Tight End, 1965:

At that time a starting engineer could expect to make ten thousand dollars a year salary. When the Packers offered me five hundred dollars to sign and nine thousand dollars to play for six months I changed my mind. I figured that I would make almost a year's salary in six months so it made sense to delay my engineering career for six months and that it what I did. It never occurred to me that I had to make the team to have to contract take effect.

I found myself with sixty other rookies in the same boat as me and began to question my decision. As it turned out, I was one of six rookies on Vince Lombardi's 1961 championship team. I would not exchange the experiences for anything and will carry my memories of my colleagues and coaches with me to the grave. I have lived my life to date attempting to apply the lessons learned during my football career.

Roger Pillath, Steelers Offensive Lineman, 1966-1967:

I was traded. Somebody in Pittsburgh didn't want to be there so we both got traded. It was an even switch of players. I liked the defensive line guys in L.A. – some of the offensive line guys I didn't like. And I didn't like Hollywood – too many phonies. I was glad I was out of there.

The bad thing was that right before I got traded I went up against Doug Atkins in a game – he was an animal. He beat the tar out of me and put me in the hospital. Then I was traded. So the next game, I had to go face Doug Atkins again!

John Brown, Steelers Offensive Lineman, 1967-1971:

Well, I wanted more money so they traded me. Pittsburgh needed a lineman and I was only twenty-seven or twenty-eight years old.

My wife was still in Cleveland – she went to school there. So after every game no matter where it was I'd drive back to Cleveland. After the school year she moved to Pittsburgh with me.

When I first came, Art Modell would let me ride back to Cleveland on the team bus…when I played against Pitt in Pittsburgh, I told Ernie Davis (teammate at Syracuse) that the city was a dirty, sooty place. I never wanted to live in that city, I told him. Be careful what you say!

Ralph Berlin, Steelers Trainer, 1968-1993:

I was a friend of Art Rooney Jr. Art traveled a lot to scout teams and I was the trainer at the University of Kentucky. We had a good football team then – we had three number one draft choices.

I became friends with Art and when the Steelers trainer job opened up, I called him and asked if he could help me get the job. He said no, but he did help me get an interview.

I interviewed with Dan. I'm not sure why he chose me, but I'm glad he did. It was always my desire to be a trainer for an NFL team.

I traveled the country looking for guys – they told me where to go. That wasn't uncommon then. Staffs were small – we only had seven coaches then. Noll coached the quarterbacks and special teams and we had three for offense and three for defense.

When I was hired I was the nineteenth employee. Now, there are over two-hundred. So, we were all involved.

There were also no limits to the number of free agents and players then. You could sign as many as you wanted. There was one bus leaving with the recent cuts at the same time another bus was coming in with new signees. There were six exhibition games then and guys got cut after the first game. There was no formal taxi squad either.

It's so much more advanced now. We had nothing like that in the mid-70s. Then we had three combines. We got to bring the kids in for two or three days and measure their height and weight and talk to them. That was basically it. And all of that information was kept private by each team.

The NCAA stepped in and said we couldn't do this. It was taking the kids out of school for too long, so they forced the NFL to combine the three combines. Now, we all get the same information.

Only three teams then scouted the smaller Black schools. The other teams didn't look at them. Bill Nunn knew those guys. Blount, guys like that, only Dallas really looked at them besides Pittsburgh.

L.C. Greenwood, Steelers Defensive Lineman, 1969-1981:

Bill Nunn covered the SWAC at the time. Not sure what influence he had if any in me being drafted by the Steelers. He signed me but Art Rooney was the guy who saw me.

I didn't know who he was even until I got to Pittsburgh. Scouting just wasn't that refined then. I remember Art Rooney from a game in Jackson, Mississippi. Played the Jackson Tigers – I had one of those games every player likes to have. After the game I was all banged up – bruised sternum, pulled groin and was all wrapped up with bandages when Art Rooney and a bunch of guys from the press were there. It was my first encounter with the press really. I didn't take off my uniform – I didn't want them to see all the bandages and how banged up I was.

Bob Adams, Steelers Tight End, 1969-1971:

I was not drafted and naturally I was disappointed. Late in the night of the draft I had a call from the Steelers new head coach, Chuck Noll. Chuck was very positive and said he had hoped to draft me but had to pick for other positions first.

Signing with the Steelers was a smart move. Art Rooney Jr. had scouted me and was a very nice, sincere man. I had no idea who Chuck Noll was at the time, he'd been an assistant at San Diego last and before that the Colts and Browns I believe. Little did I know that he would be one of the most influential teachers I would have, a four time Super Bowl Champion and a well-deserved Hall of Famer.

The Steelers front office sent me a brochure on Pittsburgh produced by the Chamber of Commerce. It named Pittsburgh the "Sister City" of San Francisco, my birthplace. It showed a picture of a cable car going up a hill and tunnels and bridges across the water. The Golden Triangle was our Golden Gate.

Strange as it sounds the brochure made me feel more comfortable. I signed with the Steelers a week later. I received a one thousand dollar signing bonus, which my wife and I used to go to Hawaii for our honeymoon just a few weeks later. Things looked promising. I have on file the contract signed with Dan Rooney.

Dan negotiated my four contracts with the Steelers. I had no agent…I had no chance until my third year. I calculated why my request for a raise was justified. I devised a chart devised by using calculus. I had drawn the graphs based on my stats for receiving, third-down blocking and conversions and fumble recoveries. I think I confused him enough he finally gave in and gave me the raise. So to that degree, college paid off.

Terry Hanratty, Steelers Quarterback, 1969-1976:

It was tough. Those were great teams and great guys. It was like going home week. People ask me if there was free agency, would I have gone elsewhere to try to start or stayed as a back-up in Pittsburgh. I really don't know. Those were just great guys – and great owners. I mean, what other team has just three coaches since 1969? It's incredible. Some of these new owners, some who probably want to be coaches, should sit down with the Rooneys for a few weeks to see how it's done.

People probably realize it, but it's a family-owned business that really has the public in mind. They are charitable to the Pittsburgh community, they have a great facility and stability in the franchise.

John Rowser, Steelers Cornerback, 1970-1973:

It's a mercenary game. You go where you are paid. There was lots of good camaraderie I had with those guys. We should have won a Super Bowl when I was there. Of course they had to win it after I left. Bradshaw came around – made less mistakes to help them win it.

I made more money in Denver though and played with some good players there too. You can't bemoan the situation – you just take advantage of it. In Denver I helped the team develop the Orange Crush defense. Denver really valued me there as well.

Pittsburgh had a new coach – Bill Austin. He hired Tom Fletcher from Missouri as one of his coaches – and Fletcher knew me from my playing days there as well. So, Pittsburgh was working out a trade with Philadelphia involving Gary Ballman and Earl Gros. Fletcher told Austin they should have Philadelphia "throw me into the deal," and they did.

It was the best thing that happened to me.

John "Frenchy" Fuqua, Steelers Running Back, 1970-1976:

My second year in New York – I thought that would be my best season. They had two backs – thirty year-old Frederickson, who had bad knees, and Duhan, a newer guy. They brought in James Coffey from Atlanta but he had two messed up knees too. I was living in Baltimore then – it was close to where I went to school. I was selling insurance in the offseason. I remember I was in the office Monday, getting ready to head out into the field. There were twenty-three agents then – all of us in one huge room. We had phone operator then in the front of the room that ran the switchboard. Well, the operator gets a call, and instead of sending it back to me, she takes her headset off and yells back, "Fuqua! The New York Giants are on the phone for you! It's Alex Webster." Well, everyone starts to crowd around my desk. We didn't even have cubicles. So I say hi to the coach, He says, "I've got good and bad news for you." I said, "Ok." He says, "The Giants made a move today that I think is good for you. The Giants traded you…" Now, all are looking at me in the room, my mouth hanging open. I asked where to. He told me, "To Pittsburgh. Good luck – you probably heard we traded for a running back – Ron Johnson – today?" I didn't know that then. I knew Ron actually – from Baltimore.

At the time, they had Earl Gros and Dick Hoak "Rocky" they had a lot of veterans there. They paired me up with Preston as his fullback – said I probably wasn't going to make the team anyway! But by the end of the exhibition, Preston and I became the starters, and Hoakie became the running backs coach.

Bob Leahy, Steelers Quarterback, 1970-1971:

In 1970, the strike was about to happen. That's what was happening. Teams needed to fill their rosters with as many players as they could for training camp. If there wasn't a strike, I probably would have never had the opportunity to play professional football.

Back then they had the college-NFL All-Star Game. I was the only quarterback in Latrobe and that helped me. Hanratty, Nix, Shiner were all out for the strike and Bradshaw was at the All-Star game. I was the only quarterback for both of the offensive teams in practice. It indoctrinated me right away. I loved it.

Noll and I formed a good, solid relationship. Noll was brilliant. He won four Super Bowls and to my knowledge never won the NFL Coach of the Year. That blows my mind. He wanted it all for the players – he never took endorsements. He didn't want the limelight. When I look back on my appreciation for coaching, I look back to Chuck Noll.

Tom Sorensen, Steelers Kicker, 1970:

I was the kicker for the Montreal Alouettes, there was a quota for U.S. citizens at the time, and I was to be cut or have to play another position, so the coach – Sam Etchevary, a great guy – made a call to people he knew in Pittsburgh and I was soon contacted by them.

I was brought in for a day of try out at Forbes Field with a couple of assistant coaches. I did some running, and field goals, and kickoffs for them, and they signed me. I got to personally be signed by the original Mr. Rooney, in the old hotel downtown. He gave me a cigar, wished me luck, and gave me a room key for the night. What a thrill!

Chuck Allen, Steelers Linebacker, 1970-1971:

In 1971, near the end of the season, I received a severe knee injury. My spirit was willing but my knee was weak and my speed was slower. So just before the last preseason game of 1972 they placed me on waivers.

At that same time, Coach Khayat in Philadelphia got two linebackers hurt so I was claimed on waivers. Philadelphia flew me in to Buffalo to play in their last preseason game. I went over their defenses on Friday night and played most of the game on Saturday. When we returned to Philly, Coach Khayat told me to bring my family in from Pittsburgh. I would likely be starting versus Dallas on Sunday.

I opened the season in Dallas and it was about 117 degrees. The next week, our middle linebacker got healthy so I was only a spot player plus special teams player for the rest of the season. The best part was I received another year's salary and another year's pension.

My health is pretty good for a seventy-two and a half year-old and twelve year veteran of the NFL. My dad was a coal miner for about thirty years and not too many jobs were tougher. So why should I ever complain?

I've always adhered to the saying "Toughness is a quality of the mind." When I start hurting from some old football injuries I just think of how my dad had to tough it out.

Lou Riecke, Steelers Strength and Conditioning Coach, 1970-1980:

I got a call at the office and it was Chuck. He said "Hi, it's Chuck Noll," and I asked what I could do for him!

He said he wanted to talk to me about putting in a weight program in Pittsburgh. The Steelers didn't have a weightlifting program then. They didn't even have a weight room. When he was the Assistant Coach in San Diego he saw what a weightlifting program did for them and one of the guys there recommended me to Chuck, so he called me.

He told me to get a first class ticket to Pittsburgh and charge it to him. So I went to Pittsburgh and we talked for a couple of days, first on how to do it. I was the weightlifting coach for the New Orleans Athletic Club and I got a free membership to the club for that. But that was really my coaching history before then – I never thought of doing it for football.

Ocie Austin, Steelers Safety, 1970-1971:

In 1971, I was looking at practicing in Three Rivers. That synthetic field was responsible for the injury I suffered, so I decided not to sign a contract and become a free agent. I was actively negotiating with the team - there was still a possibility I would sign, but I felt I would have a longer career playing on natural grass.

I was traded to the Redskins prior to becoming a free agent. In those days, contracts had a provision that you lost ten percent of your salary if you didn't sign a contract and became a free agent. So I asked Washington for a signing bonus to cover that ten percent and they said no. So I became a free agent.

It was not as easy as I thought it would be to get on another team. My agent said by the time Washington made their decision and I became a free agent most teams had already filled their rosters.

But it turned out lots of players like me found themselves in the same situation – no one was signing them. I sat out that season and then became a member of the lawsuit against the NFL. The lawsuit was spearheaded by John Mackey. It was an Anti-Trust suit – ten of us originally who sued the NFL for not allowing us to exercise our right for free agency and to find employment. We charged there was collusion by the owners.

In 1977, after going through the courts in Minnesota, the NFL settled out of court and made changes to the language in the contracts from then on. The players in the lawsuit received smaller monetary awards than we would have liked but it was an acknowledgement that the NFL colluded to stop us from gaining employment.

I would have rather played football. It was a tough time – they took the game of football away from me. By 1977 I thought I could release the anger and disappointment but I still felt upset. I was a four-year player so I wasn't vested in the pension – the pension then was for five or more years. It was hard to accept that.

Jon Staggers, Steelers Wide Receiver, 1970-1971:

I was going through a big transition of my own at the time. I had dislocated my shoulder right before the Orange Bowl. I played in the Orange Bowl and then in the Hula Bowl before getting surgery.

Interestingly, at the time I was drafted by the Steelers and graduating from college, I was also drafted by the Army. I got my physical and the Army told me to come back in six months due to the shoulder operation.

That was also the first year back for Rocky Bleier. They really took care of him – he wasn't practicing yet – he was at the facility getting healthy. Well, my six months was up and I took my physical and was ready to enter the Army when the Steelers got me into the Army Reserves. I was unbelievably grateful and, in a great sense, very naive. I would have gone to Vietnam. My college friend and future teammate in Green Bay, Ron McBride had also gotten out of the Army but had to do so by writing a letter to his congressman.

Ed Bradley, Steelers Linebacker, 1972-1975

Now, my son Jeff Bradley signed as a free agent with the Steelers back in '09. I told him to pay attention. Keep his eyes and ears open, soak up everything you can like a sponge and bust your ass…and lastly, that you better have a "thick skin". Well, he calls me one morning from camp and says "Dad, you were right. You gotta have a thick skin. They released me today."

Such is Pro-Ball…

Gordon Gravelle, Steelers Offensive Lineman, 1972-1976:

Unfortunately, during my career I had a few injuries that required surgeries. After my fifth year with the Steelers I was slowing down a step and Coach Noll was able to trade me to the Giants for a second round draft choice.

It was a very difficult time for my young family and I to uproot from Pittsburgh and the Steelers to a new city and an organization that was in total disarray. The Giants of the late 1970s were the most dysfunctional organization in the NFL with two factions of the Mara family fighting against each other on a daily basis for control over the team. It filtered down into all aspects of the organization and really affected the performance of the team.

My experience with the Giants, especially after being with the Steelers, was a nightmare. As I mentioned above, the Steelers are the epitome of a first class and model organization where an environment has been created in which their employees (players) can excel and perform at their best.

I played for the Giants for two years, 1977 and 1978. I officially retired after the '78 season but was asked to come back late in training camp in 1979. The Giants had a new coaching staff in place by then. I had moved back to California and was running an aviation business I owned when I agreed to go back to N.Y.

After I arrived, I was informed that I would be fined for every day I had missed. I filed a grievance through the players union. After about four weeks the hearing was scheduled in Washington D.C. The day before the hearing the head coach called me to his office, gave me a reimbursement check for the money they had fined me, and then released me.

I returned home to California to run my business but then received a call from "Bad Rad" checking to see if I wanted to come down to the Rams and help them out as a reserve. By 1979 Bud Carson, Lionel Taylor, and Dan were with the Rams. As I mentioned above, Dan is the best position coach I had ever played for. Bud and Lionel were equally good coaches. I knew the Rams were a good team and with those three coaches there I knew the Rams could have a successful season. I felt enthused again and went down and joined the Rams. Little did anyone know, especially me that the Rams would end up in Super Bowl XIV against the Steelers.

I had a blast playing against my old teammates. It turned out to be my final game in the NFL, very fittingly I might add.

Barry Pearson, Steelers Wide Receiver, 1972-1973:

My decision to sign with the Steelers wasn't really difficult. I had a number of teams that wanted to sign me and I selected the Steelers because Lionel Taylor, the receivers coach, had come to Northwestern and watched me practice and spent time talking to me and actually called and wanted to sign me, not some scout that I had never met.

As far as making the roster, you hope you get enough opportunities to show that you belong and I guess I accomplished that.

There is no doubt that trying to make a NFL roster is stressful. I dealt with it on a day-to-day basis because I had to critique each day on how I felt I performed in practice and hope to get feedback from my coach and then go through the agony of the days when they were required to trim their rosters.

I have to say the worst day in your life is that final day when they decide which forty-five guys stay.

Woody Widenhofer, Steelers Linebacker Coach & Defensive Coordinator, 1973-1983:

The one area the team was ahead of everyone was in the draft. Chuck and Art set up what they wanted to do and the coaches were involved in the scouting, which was unusual. We worked out the players too with the scouts. The coaches and scouts both went to see the players work out and did write-ups on them that we gave to Art. We also used the BLESTO Scouting Service then, so we had information from scouts, coaches, and BLESTO. We were ready for the draft.

I remember one situation. During the draft we had fifteen seconds left on our pick and we were still discussing it. The choice was between Lambert and another linebacker, Matt Blair from Iowa State. Finally, Chuck looked at me and asked me who I wanted since both were linebackers. I said I wanted Lambert.

Lynn Swann, Steelers Wide Receiver, 1974-1982:

You look at the past. Pittsburgh has released starters – Hall of Fame players who may have been injured or who they decided were done. Bradshaw and Lambert for example. Some decide on their own to go on to another career – myself included.

Those that still wanted to play usually wanted to do so for a competitive team – Porter and Harris were examples. Bill Cowher may have released more starters than both Chuck Noll and Tomlin. It took him ten years to get the right mix of players to win the Super Bowl.

At the end of the day, you can't argue with the consistent success of the Rooneys. It's an emotional decision for fans watching their favorite players and then seeing them gone.

But the teams move one and don't waste any time doing so! Noll once said "I can't coach players that aren't here."

Montana – I think it was him – once said to me "If playing in professional football is like a scholarship, stay on scholarship as long as you can." Once you leave the sport – because of injury or age – you can't come back. It's gone. Someone once told me that "It's better to play two years longer than you should have than one year less than you could."

Dick Conn, Steelers Cornerback, 1974:

Making the Pittsburgh Steelers team was a great memory. All of us rookies would know when the cuts were and would sweat it out every time. You would have to go by the trainer [Ralph Berlin] on the way to the locker room and he was the one that told you to get your playbook and go see Coach Noll. The last cut I was a nervous wreck!

Dave Reavis and I stopped before we went in to the training room and gave each other one more good luck hug. Dave went first. I waited and he didn't come back out. Then I took a deep breath and entered the training room. I got to Ralph and he stopped me…he said get some sleep, and I said here or at home and when – he said here! I knew I had made it. I ran in the locker room to see Reavis and I had both made the team.

After Coach cut me it was tough to go somewhere else because the rosters had been reduced by four players. There were a lot of good player with nowhere to go. I went to the World League in Jackson until they folded three games later. The Giants had called and I was headed there when Pete Rozelle put a ban on World Football players from coming back in to the NFL. In the meantime my good friend from college (Andy Johnson with the Patriots) told the special teams coach with the Patriots that they needed to call me. They did and I signed with them.

I was there for five great years and even came to Pittsburgh and beat the Steelers in 1976. It was a weird feeling to come back in that stadium and again the emotions ran high.

Reggie Harrison, Steelers Running Back, 1974-1977:

I hurt my hip and had to take medication. The medication knocked me out and I missed the training session. He cut me. No discussion. I was gone.

He never knew what happened. He never heard my side. I broke the rule and that was it.

I went to Green Bay after and finished up the year there. That was another team with great athletes but they could never out it together. Bart Starr was no Chuck Noll.

Dick Conn, Steelers Cornerback, 1974:

It was strange to come in to camp in a cab from the airport and have current players, I remember John McMakin, beating on the cab and calling you a scab as you came in to the practice facility.

As rookies we had no choice because we didn't have a job yet. The strike helped the rookies that year get playing time that we wouldn't have had otherwise. We had fourteen rookies make the team and it probably would have been four or five if not for the strike. I probably wouldn't have been in that four or five!

Ray Pinney, Steelers Offensive Lineman, 1976-1982, 1985-1987:

Leaving the Steelers was difficult because of our success and I really liked the ownership, my coaches and fellow players. I left for three years to play in the USFL after the 1982 NFL season. The reason I left was I doubled my salary. It seemed like an easy decision for me at the time.

Looking back on things, I think I made the right decision. When the USFL ended, I rejoined the Steelers for the 1985 NFL season. I guess the Steelers felt I could still contribute to the team and ended up playing three more seasons with them.

In 1985, my year with the Michigan Panthers of the USFL started training camp in Phoenix, AZ in January. I went through pre-season, an entire sixteen game regular season, and the to the championship game. Then in the fall of 1985 after the USFL went bankrupt, I rejoined the Steelers playing all but two of the NFL games that season.

Between the two leagues, I played about thirty-eight games in 1985 and it took a toll on my body. That was definitely too much football in one year.

Neil Graff, Steelers Quarterback, 1976-1977:

I found it hard to leave the Steelers in 1978 because I had grown to feel like part of the family. When you are winning it is always fun to go to work and that is not an environment that very many NFL teams find themselves in. By that time in my career I had realized the realities of the NFL and knew that my career path could change at any time.

After being a back-up QB for six years I realized that I had to soon make the transition to the top level of QBs or my career would probably be over. Although I hated to leave Pittsburgh, I viewed going to the Packers as an opportunity to perhaps move up the ladder.

Dennis "Dirt" Winston, Steelers Linebacker, 1977-1981, 1985-1986:

I had a contract dispute with the team. I was told they were going to renegotiate my contract, but then the ownership changed. The new owner, Tom Benson, refused to negotiate with anyone. After walking about a couple times they decided I wasn't needed I guess and released me.

Shortly after that I got a call from Tony Dungy and he asked if I still wanted to play football.

Bryan Hinkle offered me my old number fifty-three, but I said no and wore number fifty-five after that.

Sydney Thornton, Steelers Running Back, 1977-1982:

The NFL is a business. When they decide you don't fit into their plans, then you go. That's how it was. There's no sense trying to talk to the coach about it. It's done.

I felt I had one or two more years left in me and went to the USFL. I played with Doug Williams there – took handoffs and caught passes from him. I was successful in that league but the league didn't last.

I didn't understand how fortunate I was to be a part of a situation and organization like the one in Pittsburgh. People play so many years without ever getting to a Super Bowl and I got to two.

I wish I had been wiser to understand the professional side of sports though. I came from a small college – football was big but not like the NFL. When you get to the NFL you had to adjust to that lifestyle – you have to handle it like a business. I didn't have the right guidance and an agent I could trust.

It hurt me a lot. I didn't have the right person to negotiate for me and didn't have the power I needed off the field to help me. In my third season it was my renegotiation year and it was a Super Bowl year too. But I had no idea what I was worth. Imagine that.

The NFL is a business. When they decide you don't fit into their plans, then you go. That's how it was. There's no sense trying to talk to the coach about it. It's done.

I felt I had one or two more years left in me and went to the USFL. I played with Doug Williams there – took handoffs and caught passes from him. I was successful in that league but the league didn't last.

Robin Cole, Steelers Linebacker, 1977-1988:

I was in camp in Pittsburgh for seven weeks – through all the preseason games. I got cut the Monday of the first week of the season. So, what do I do now? I was in shape – I might as well play. I got claimed by the Jets that Tuesday – they lost a couple of linebackers to injury and they needed an experienced back-up linebacker. But then the starting linebacker got hurt so I ended up starting at linebacker.

But, I dislocated my toe versus Pittsburgh in the first game the Jets ever beat Pittsburgh. I caught it in the Astroturf and tore tendons…

Tom Beasley, Steelers Defensive Lineman, 1978-1983:

I was told when I was drafted that I was brought in to replace Joe Greene. Banaszak was there to replace Dwight White.

It's a young man's game. Joe, L.C., Ernie and Dwight were getting up in age. When I played the average career lasted 3.2 years. It's a very short career. Lots of things happen to you as you age. You get a step slower and your body recovers more slowly. At twenty-two, I could play every day. At thirty-two, I wasn't ready to play until Thursdays.

Pittsburgh had additional picks due to trades. They were obviously looking down the road to replace the Hall of Fame and

All-Pro players. Chuck was very proactive – he wanted us to get used to the system and get tutored by the best.

Rick Moser, Running Back, 1978-1979, 1981-1982:

I actually left the Steelers three days after Thanksgiving in 1980. My third year (1980) I broke my collar bone against the Giants in the first preseason game. I was put on IR (Injured Reserve) for the year.

I had healed and was practicing with the team in November. The coaches wanted to reactivate me to help the team on Special Teams so they had to put me on reclaimable waivers for a twenty-four hour period after which if no other team claims you – the Steelers could reactivate you. Well long story short, Miami claimed me (and Thom Dornbrook) two days before Miami was to play the Steelers in Pittsburgh. We had to move our equipment over to the Visitor's locker room. I talked Don Shula into letting me in on kickoff team and I made Gregg Hawthorne fumble the ball which Miami recovered. Pittsburgh won the game.

I finished out the season with Miami. I hated it there. I wanted to get back to Pittsburgh. I was spoiled from winning back to back Super Bowls and was feeling I wasn't finished there so the following preseason in Miami (1981) I had Shula fail me on my physical. My lower back was giving me problems but nothing serious. He knew I wanted out and he waived me. Pittsburgh didn't pick me up – the Raiders did. So I went to their training camp in Santa Rosa, CA and knew after a couple of days I had no chance of making their team. I lasted a few weeks – got cut – went back home to Thousand Oaks, CA and began going back on interviews/auditions in Hollywood.

I finally landed a good role in Tom Cruise's first starring role movie "Losin' It". It was 2-3 weeks of work. I had a contract. But one week before my start date – I got a call from the Kansas City Chiefs who had a spot open due to Art Still getting injured. I had a big decision to make. Do the movie with un-known Tom Cruise that could lead to who knows what else or go to the Chiefs for who knows how long. I decided to go to the Chiefs and try and get two more years in the NFL so I would qualify for pension. Hollywood could wait – the NFL doesn't. Well, I got two more weeks at Kansas City who released me when Art Still was ready to play again. I went back home to Thousand Oaks and started back into Hollywood. One day while driving home from an audition I heard on the radio that Cliff Stoudt broke his hand or wrist on a punching machine at a bar in Seattle.

The Steelers were fogged in after their game in Seattle and had to stay overnight. Cliff and the boys apparently went out and his misfortune was my gain. There was a roster spot open. I called my agent who contacted the Steelers who told me to come in and if I ran a decent forty and looked in shape they would sign me. I passed and was a Steeler once more. I played out the season and returned the following season – 1982. The guy who replaced me in the Tom Cruise movie – Rick Rosso-vich went on to do "Top Gun" with who else – Tom Cruise. Not saying that would have happened to me but – who knows. Anyway, I got five years in the NFL and qualified for pension. That was my goal.

Thom Dornbrook, Steelers Offensive Lineman, 1979-1980:

I didn't want to leave Pittsburgh. I was practicing at left guard to play Miami – it was over Thanksgiving weekend. I was put on IR before, and the only way to get back to play was through waivers. Chuck put me on waivers the night before Thanksgiving. The next day while I was practicing they came down and told me I had a call I needed to take. I walked in my gear all the way to the office to take the all…and that's a long walk. When I picked up the phone, Don Shula was on the line and said "Welcome to Miami!" They picked me off of the waiver wire. I took my stuff to the visitor's locker room and played for them the rest of the year.

I felt like a piece of meat in a locker. I grew up in Pittsburgh and wanted to stay with them.

- 185 -

Tunch Ilkin, Steelers Offensive Lineman, 1980-1992:

The hardest thing was the '87 strike. That year four captains crossed the picket line. These were good friends – it was hard. I didn't blame them – Dunn, Stallworth, Webby and Shell were in their last seasons. I understood it. But I thought I would lose more guys.

It really stretched me. I took the impact of my position on the labor movement seriously. My responsibility was to keep those guys together and it was a heavy burden. They had so many worries about making ends meet and getting paychecks. It was the biggest challenge I ever faced as a leader. I wanted to present all the information to them - I didn't want to miss anything.

I felt very strongly about the '87 fight. I made a statement early on that even if there's only one guy left on strike I'm staying out. At the end guys were worried and didn't know if they could hold out any longer. I kept telling them just to hold out a little more. Gene Upshaw then told us that by Friday, either we have an agreement or we all would cross together.

On the conference call the day before Gene told us he had bad news. There was no deal – and, he said we don't have any place to surrender to either. I called Wolf and told him there was no deal. It was 2 a.m. and we were all meeting at 8 a.m. that morning. I told him I couldn't go in. He told me my agent told him I'd be a martyr and told me to stop being a martyr. I believed in what we were doing, I told him. Thirty minutes later after going back and forth, he just asked me if he should bring in the donuts and coffee, or should I…

The next morning I told the guys that if they want to go in they should, but I couldn't. One by one they all said they wouldn't. It was crazy – these were private meetings, but the media was always there, no matter where we met. I don't know who our leak was…those were crazy times.

Tunch Ilkin, Steelers Offensive Lineman, 1980-1992:

The Steelers drafted Leon Searcy in '92. That was the first year for Bill Cowher there and it was strange. I was the same age as the head coach. When the season ended, in my exit meeting with Bill he told me thanks, but he wasn't sure about next year. He said they had to make sure Searcy could play as they were paying him a lot of money and he was a first round pick.

Later I called him after I didn't get a contract yet and he said I should probably look somewhere else. Green Bay called – I wanted to finish as a Steeler but I understood. So I called Jim Boston – the Steelers' business manager – and told him Green Bay offered me a contract. I just wanted to know what was going on – I wasn't asking for money. He told me he and Mr. Rooney spoke and that I should probably take the Green Bay deal.

Sam Washington, Steelers Cornerback, 1982-1985:

I still don't know what happened. Roger [Trainer] told me to go see Chuck – I went to my locker first and there was nothing there. When I went to see Chuck he told me I was traded and I needed to be in Cincinnati by 1:00 p.m. tomorrow. I don't know why or what they even traded me for.

I played against Houston after only three days of practice in Cincinnati. Then the next week we played Pittsburgh and Cincinnati didn't even dress me. They never told me why. I wasn't one to ask questions, but I played every game afterwards.

I cried like a baby. In my mind I knew the Steelers offense from running the scout teams. I knew when the slant was coming and would have had a big game against the Steelers. The coaches definitely picked my brain before the game though.

Edmund Nelson, Steelers Defensive Lineman, 1982-1987:

Free agency was a huge sticking point back then because player movement wasn't really allowed unless a team decided to trade you. We fought for it then and again in 1986 when we had a little victory and since then free agency has blossomed into what we have now.

The players were united in 1982 but the league basically broke us in 1986 when they signed the scab players and many players lost their jobs when we finally went back to work. We also had a lot of defectors cross the picket lines, many were well-known and popular players nearing the end of their careers and they wanted to make sure they didn't miss any paychecks.

Eric Williams, Steelers Safety, 1983-1986:

I started the last preseason game of the season. I went into the locker room and all my stuff was cleared out.

Like I said, you're here one day, gone the next. There's no security. They drafted Thomas Everett that year and had big plans for him, even though he was hurt and didn't play much of the preseason. I think they wanted a more physical hitter. That wasn't my kind of game so they went in a different direction.

I'd seen it with so many guys over my four years. I wasn't devastated at that point.

Pete Rostosky, Steelers Offensive Lineman, 1983-1986:

Being a Pittsburgh local I naturally watched the Steelers every Sunday. They were my heroes. It really was a dream come true!

After the second day of the draft, my college roommate answered the call while I was out, and when he told me the Steelers called me for a tryout, I thought he was just joking around. But when I called the number back, Dick Haley answered the phone and invited me to come down for a tryout.

I went home to our farm in Monongahela, PA, and when the day came for the tryout, I remember my dad driving me down Route 51 and actually stopped at Century III Mall to buy a pair of turf shoes because I never owned a pair. We were both so excited to walk through that tunnel onto the field for the very first time ever in Three Rivers Stadium! What a thrill!

Craig Dunaway, Steelers Tight End, 1983:

Tony Parisi taught me some things, too. One was that when you're time is up, it's time for everyone to move on. That all came about because I was interested in getting the same number I'd worn in high school and college. My junior year at Upper St. Clair High School I chose number eighty-eight because I admired Lynn Swann. At Michigan, they gave me that number without me even asking for it. So when I went to the Steelers, Swann had just retired. The number was available. Only problem was, I thought they might be thinking about retiring number eighty-eight. When I talked to Tony, I remember telling him I'd love to have number eighty-eight but would understand if they didn't want to give it out, especially right away. He seemed to scoff at the idea. Next thing I know, I'm number eighty-eight.

Steve August, Steelers Offensive Lineman, 1984:

I had been a starter in Seattle since my second year in 1978 and was very happy making the Pacific Northwest my home but Seattle decided I was expendable even though I was the starting right tackle the day I was traded.

Pittsburgh had a great right tackle in Larry Brown but he had been hurt and was actually in the hospital the day I arrived in town, so they had a need and worked out a trade with Seattle to acquire me.

I was very excited to be able to come home and play in Pittsburgh; it couldn't have worked out any better. I have been a Steeler fan since my youth football days when I started watching professional football games and to be able to put on the Black and Gold was a dream come true.

I did really well on my tryout, and they signed me right then with a whopping one thousand dolla signing bonus! How things have changed.

John Swain, Steelers Cornerback, 1985-1986:

My sixth year I hurt my knee in a preseason game versus the Redskins. I had surgery and was out for six games but started the last eight games. But it was a two-year deal. My contract was up and Pittsburgh only offered me $150,000.

My agent and I thought I should get $300,000 – especially with Woodruff out with an injury, so we refused the offer. They countered with an offer for $180,000 but we refused that too. They went to $190,000, but then the draft came and they drafted Woodson and Delton Hall and let me go. I was picked up by Green Bay right after.

Preston Gothard, Steelers Tight End, 1985-1988:

Earnest Jackson was like a huge car salesman. His contract was loaded with incentives. The Steelers didn't pay him much money but he got incentives for everything. If he tied his shoes correctly he got money. I remember he and Rich Erenberg sitting with the playbook, a calculator and a briefcase figuring out how much money he could make on every play and game!

Hardy Nickerson, Steelers Linebacker, 1987-1992:

I left in free agency. It was the first class for NFL free agency. It was tough. As a player, you want to be with the same team your whole career. But that's the financial part of football.

A number of teams contacted me. It was like being a college kid and I just felt at home in Tampa Bay.

It felt good to be recruited, yeah! The city didn't have a winning team in a long time. I got a warm welcome. My wife and I flew in and arrived at midnight. Sam Wyche was there at the gate with five hundred fans with Hardy Nickerson jerseys chanting my name!

Rodney Carter, Steelers Running Back, 1987-1989:

When they let me go, I was the last guy on the team to get cut. I wasn't expecting it. We played the Giants the last preseason game and I beat Lawrence Taylor for a big reception and took it near the goal line. My locker was next to the training room. Chuck Noll came to me – and he didn't say much to players – but he told me I should get ready for next week's game. I said "wow" – I thought I made the team. It was a big deal – there were only forty-seven players then – no practice squads. That Monday we were all doing the math to see if we were close to making the team. I knew they liked Dwight Stone and Merril Hoge. Then there was Pollard, Earnest Jackson and Abercrombie. That's five right there. They called you early Monday morning if you were going to be cut. Well, I waited for the call: 6:30 a.m., 7:00, and 7:30…no call. At 8:00 a.m. I decided to head down for the 9:00 a.m. team meeting they had. I got there at 8:15 but I wouldn't get dressed for the meeting – not until I knew for sure if I made the team. At 8:45, still nothing. So, I started putting on my shorts, then at 8:50 a.m., I was told to go see Tom Donohoe and talk to him. He gave me the usual talk – I was a hard worker, stay in shape…I didn't want to hear it. I was just like, whatever. I just wanted to get out of there. All the reporters were gone by then so I could just leave quietly.

Lorenzo Freeman, Steelers Defensive Lineman, 1987-1990:

It was the year of the strike – I was the first defensive lineman drafted by Green Bay that year.

Charlie Martin was the player ahead of me in camp, but he got in trouble the night before the strike and was released. They wanted me to play in place of him in a game later, and because of the strike I decided not to play. They looked at that negatively. I made it a point to try to prove myself after, but it was too late.

It was a blessing. I worked out for the Steelers and Coach Greene asked me what happened in Green Bay. I told him the start of it and he told me he understood. I said to myself, he didn't need the details. He understood.

Buddy Aydelette, Steelers Offensive Lineman, 1987:

To me it was just 1987 and I wanted to continue to play football. I was in camp with the Vikings in 1987. I was there because Rollie Dotsch was now on their staff. I was released the week of the last preseason game in Minnesota and had a long drive back to Alabama.

I thought that was the end of my playing days. When I got home my wife said get a good night sleep you have a plane ticket to Pittsburgh waiting at the airport. I really don't remember who contacted me (through my wife, of thirty-two years now).

We used a lot of Steelers terminology in Birmingham because of Rollie. It was like the USFL's version of Pittsburgh, really.

It was a good fit, yes. No doubt it helped me. It's like learning a new language when you go to a new team – you do the same things, but they are called something different. Not having to learn something new was very helpful.

Thomas Everett, Steelers Safety, 1987-1991:

I told the Steelers I'd take their numbers for two years, but not the option year after the two years they insisted on. That wouldn't have been fair. But they wouldn't budge or look at our numbers. Then they said some bad things, we probably did too…no one would budge. My thing was, at least be men and talk – negotiate. They have their right not to I guess – but I had no rights. There was no free agency then. They just said take it or leave it. So I said this is it and I wouldn't play. I'm, not coming – I'll sit out. I didn't have any other leverage at the time.

After that, Chuck Noll stepped down and Bill Cowher was hired. He called me that afternoon and said that "Thomas. You're my free safety! We want you here." I liked the staff they put together there. Cowher, LeBeau as the secondary coach and Dom Capers as the defensive coordinator. Cowher told me they'd figure a way to get things done. So I went up for mini-camp. I tried to do all I could to show them I wanted to be there. I didn't want to go – I was excited about the new coaching staff and built great bonds with the players there.

So, back to camp…after I sat out the first three preseason games and kept training in Dallas, I watched a Monday Night game and AL Michaels started talking about Reggie Brown and the start of what would be free agency. I think the Steelers panicked – they were afraid they'd lose me for nothing and traded me to Dallas. It's funny. When I think of the dollars we were negotiating over then versus what players make now – it was like pennies!

Michael Minter, Steelers Defensive Lineman, 1987:

I was signed as a free agent in 1987 before the strike but I was released during training camp due to contractual issues. I was attending college in Texas when the strike began and Pittsburgh called and offered me a contract as a replacement player. I felt that would be a chance for me to get my foot back in the NFL door.

It was an easy decision for me to play during the NFL strike. It was a second chance for me to make a living by playing the game I loved. Pittsburgh was my favorite childhood team, so I could not imagine turning down that opportunity.

I was one of a few replacement players left in camp when all of the veterans returned to work. There was not enough locker space available, so I was assigned to share a locker space with the late Terry Long. I remember that he was not too happy when he found out about that decision. He attempted to take it out on me on the practice field. I think I gained his respect after a few battles.

He wanted to bring me back to camp in 1988. My hopes were to remain in Pittsburgh and make a name for myself. I thought that I could continue to be a help on the defensive line, so I was disappointed to be released.

The Steelers brought me back to camp in '88 as they said they would, so I still had hope.

Danzell Lee, Steelers Tight End, 1987:

I remember being in the training room and coach Chuck Noll came in. He looked at me and my foot. He said "man this thing has really been bleeding out." He then looked at the other foot and then said "wait a minute, this foot looks exactly the same."

He then walked out. I don't know what he meant about that comment, but it didn't feel right. I was experiencing some severe pain. And I tried my best to do what I could to get back. It just wasn't happening. Soon after that exchange of events, I received a visit from the tight end coach. He expressed to me that the team was not going to place me on IR because they didn't think the injury was severe enough to do that. He then expressed to me that I needed to do whatever I needed to do to get back to practice.

Well, to make a long story short, I reluctantly did what I needed to do. Days later I was able to get to the field without too much pain. I was able to get through one or two practices and get on film. The next day, I was called to the office and told I was going to be placed on waivers. The team was going to go in a different direction. This is how I left the Steelers. I was placed on waivers during the '88 season, just before returning to the active roster. Not sure why…I did try to meet with Chuck Noll about it, but felt like he wasn't straight with me. He said all the right things and complemented my efforts and abilities. But, I was still placed on waivers.

Jim Boyle, Steelers Offensive Lineman, 1987-1988:

I was out of football for two years when the strike season occurred. I had just finished graduating from Tulane when I got a call from the Steelers to join their strike team. They were in need of offensive linemen to begin with and they promised me a good look even if the strike would end.

I was apprehensive at first to sign but it allowed me to get back into football after what I considered a bad experience with the Miami Dolphins.

A few of the Steelers main guys didn't go on strike. Guys like Mike Webster and John Stallworth set the examples on how to carry yourself on and off the field. Once the team was set the practices and meetings were the same as if it were regular season play. Johnstown, PA was the camp site. It was kind of neat visiting there and finding out more about the Great Flood that occurred there.

John Jackson, Steelers Offensive Lineman, 1988-1997:

It was real hard to leave. I would not have done the same thing again. The offer – I just couldn't refuse those numbers.

I talked to Mr. Rooney and Cowher and told them it wasn't personal, that I had to take care of my family. Both understood. Mr. Rooney told me that when I was ready to come home, to let them know. That meant a lot.

Cowher said "You might want to take the money!"

All teams try to get fair market value. In negotiations, all have to come to the middle road. For the Steelers, loyalty is paramount as far as the players they represent and develop.

They shoot straight in negotiations and hold no punches. They pay players their worth but want to surround them with talent so they can win games. Most teams, their pay scale is skewed. The Steelers philosophy is to have the right people in place, sacrifice some value but not to sacrifice character.

Tim Worley, Steelers Running Back, 1989-1993:

Actually, during the 1993 season, I had already asked Coach Cowher to help me find another team that was looking for a running back. My mind was about looking for another team, but my heart was still in Pittsburgh and I wanted to play for the Steelers.

My mind led me to want to leave because I wasn't playing that much. Barry Foster was doing his thing and, after my 1992 suspension, I was in a position of needing to be humble and taking the back seat so I could earn my way back. But I didn't know how to do that. I was busy complaining while sitting on the bench in a very privileged position.

Jerrol Williams, Steelers Linebacker, 1989-1992:

It was the first year of free agency – it was very hard to leave. I didn't know a lot about the business of football and listened to my agent. I never wanted to leave. It looked like it was about money to some, but really I just listened to my agent. I wasn't from a football background and my agent said Pittsburgh didn't make an offer close to San Diego's.

They had Neil O'Donnell to take care of. I really should have been more hands-on. I could have worked out a deal with Pittsburgh. I just didn't understand the business – I just wanted to play football. I should have communicated with Coach Cowher at least. San Diego was closer to home and there were other factors, but yeah, I should have stayed.

Terry O'Shea, Steelers Tight End, 1989-1990:

It's a funny story. I got called back after I got cut because they needed someone for a week for practice. On the practice day I went back and found my shirt in my locker – it had my number eighty-five but no name plate. It was just the shirt with no name. No one said anything, so I just went out to get the photo taken. Mularkey walked with me and asked me if I thought having no name on my jersey was any indication I wouldn't make the team!

Sure enough, after practice, Donohoe came up to me and said thanks for the week of work.

I tried out after that for San Diego. I walked out with this other huge tight end and we introduced ourselves. The coach looked at both of us then said to me, "Terry, I thought you were bigger than that..." I was like, should I just go home now?

I wanted to play in Barcelona. I wasn't going to get much playing time in the NFL not starting. I thought it would be good to take a slight step back, get playing time and build up my confidence, even though I had received an offer from Buffalo.

Playing there was fantastic. I was above average as a player there. All my confidence came back – I had six catches one game. We had a hotel on the Mediterranean Sea overlooking a beach. It was crazy. We played an hour away from Barcelona the year of the Olympics. We only practiced three days a week. That was opposite of Chuck Noll's practices.

It was a lot of fun. The little town we stayed in had a siesta every day so we'd nap then go out. I remember we played beach volleyball the day of a game with a bunch of the girls. It was the opposite of the NFL. It was a lot of fun and less pressure.

Unfortunately, I got hurt around the fifth game – a herniated or bulging disk in my back. I got back in time to play one playoff game, then that was all she wrote for me.

Barry Foster, Steelers Running Back, 1990-1994:

I saw the writing on the wall though. In the '95 season I had a two and a half million dollar price tag and Bam Morris had a $500,000 price tag, and we had split carries in '94 with the same output because of my injuries. So from just the yardage standpoint, we were the same. I thought I'd get one more year to help keep stability there and be kept one more year, but that didn't happen. I wasn't angry, just disappointed and surprised.

Chris Calloway, Steelers Wide Receiver, 1990-1991:

When Bill Cowher came in, he gave me an opportunity to stay or test the Plan B market. With myself and advice from my agent, I decided to test the market which eventually made me more money. Who knows what would have happened if I would've stayed (Super Bowl?), but I was happy with my eleven year career.

LeRoy Thompson, Steelers Running Back, 1991-1993:

I was pretty well prepared fundamentally for the pros and big time competition did not scare me having spent my career at Penn State battling for carries with the likes of Blair Thomas, Gary Brown, Richie Anderson, and Sam Gash. All of whom went pro and had solid NFL careers. What was crazy my rookie season, was that I held out of camp for two weeks as a sixth round draft pick. This was unheard of and Chuck Noll kept saying in the paper that there was no reason for me to even come to camp because I would be cut. However, Pittsburgh was trying to pay me fifty percent of the pay the same player in my slot was drafted the year before. My agent Brett Senior cautioned that I should not take the deal and go in if I was confident that I could compete and make the team. I told him that not only would I make the team, but I would play a significant role. We got the deal done two weeks later which was a whopping $115,000 base with a $45,000 signing bonus!

You could not tell me I was not the richest guy in the world when I signed. I came into camp and in the first practice I fought with Hardy Nickerson (I mean I got beat up by Hardy Nickerson), faked out and broke Greg Lloyd's ankle for a TD, and made a crushing block on pass protection and all was forgiven by the Coaches. They knew they had a player from then on in.

The trade was all my fault.

I had just led the team in rushing, returns, and pass caught by backs in '93 when Barry Foster went down. I was a restricted free agent which meant that if a team signed me, they would have to give up a first round draft pick, which was not likely. I wanted a significant pay raise so my agent went in after the season and said pay us or trade us! We were bluffing! The next thing I know, I am on a plane to New England and Bam Morris was getting all of my snaps.

As I look back, I never should have left Pittsburgh nor New England for that matter. I ended up second on the team in rushing at New England that year, caught sixty-five balls, and led the team and returns. I became a free agent and signed with Kansas City to replace Marcus Allen so I thought. When I got there, Marcus had the best year that he ever had as a Chief and I was off again. I never found the right fit in an offense again for my style after leaving New England and the Steelers. I should have played for at least ten years with those teams.

Ernie Mills, Steelers Wide Receiver, 1991-1996:

There were a lot of reasons I left, but ultimately, I wanted a change for the grass field surface and my ACL knee injury in the Super Bowl. It didn't respond the way I wanted it too in 1996, the last year of my contract. So I went to Carolina because it was grass and a familiar coaching face (Dom Capers).

It was really hard to move on and especially difficult when the offensive system I was used to didn't fit my style of play. So I only lasted a year there. Dallas, my last two years, was great because Chan was the coach and I was truly a veteran at that point.

Definitely wish I had stayed in the 'Burgh.

Levon Kirkland, Steelers Linebacker, 1992-2000:

It did surprise me [being cut by Steelers]. I really had no warning – I guess it was naive on my part. I thought I had bounced back that season and played like the Kirkland of old.

It was more of a money issue, I realized later. It hits you then as a player – it's a business. You got to be loyal to the team as a player, but you have to be loyal to yourself too. It can happen to anyone – no one, not even Montana – is immune to it.

I got nine years with the team though. They drafted me and extended me two times. But it was time to move on.

I loved the team dearly, but Seattle offered me a good deal. It helped to move far away, to see other things and meet new people and add to my career. I wanted to stay and probably would have taken a pay cut. I felt strongly about being a Steeler, but they did what they thought was best.

Kendall Gammon, Steelers Long Snapper, 1992-1995:

It was awful. It was the hardest thing I had to do, leaving the team, except seeing my kid in the NICU unit for two weeks. I got a phone call during my nap when I went home after practice asking for me to come in to the Steelers office. My wife asked me what was going on and I knew right away they were calling to tell me I was cut.

They brought in Kirk Botkin from New Orleans to replace me. They wanted a position player who could also snap. I was in tears, I'm not embarrassed to say. The next day, New Orleans signed me to replace Kirk Botkin – the guy that took my place in Pittsburgh. I think Pittsburgh cut Botkin a couple of weeks later, too. It's funny…that's the NFL.

Leon Searcy, Steelers Offensive Lineman, 1992-1995:

Cowher called me and said that no matter what you hear management say about me, he wanted me back and to be a Steeler. I told my agent – Drew Rosenhaus – that I didn't want to leave Pittsburgh unless there was a mind-blowing offer. I had unfinished business in Pittsburgh – we just lost the Super Bowl and we had a good team.

Well, I was visiting my family when Drew called me and said Pittsburgh was dogging me out. Saying I wasn't even their best offensive tackle. Now, I remember what Cowher told me and I told Drew that. So he told me he'd call Pittsburgh and put me on a three-way call, without Pittsburgh knowing I was on the line. So I'm not sure who it was on the Steelers line, but he just blasted me. Saying I had only started for two seasons, that my first year was horrible, that I was much too young to be asking for that kind of money especially as a two-year starter with just one good season.

Now, I was young and didn't understand anything about negotiating. It all rubbed me the wrong way. I hung up the phone after fifteen-twenty minutes of assault. My agent called me back and I told him I wanted to prove I could have success elsewhere. I thought the Steelers was the right place and system for me, but now the hell with that. I told him to find me a new team. I overreacted. I was angry and made a decision emotionally. Two days later my agent came back with a contract from Jacksonville – that made me the highest-paid offensive lineman in the NFL. Now, did my agent set me up? He probably did looking back on it. Maybe he used me…but that's the kind of lesson I want to teach others about now.

Chad Brown, Steelers Linebacker, 1993-1996, 2006:

They flew me in before the draft and had me watch film with Marvin Lewis. The film we watched was of outside linebackers – he was probing me on that spot. But they signed Kevin Greene two days before the draft. Maybe I said the right things to help them think I could move inside or maybe the film of me they watched was enough for them to feel confident in me.

I was the only inside linebacker that was also a third-down pass rusher in the NFL then. The staff did a great job seeing my value was in more than just one spot.

It was super tough leaving Pittsburgh. Being a Steeler was special – I knew that even though I hadn't played anywhere else. Every hotel we went to was crowded – there were crowds everywhere. You didn't have that with other teams. Every team doesn't have Super Bowl trophies you walk by every day.

But, football is a passion and a job. The Steelers were limited money-wise. They just re-signed Lloyd. They didn't have the new stadium then that would get them more money. They didn't have George Allen. And, they needed to re-sign Jerome Bettis too.

It was a no-brainer financially for me. It was just shocking how different it was. Seattle fans would ask me if I was still playing – I just made the Pro Bowl that year! It was like playing in the Canadian League.

Reggie Barnes, Steelers Linebacker, 1993:

My agent, Ralph Cindrich, was based in Pittsburgh, and as soon as the draft was over I got four to five calls from teams that were all wanting me to sign with them. My thought was, "why didn't you call me an hour ago and draft me?" I knew they were all trying to entice me to play and I was processing it all. The agent said Pittsburgh has some veteran linebackers, like David Little, and he thought that would give me an opportunity to have an impact as a rookie because some might leave. You don't get to do research on the teams. You have 30-40 minutes to make a decision. So I left it to the agent's expertise. I was also a Pittsburgh fan even though I lived in Dallas, so when I had a chance to play in Pittsburgh it was exciting. I even played against Joe Green's son when I played football in high school in Dallas.

Myron Bell, Steelers Safety, 1994-1997, 2000-2001:

I was always struck at how Rod, Carnell, and Darren would come to work every day wearing Dockers and carrying a briefcase; they treated what they did as a business and carried themselves like business men.

For three years during away games, I was assigned a seat in the same row as Rod's. During that time he shared a lot of knowledge and wisdom. There were no limits to where the conversation would go about life's experiences.

Ray Seals, Steelers Defensive Lineman, 1994-1996:

In 1993, I became a free agent and wasn't going to re-sign with Tampa Bay. I got a concussion in practice and the doctor put me on the sidelines. One of the coaches – Floyd Peters – saw me there and told Coach Wyche I took myself off the field. Wyche put me in front of the whole team and embarrassed me – chewed me out and made me practice in front of them all.

I was embarrassed and left the team.

I never thought of Pittsburgh as a team that would be interested in me – we never played them. But Drew Rosenhaus called me and said Pittsburgh wanted to bring me in! I was amazed.

Brentson Buckner, Steelers Defensive Lineman, 1994-1996:

I was traded, yeah. It was a shock. I was a Steelers fan since I was five years old. My father bought me Steelers pajamas, sheets…when I was drafted, I was a fan living a dream.

The day I was traded was one of the darkest days of my NFL career. I had nothing in common with anyone in Kansas City. It was a shock to go from Pittsburgh, where I had a lot of friends and we expected to win, to Kansas City.

It reflected in training camp. I felt I got a raw deal. I didn't know if I wanted to play football any more.

Dick LeBeau knew me from Pittsburgh and brought me to Cincinnati. I knew him well and had a comfort level with him. It jump-started my career. I played the year out then signed with the 49'ers. The rebirth of Brentson Buckner started there.

Myron Bell, Steelers Safety, 1994-1997, 2000-2001:

It was hard to leave the Steelers, but I had gone through the process of becoming a starter in the NFL. I had to go where I thought I had the best opportunity to play. The Steelers were set at the safety position. Things didn't go the way that I had planned for them to go career wise or financially as a free agent. At this time in my life, I really had to do some soul-searching personally.

My agent stayed in contact with a player personnel guy during the 2000 season. Doug Whaley brought my name up to Coach Cowher and they agreed to sign me back. Coming back to the Steelers was a breath of fresh air and I was welcomed back by everyone. First of all, the Steelers didn't see the Bengals as a rival. The Bengals were the team that viewed the Steelers as their rival team.

Earl Holmes, Steelers Linebacker, 1996-2001:

To this day, the best time I had was in Pittsburgh. I offered some advice to Joey Porter when he went to Miami. It's a business. The contract thing – you don't always have to go for it. At the same time, I know I called Cowher after I left and told him I made a mistake. He told me it's not like this everywhere – that I should think before I left to play for Cleveland. I didn't understand then.

There was no Coach Cowher, Mike Archer, LeBeau, or Tim Lewis in Cleveland. I was fortunate to have Coach Butler. But it was different. I called Joey – told him I knew Miami offered him more money but you have to be happy. It's more than just about football – you have to have that family. You miss that. My wife still asks me today what it would be like if I stayed...but when you are young, those are business decisions. You don't realize the other stuff as much.

I never forget it now. I tell my kids - my rookie year in camp I introduced Coach Cowher to my family. After the second home game, my family, me, and Coach Cowher were riding the elevator – he knew all of their names and spoke to them the whole time. I was like, "Wow! How did he do that with all of those guys on the team?" That impressed me the most. It was a family. I was so impressed with that – that did so much to me.

I left making a business decision. My heart though was in Pittsburgh. I got ten years in the NFL – I got the chance to meet a lot of people – but the playoffs, the family atmosphere – that was the norm in Pittsburgh. The Browns made the playoffs once – my first year there. They haven't been there since!

You miss that winning. That great organization – the people, fan base, owners...they've been doing it for a very long time. When you get to other teams it's so different. Once I left and looked back, I see that's what Cowher was trying to tell me.

Nolan Harrison, Steelers Defensive Lineman, 1997-1999:

Jim Haslett was the defensive coordinator for the Steelers then. He was also the linebackers coach for the Raiders when I was there. He called me to Pittsburgh to offer me the position. I met with him and Coach John Mitchell, who as you know has coached many Pro Bowl lineman.

What convinced me to come was when Coach Mitchell showed me the film of nose tackle Joel Steed destroying various offensive lines. I knew that I wanted to play next to that guy!

The Steelers decided not to re-sign me, but we had practiced, scrimmaged, and played against the Redskins the past two seasons. They knew me, and knew what I was capable of. Coach Terry Robiski was also on the staff of the Redskins. Coach Robiski was on the Raiders staff as well when I was there so that made the transition easier.

Courtney Hawkins, Steelers Wide Receiver, 1997-2000:

Mentally, I was not ready to retire. Physically, I had fifteen surgeries – nine knee surgeries. Nothing post-football at least.

They slowed me down, I guess. It was a decision made by the teams – it took me a while to accept it. I worked out for a year hoping someone would call. Some did but nothing materialized. It was evident that it was time to move on – to go on to that next stage in life.

Being in the NFL is a rollercoaster ride. It's a heckuva two minutes, but after the ride stops it's over and then it's off to the next ride. This is the business side of the NFL and it can be cutthroat. Teams will let you know when you are done.

Dewayne Washington, Steelers Cornerback, 1998-2003:

Denver definitely offered more, yeah. But I knew I had a chance to go and learn from some excellent backs in Pittsburgh like Darren Perry and Carnell Lake. I was in my fifth year but I was still trying to learn the game. I knew Lewis was a good coach too and Woodson just left so I was taking his place.

And Coach Cowher was definitely a bonus. It was good he was a fellow Wolfpacker!

I signed in the second week of free agency. It felt like two months! Jerome and me were good friends so it helped knowing him too. Pittsburgh were winners – I think they lost the season before in the AFC Championship. I was sold that they needed a cornerback to make the Super Bowl. I wanted to be that missing piece. We struggled a couple of years at first before we turned it around.

It was definitely hard to leave. It was my tenth year and it was tough. I saw myself finishing in Pittsburgh. When your game slips…it is what it is. I'll be honest, I didn't have a good year and the Steelers don't hesitate to move forward. They just drafted Ike Taylor and had some guys they needed to play.

It's always tough. It was home for me, but that's the nature of the business. I just wanted to win one. I was so happy for those guys in 2005 – many of those were the same guys.

Bobby Shaw, Steelers Wide Receiver, 1998-2001:

In my second and third year I put up good numbers considering our run-oriented offense. I had the highest yards per catch, and was near the top in receptions and touchdowns too. In my fourth year, we switched offensive coordinators from Kevin Gilbride (now the New York Giants coordinator) to Mike Mularkey, and my playing time and numbers were drastically cut down.

I felt I wanted to be a bigger part of an offense. That's the tough part of the business – weighing comfort versus doing all you can do to be all you can be, re-signing would not have allowed me to do that. I didn't want to take the safe route in my career.

I had a career year after that in Jacksonville, and then Buffalo after that. I was able to accomplish a lot of my goals by leaving, but it was still unfortunate. I don't regret it though.

Hank Poteat, Steelers Cornerback, 2000-2002:

What you see on TV and in the media – it's all hype. It's not real. They talk about the guys making millions, but you never hear about the Hank Poteats and the guys that play for minimum salaries and the guys that get cut. And those are most of the players.

The majority of the players don't make millions. Many live from check-to-check. That world is fake. Most are regular guys. I remember the first time I got cut – it was on my birthday. Almost every time I got cut it was on my birthday actually. I was about to start eating pancakes with my wife when some guy from the Steelers called me and told me.

The first time I got cut I had a house in Delaware and an apartment in Pittsburgh. I couldn't get out of the lease so I had two payments. Then Tampa Bay picked me up so I went out there and got an apartment there. My first game there I hurt my hamstring and got cut after four weeks. So, now I had two leases and a mortgage payment – and no pay.

That's what happens. You get signed a few weeks in so your kids are in school and you're playing in another city – so you have to leave behind your wife and kids. And because you are signing one-year deals you can't buy a home with no job security.

There are so many guys that deal with this stuff week in and week out. You can get cut any time. But I maintained that for ten years. I had a strong mindset and belief in myself. I didn't

worry about the media, blogs, friends who turned their back…
I didn't worry about it. I kept pushing for my dream. I'm thankful for Erci Mangini – he saw that and took me everywhere he went – Cleveland, New England, and the Jets.

Tommy Maddox, Steelers Quarterback, 2001-2005:

I would be lying if I said that it didn't surprise me [when they drafted Ben Roethlisberger]. When I left the facility that Friday they told me they were probably going to draft an offensive linemen. It was tough for me, but I think that it would be hard to say that they didn't make the right choice. It is always hard to lose your job to an injury, but let's face it, it was only a matter of time. Ben has had a great career and I still root for him and the Steelers every week.

Rodney Bailey, Steelers Defensive Lineman, 2001-2003, 2006:

I was a restricted free agent at the time. I had the offer sheet and it paid me considerably more than what I would have made otherwise. I was difficult to leave behind a family and go to a new team. Many don't realize how difficult it is.

We won a Super Bowl, which was one of the coolest things. Then the following year I lost the Super Bowl after I signed with Seattle and we played the Steelers!

I came back to afterwards to where my career began – in Pittsburgh. I am a Steeler. Black and Gold is what I bleed. What you are is where you come from.

The greatest thing about the Steelers is that it is a family. You're treated well – if you were a first round pick or a free agent, you're a family member. No matter if you played for one year or twelve years, you're a Steeler for life. That's unique to most NFL teams. My time in New England, Seattle, Arizona...I'm still remembered as a Steeler. That's due to a great fan base and locker room.

Mathias Nkwenti, Steelers Offensive Lineman, 2001-2003:

I hated the politics of the game. Like some guys were running for player rep or something. It's a business and I get that. But I didn't kiss ass. If you respect me I respect you. The NFL is like a completely different kind of corporate job and you need to remember that.

I remember the scouts – I made friends with some of those guys. They know everything – they are like gnats on the walls. They'd tell me all the things people said about me when they wouldn't say it straight to me. What were people really saying? It was like women gossip stuff. If I was sucking or letting up sacks I'd understand more, but that kind of politics bothered me. If I didn't like you, you'd know it. I'd tell you to your face, not behind your back. My father hated the politics and I did too.

Kendall Simmons, Steelers Offensive Lineman, 2002-2008:

Well putting those feelings [about being released] into words is still very hard. It hurt and I really didn't see it coming. It is difficult to get over until you realize football is a business.

Once I became a free agent, I had two options New England and Buffalo. The time I spent with the Patriots taught me to lean on God more and to realize that the grass isn't always greener on the other side.

I felt as if I fit in at Buffalo from the time I got there. Sean Kugler was the offensive line coach while I was there. He made the transition easier for me. Neither team compared to Pittsburgh.

Antwaan Randle El, Steelers Wide Receiver, 2002-2005, 2010:

Leaving came down to financial reasons. It wasn't even close, but it was hard.

My last contract year, the Steelers offered me $2.2 million, then after camp, $3.6 million. I was a starter and felt I was worth more so I didn't sign the contract and played out the year. That year, I threw a touchdown in the Super Bowl, had three punt returns for touchdowns and had a good year receiving. I felt like I was playing poker and had the best hand. But they couldn't come close to the Redskins offer. I had two kids…I wanted to stay, especially after the Super Bowl success, but the offer just wasn't close.

When I returned, the guys that still knew me said I got my money, so welcome back! Deshea [Townsend] wasn't there, and that was weird. It was always Deshea and Hines. They brought Foote back, and that was good.

I actually talked to Tomlin when I worked for the NFL Network in 2008. After the championship, I interviewed him and said then that I'd come back home if there was a chance, and it came down to it.

Chris Doering, Steelers Wide Receiver, 2003-2004:

As a player in the NFL, it's all about opportunities and coaches that like you. I was a later round draft choice by Jacksonville who probably drafted me because I was a Florida guy. I didn't fit well in the Jacksonville offense, and I went to the Colts for two years. When Spurrier came to the NFL and DC, I was probably the only Florida guy that was happy about it and was signed by him. But Snyder made sure a lot of us Florida guys in DC were not re-signed that second season – he was unhappy Spurrier brought so many of us in.

Mularkey was a former Gator – he then brought me into Pittsburgh and I played there for two years. It was my favorite two years in the NFL – both on and off the field.

I was fortunate to play in Denver, Washington, and Pittsburgh. Those three – and maybe Green Bay and a couple others – have the best football fanbases. The smaller big city thing and the passion of the fans plus the opportunity to be a part of something meaningful to all of the fans – it was a special feeling.

Najeh Davenport, Steelers Running Back, 2006-2008:

Unfortunately, the Packers cut me, and I thought my pro career was done. I remember trying to update my resume the next day.

That night my agent called and told me the Steelers were interested in bring me out. When I arrived in Pittsburgh I had a twenty minute meeting with BC (Bill Cower) and he shook my hand and told me welcome to the Steelers.

Oh man. It was the hardest thing I ever had to do in my life. The situation was about money really. I was getting older and they drafted Troy [Polamalu] that year. It's part of the business – you can't play forever.

Denver had Shanahan at the time. They were more offensively geared – where Pittsburgh was more about defense. It wasn't like Pittsburgh. It was a great organization, don't get me wrong. But my blue-collar mentality was perfect for Pittsburgh. In Denver we practiced at most one hour a day. You sit on the field with the view of the Rocky Mountains and it was like a country club.

It was just different. I missed the camaraderie with the guys I pretty much grew up with. We had a stable team for those eight years – a lot of the guys I was drafted with left or retired when I did. It was like leaving your family and I was just a stepchild in Denver.

I'd tell all the guys if I could now that in free agency, if you are contemplating leaving, it's not going to get any better than Pittsburgh.

John Norwig, Head Trainer, Steelers:

In college, we dealt with the players, coaches and parents. We tell the coaches and players and offer to call the parents.

In the NFL, it's much more political. We deal with players, coaches and agents. Agents may want their players to play for incentives or want you to operate a certain way and require you to get second opinions. When that happens we'll have to fly them to see other doctors.

The political issues usually take care of themselves by us being brutally honest and by working well with those other doctors.

Ralph Cindrich, Pittsburgh Sports Agent:

My advice to players: in Professional football, finding a good home where you are happy, have success, and enjoy getting up and going to work is not the rule. When you find it, you don't easily throw it away.

You look at it after tax dollars and weigh that with the unknown of another team and you think twice about. I think about some of the great players with the Steelers that left here and fizzled. Maybe a shot at the Hall of Fame if they had stayed, who knows? If the money is so large that you get a nose bleed, a gift from God, take it and the crap that likely goes with it.

Religion/Spirituality:

Much like with race, religion was also an individual driver for players, as well as the means by which players bonded. From group prayer, Scientology and Breem, players found their own ways to spirituality that helped some cope with the stress of the game, temptations of being a "local celebrity," and the absence of family as the spent the majority of their time with team.

The Steelers focused on drafting high-effort, high-character players. For many of those drafted players, their spirituality is what helped them develop those characteristics. It's unlikely the Steelers considered any form of religion in the drafting/acquiring of players. It was more an inherent characteristic that many of the players possessed. Again, high character players often had the foundation of that work ethic rooted in the values of their religious upbringings. It's little wonder that religion become a bonding force for the team and a means for bringing players together across racial and geographical divides.

Bill Kisher, Steelers Offensive Lineman, 1958-1959

I came into the NFL committed to the Christian faith. I guess I was a goody, goody guy, I didn't drink or smoke. But I was big enough that no one would mess with me when I said no. Race was a big deal then too – though I was color blind to it all. So I just said no to those things and moved on.

I actually started the chapel service in Pittsburgh for Protestants. Rooney came up to me when I did and said "You can do that, but you have to start one for the Catholics too!" So I held two chapel services for home and away games. I helped start the FCA chapter in Oklahoma – I was always very involved in my faith. I had the privilege of starting it with the Steelers. It was exciting to see the respect the players had for the chapel.

John Campbell, Steelers Linebacker, 1965-1969:

I am presently the lead Chaplain for the city of Burnsville and Bloomington Police Departments. I have been a police Chaplain for eight years and have been an associate pastor at a Bloomington church for the past fifteen years. Before that I worked for our National Denomination (Church of God – Cleveland, TN) as a speaker for the Department of Lay Ministries. I served in that capacity for twenty-two years.

Unfortunately, all this positive effort came after my football career, so if my teammates have a little difficulty taking all this in, I understand as I would not have been a likely candidate for the Lord's work during my days in Pittsburgh.

To say that my goals and ambitions in life were a little less than heavenly focused, is a true assessment.

Jon Kolb, Steelers Offensive Lineman, 1969-1981:

I know what I read in the Bible. We must practice our faith. I like it when I hear about people practicing medicine, practicing law. Well, we practiced our Christianity and do so still every day and are tested every day.

In that same way, we practiced football. Tunch, Craig... in practice every day we were also tested. We became better athletes because of it. Better balance, technique...that was the brilliance of Chuck Noll. He didn't leave any of that out – we were tested every day.

You run to win. That's what the Bible tells us. Jeremiah tells us, "If you raced with men on foot and they have worn you out, how can you compete with horses?" Well, we give participation trophies today. The Bible says it matters if you win or lose. But we preach in the United States that it's not whether you win or lose, it is how you play the game. So which is it?

I heard Bud Wilkinson, the head coach at Oklahoma, once say that his definition of football was "Forty young men running on the football field desperately in need of a rest. And forty-thousand fans in attendance in need of exercise." We train to run, to win. It's radical for the Church when we say play to win, but we watch football which is all about playing to win." Again, which is it? We need to train these men to use their might to do right and win that battle.

Bob Adams, Steelers Tight End, 1969-1971:

I stuck with Scientology during and after my career. I decided eight years ago to go full time as an executive with the Church. I am now the Vice President of the Church of Scientology International and live in Los Angeles, where we have our world headquarters.

In short, Scientology is an "applied religious philosophy." You can be any religion and use Scientology, or have no religion. The word means Scien = knowledge; and ology = study of. So it is a study of knowledge. Not just data, not facts. Knowledge is something you really know to be true for yourself in making life better, more understandable. It offers tools you can use every day to get along better in life. The best thing to do to understand any subject is to read a book on it. If people are interested to find out more, I advise them to read *Dianetics*.

The first thing I learned in Scientology was a very tough course on interpersonal communications and classroom management skills. I had just gone through a divorce; I had a young child and was teaching in the off-season. I had some time and used it to advance myself spiritually. I had not heard of Scientology or Dianetics or L. Ron Hubbard. I went into it to learn something if there was something there to learn. I read Hubbard's books while doing the communications course. I saw there was a lot to this and took it to the football field.

The big changes in my play were in my ability to concentrate or focus on the ball in flight. I really learned what this thing called concentration is made of and now I could work on improving it by doing drills I found profoundly similar to drilling in athletics. Communication requires component parts that haves to happen or you "drop the ball" when omitted. Catching and running with the ball was much simpler and easier. Things I learned from Lionel Taylor made more sense than ever.

Scientology is not a passive approach to living your life. It is about action, setting and completing goals, knowing what your purpose is and going for it, which was real to me as an athlete. I took it to the classroom also. I was a better teacher because I could recognize and diagnose a student who was having trouble and really help him or her.

It took the stress out while I was in the classroom and I was more cheerful and my classrooms, were much more productive and the kids felt they were learning and felt good about that.

My relationship with my ex-wife improved greatly. Actually I could see I was becoming a better person. What I liked most, I could offer effective help to others, even those who I did not particularly know or even like. I now understood how and why I could become stressed out. For me, Scientology works. I had compassion and tolerance for others but that improved too.

My son, then a toddler, and I were very close and Scientology, as I applied to my life, helped me understand him. Parenting cannot be perfect, but I made improvements in handling my kid and our relationship was and is very strong. He now has two kids himself and is a fantastic parent for which I am very proud.

Jon Kolb, Steelers Offensive Lineman, 1969-1981:

Dave, my accountant friend since I was twenty-two also helped me. We were playing in New York once that second season and the guy that did the chapel service before the game said we need to go through life like "this" – and he put one hand up over his head and one hand down. One hand down for bringing others up, and one hand up to those who have been there before and who can give guidance.

Well, I thought about that. I didn't have a single person to reach up to. I had plenty of the "hands down" people. So I called Dave and met with him. I told him I need more of "this" – and showed him the hands up motion. He said "What?" I explained that to him and then he took it seriously and helped me.

The idea isn't that you run around like Mother Teresa. You are just there for others when they need you.

I teach class at Butler Community College. Each class has to do a term paper. Twenty-one of the twenty-eight students in the health sciences class wrote about suicide and drug prevention. It says there's a need out there and that if you are open, you'll find those to help.

Jon Staggers, Steelers Wide Receiver, 1970-1971:

Breema is about self-understanding and self-realization. It's about being present in the moment – it helps to support the finding of meaning and purpose to life by being in harmony with the mind, body, and feelings. Finding harmony with life.

You can ask the mind to participate with the body, but you can't control your feelings. In high school and college, you're mostly working with the mind. As an athlete, you work with the body and ask the mind to participate. The feelings come naturally afterwards.

Sports gave me the feeling of exhilaration. Or was it because the body and the mind and the feelings were all working together in the present moment? It's all about experiencing something you love.

My father was a coach – both in high school and college at some of the small Southern Black schools. I've been around athletes my whole life – I carried the helmets of the players he coached then. My uncle was a sociologist – they both had big influences on me. I searched for meaning in my own life using those influences and met many master teachers, and through them landed with Breema.

Brad Cousino, Steelers Linebacker, 1977-1978:

The younger linebackers such as Robin Cole, Dirt Winston, Dave LaCrosse, and I would hang around together since we were all linebackers. What really stands out is that a small group of the players met many mornings during 1978 summer camp (Donnie Shell, Tony Dungy, Mel Blount, Jon Kolb, John Stallworth, myself, and occasionally a few other players) for a Bible study of different books of the bible, such as the four Gospels, Book of Romans, Ephesians, Colossians, etc. Football camp is exceptionally tough mentally, physically and spiritually so it was good to "refresh" and share from the word of God with others who believed as I do.

Tunch Ilkin, Steelers Offensive Lineman, 1980-1992:

We'd also go out to Beasley's farm and go deer hunting and ride three-wheelers on the trails. Beasley, Dunn, and Wolfley would take me up these crazy trails – I didn't know what I was doing and would get all beat up, flipping backwards…when I caught up to them and they were all laughing at me.

In fact, me, Kolb, Webby, Peterson, and Wolfley all got baptized at Beasley's farm.

David Trout, Steelers Kicker, 1981, 1987:

After I was with the Cowboy's I was working out with getting ready to go back to camp with the Kansas City Chiefs and prayed if God had a different direction for me with my life. The next night I kicked off and the tee rolled out in front of my follow through and I broke my ankle and decided to go into missions.

Carl Peterson offered to put me on IR but I decided to follow a different path. I then worked on missionary homes in Florida and then went into Youth Ministry where I was a Youth Pastor at St. Johns church in Turnersville, NJ. I then went to Piedmont Bible College in North Carolina where I received my Airframe and Powerplant License to build and fly aircraft in 1994 to 1995.

I then took that to UIM Missions where I was a Missionary Busch Pilot flying in and out of Mexico landing the small plane in "Red" areas and was often held at gun point by Mexican drug lords. The air strips were in mountains and extremely small to land the planes to bring supplies to the Mexican people and the gospel. After our family left the mission I went back to New Jersey and built houses in the area for work.

I am planning on possibly going back to Bolivia where I grew up at, where my parents were missionaries in the Amazon where I groomed my leg playing Pro-soccer at the age of twelve.

Dwight Stone, Steelers Wide Receiver/Return Specialist, 1987-1994:

After visiting the Steelers, I prayed and read my Bible too and asked the Lord to give me a sign on how to choose a NFL Team...the following day I saw a gentleman selling pictures on the side of the road in Murfreesboro, Tennessee. The first picture I saw was a picture of Pittsburgh on the front of all the other pictures.

Tyronne Stowe, Steelers linebacker, 1987-1990:

Running through the tires and daily drills is what makes big plays possible. Stay focused on the goal, and forget about the past or the last play. Concentrate on today and the next.

Paul says in Philippians 3:13-14, "But one thing I do, forgetting those things which are behind and reaching forward to those things which are ahead, I press toward the goal for the prize of the upward call of God in Christ Jesus. Knowing that God have given us everything you need to succeed." Make the most of your opportunities that life presents and be successful. I was cut four times from the NFL. I didn't quit, and am now receiving a retirement check, because I keep my eye on the prize or goal.

Tim Johnson, Steelers Defensive Lineman, 1987-1989:

Draft day is a very nerve racking experience because after all the hard work the decision about your career and future becomes uncertain on that day. To avoid being overwhelmed by anxiety and uncertainty I actually went to a prayer meeting at my local church as a way of demonstrating my trust in Christ to lead me where he wanted me. When I finally got the call that I was drafted by the Steelers, I was excited to have an opportunity to play for another championship organization, even though we didn't win a Super Bowl during my time there.

Tim Worley, Steelers Running Back, 1989-1993:

I had been speaking professionally for quite a few years after my football career was over. It was one of those gifts that I had on the inside that had to be developed by the good Lord Himself.

Once football was over for me, I went through years and years of trying to find my way and trying to find that other thing in me besides sports and being an athlete. I found out later that I had a gift for gab! God took that gift of gab and turned it into a new career and a ministry.

LeRoy Thompson, Steelers Running Back, 1991-1993:

I got involved with charities because I do not feel comfortable when I am not blessing and helping other people. So many people like my parents, coaches, teachers, and programs like the YMCA and Boys Clubs poured so much into me. My community involvement is my way of giving back to God for his blessing on me and giving back to a village of folk and programs that helped mode me into the man I am today.

Myron Bell, Steelers Safety, 1994-1997, 2000-2001:

I have been a Steelers fan since I was seven years old. However, on draft day I cried at being taken in the fifth round; though I quickly realized I was being ungrateful for the tremendous opportunity God had blessed me with. My mother reminded me of my childhood dream to play for the Steelers. I didn't really focus on who was currently on the roster; I just set out to prove I was much better than all the safetys taken before me.

Tim Lester, Steelers Fullback, 1995-1998:

My faith was very weak at that time when I was in the NFL. I was consumed too much by the NFL logo, money, fame, and women. But the little faith I had gave me confidence to play relentless for God and fear no one but God.

Whenever I played against bigger, stronger, faster players, which was every week, I would think about the story of David and Goliath and how he defeated Goliath with one small stone. Now that's faith. That little faith I had allowed me to play eight years in the NFL and start six years out of the eight years.

Today I am growing more every day in my faith. It's a battle to break away from Satan's stronghold, but I am obedient to what God has called me to do. I still drive the bus but now I drive it for God. My mission now is a lot bigger than the bus, I lead the way for God's kingdom.

Pete Gonzalez, Steelers Quarterback, 1997-1998:

One incredible memory was receiving the phone call that I had made the team! Wow! In everyone's eyes I was the camp arm, local guy from Pitt, ugly duckling of quarterbacks. God gave me a platform to glorify him with the skills he gave me! Making the team was huge!

Hank Poteat, Steelers Cornerback, 2000-2002:

Brent Alexander helped me spiritually. I was spiritual as a kid but lost it growing up. Brent was a strong man of God – I'd try to keep my distance from him – I knew right from wrong and knew some of the things I was doing weren't right. But after a couple of seasons he became my roommate in camp. After running away there he was! I think it was a message from God.

Dan Kreider, Steelers Fullback, 2000-2007:

As a follower of Jesus Christ, I found a lot of peace with my circumstances when i trusted that God had my best interest in mind. It didn't mean that everything was going to work out the way I thought it should, but it gave me the peace to work as hard as I could, play with a reckless abandonment, and see where that would put me, as far as making the team.

I had no regrets. I left it all out on the field. If God had a different plan, than who am I to fight it?

Jeff Hartings, Steelers Center, 2001-2006:

I practiced my faith before football – I went to church weekly. But I didn't have a relationship with God – God was not my number one priority growing up. I wasn't glorifying God. I thought of myself – my football career, marriage, and kids. But football wasn't fulfilling on its own – I still had a void. That's what led me to go to Bible study class after a teammate recommended it to me.

I think faith had an impact on the team, but with only five or ten of us in the study, it'd be a stretch to say it was a great impact. Nothing like it was on those 70's teams.

Antwaan Randle El, Steelers Wide Receiver, 2002-2005, 2010:

It was the journey – not relying completely on myself. I had to do the conditioning and lift weights, of course. But nothing was possible without God. I played nine years in the NFL and had no serious injuries and had been productive every year. I had down years, but won a lot of games. God allowed me to shine on the biggest stages – in Super Bowls and playoffs. That's the journey – and I wasn't doing anything on my own, God was with me the entire way.

On the field, I prayed before games, even in the midst of a play I talked to God. I had no doubts – no fear because I only fear Him. I didn't fear making a big catch in traffic, or making a big block – that was all minor. The guy I lined up against was nothing versus my fear of God.

Off the field, my faith helped me as a husband and father to five children. I'm very thankful. I'm completely committed to my wife. There are a lot of divorces in the field I'm in – eighty percent of married players get divorced I think. Even with the money and distractions, I realized I had to be a good steward to my family and God.

I've been living my life for Jesus – that's my background – I've been living for God for ten to twelve years. There's not many football camps that teach that to kids. So, I tied it to the social part – what it is to be a man. That's what we teach the kids.

I got that from my upbringing – from my mom and dad. When my dad got saved when I was a kid, everything changed in my house. God transformed my dad – he was a big drinker, heavy into the alcohol. He used to kick us out the door when it was time for church. He wouldn't go but he wanted us too. The way the household changed when he was saved – it was so different.

Now we teach the kids to follow God. Who can you help? We serve the kids this way.

Travis Kirschke, Steelers Defensive Lineman, 2004-2009:

My faith has been important to me because it has given me a perspective of life beyond football. It has been my foundation to apply to all decisions I try to make in life. It has helped me to realize that football is what I did, but it's not all of who I am. I loved playing the game of football, but I also love the doors that it has opened for me to serve others.

Roy Lewis, Steelers Safety, 2008-2009:

The Chaplain gave me a list of scriptures to read. I asked him for the list and found one to focus on and internalized it. It helped me to forget the good and bad plays. All I did – it was about getting it and moving on. That helped me to get through – to not dwell on anything and just continue to grow as a rookie.

The Fans and City of Pittsburgh:

So much of a player's motivation to succeed is driven by external factors. Steelers players have long praised the support of their fans in helping make the city a good environment to play in. One where they are appreciated, though not without the pressure put upon them by those fans to win. Ultimately, the relationship between Steelers players and fans was usually one of mutual respect. Fans respected the team because they never acted above their fan base, contributed to the community, and played a physical style of football that represented the blue-collar work ethic of the city.

Conversely, the players respected the fans because they were a knowledgeable group that didn't turn their back on the team when it struggled, and showed great enthusiasm for the team, showing up in great numbers no matter where they played, never afraid to vocalize their support.

In addition to the fans, many of the players enjoyed the city itself. The atmosphere and cultural diversity allowed players from all parts of the country and socio-economic backgrounds to fit in easily.

In all, the fans and city made for a positive environment for players. While nit sunny California or as exciting, say, as a New Orleans, it was culturally ideal for players that fit the stereotypical Steeler player. The kind the organization looked so hard to find as it built those championship teams we've come to know.

Frank Lambert, Steelers Punter, 1965-1966:

In each of the past six years or so, our two sons Talley and Will and I have enjoyed a Steeler home game in what we call our "Pittsburgh Weekend." On the last two trips, our grandson, Reid, now ten years old, has accompanied us. I cherish those times.

Every time I return to Pittsburgh, I am reminded of how fortunate I am in having had the opportunity to play for the Steelers and for Art Rooney. I go by his statue and rub his hand, sometimes with a misty eye.

Mike Taylor, Steelers Offensive Lineman, 1968-1969:

The greatest single memory I have is being drafted number one by the Steelers. I also loved the people of Pittsburgh. Lloyd

Voss, John Henderson, and I would go hunting on local area farms chasing after rabbits and squirrels. There was a warm sense of community that I felt the minute I became familiar with the area. We enjoyed our social life as teammates and were embraced by the fans no matter if we won or lost.

Pittsburgh has great heart and it showed right away. I own fond memories from my brief time in Pittsburgh.

John Jackson: I enjoyed playing, but I loved the fans. Those are the greatest and most intelligent fans. They understand the *x's* and *o's* of the game, and that younger players take time to develop. It takes time to go through the progression from college to the pros and the Pittsburgh fans understand that.

They are the greatest fans I've ever seen due to their knowledge of their team's history and the game of football. They have a lot to teach other fans. I've been on other teams, and no fans compare.

Bobby Walden, Steelers Punter, 1968-1977:

The fans in Pittsburgh made my ten years there enjoyable. Whether we won or lost they were good people – they stuck with us. I still run into Steelers fans here that remember me, believe it or not. I even still get letters asking for autographs – 7-10 a week. If I had five dollars for every one I signed, I'd be sitting on a gold mine!

Jon Staggers, Steelers Wide Receiver, 1970-1971:

Pittsburgh was a blue-collar town. If they liked you, they liked you. If not, they let you know. They are honest fans and that was greatly appreciated. As a kid you don't appreciate that. But now I do. I could care less about that now – I love myself. And that's what meaning and purpose in life is. When you look at it, man, this is a difficult planet. It's a tough place to be.

Barry Pearson, Steelers Wide Receiver, 1972-1973:

To me, being able to say that I was part of those teams that started the Steelers dynasty is truly amazing. I was able to play with some of the greatest names in NFL history and be part of the one of the greatest plays ever (Immaculate Reception).

What could be better than that?

What I find interesting is that when I tell people I played for the Steelers and the Chiefs and then they introduce me to their friend they always say I played for the Steelers and never mention the Chiefs even though I played longer for the Chiefs. That tells me that people have a special feeling for the Steelers.

For me it was honor and a privilege to play for such a great organization.

Marv Kellum, Steelers Linebacker, 1974-1976:

It's humbling. You don't realize how lucky you are. I was talking to former Steeler, Craig Bingham, I'd do it all again for free to make it to the Super Bowl.

It opened a lot of doors for me. I have two boys and two grandkids. That ring means a lot too.

I got my first Super Bowl ring in the mail. I grew up on a farm. My mom and dad opened the package and it was awesome. My dad said it sparkled – I told him the ring was over here – the sparkle is the sun reflecting off of the diamonds!

My parents went to every game growing up – they shut down the farm to watch my games. Games then were your typical Friday Night Lights scenes.

I brought my parents to the Super Bowl. I remember my dad standing in the ocean of fans. He got his feet wet in some water there and told me now he lived – he got his feet wet in the West, and now the East.

Gary Dunn, Steelers Defensive Lineman, 1976-1987:

The town of Pittsburgh is amazing. Four years ago I was able to take my kids to a reunion game and they were just amazed at the people. It was a great experience for me – the Rooneys really took care of us. When my daughter arrived by bus at the Hilton, they gave us all a police escort. She asked why and I just gave her a look and she laughed. As a dad, that's a great thing.

I look back on the friends I made – the guys I still talk to and I'm buddies with. It's a great experience and I was just very fortunate to have that time in Pittsburgh.

Calvin Sweeney, Steelers Wide Receiver, 1980-1987:

I'll tell you this – Steelers fans are the greatest fans. I played at USC in front of 110,000 fans every day but there are no fans like Pittsburgh's.

I remember when they brought the four top picks in – me, Zach Valentine, Russell Davis, and Greg Hawthorne. They put us up in the William Penn Hotel. They dropped us off there and told us we had the rest of the day free. So, the four of us went down the street looking to grab a beer together.

We tried to find a liquor store - we were going to bring six-packs back to the hotel. But there were no stores. We went down the boulevard and a lady was walking down the street. We asked her where we could find a liquor store and she said you can't find one around here and none are open on Sundays anyway. But she directed us to a place that sold beer on Sundays – the Fishnet.

So, we find the place and all four of us go inside. It's dark, so it takes time for our eyes to adjust. But when they do we see, lo and behold, it's a strip bar. We're all young, so we go in and sit down to get a beer. We're all waiting for a waitress when we see a huge shadow behind us. This big Black guy calls all of us out by name, and I'm thinking "Oh no, we're in trouble already. We have barely been in the city and we're going to get in trouble at a strip bar!"

Well he says to us, "I know you guys. You were in the paper." And he showed us the newspaper with our pictures in it! I thought maybe the team had someone follow us around to make sure we didn't get into trouble or something. But after that I said these fans are the best fans! I knew then that they followed the team tremendously.

They really are great fans. It's a great city and the greatest fans in the world!

Marvin Cobb, Steelers Safety, 1980:

The Steelers fans gave me much more grief than the players. I was released by the Bengals, just prior to John Stallworth breaking his leg and opening up a roster spot. I had always played well against the Steelers, primarily because playing against my college teammate and friend, Lynn Swann always inspired me. Unfortunately, on a kickoff return in my first game as a Steeler, I was tackled awkwardly and fell on the ball, badly bruising my ribs. By the time, my rib healed, so had John Stallworth's leg and I was released.

I read in the paper that some fans thought the Steelers losing streak in 1980 was my fault as I was the only "outsider" on the team…oh well.

Marvin Cobb as safety.
Photo courtesy of Marvin Cobb

Marvin Cobb goes up on defensive.
Photo courtesy of Marvin Cobb

Chris Kolodziejski, Steelers Tight End, 1984:

I have so many great memories! One of them was right after I was drafted I was still living in Laramie Wyoming and I got a package on ice from an Iggy Borkowski, a longtime friend of Art Rooney, Sr. In the package was a box full of Kielbasa with a note welcoming me to Pittsburgh and the Polish community. What an amazing welcome and gift. He was one of the first people I met when I arrived at Pittsburgh.

The Steelers have the best fans in the world because they are a part of that team. I think that's the part we need to share with others...that sense of belonging. I think mentoring, coaching, and serving in the communities we live in are all wonderfully impactful things we can do to make a difference.

Dan Reeder, Steelers Running Back, 1986-1987:

I am very thankful for my opportunity in Pittsburgh. It was a great town to live in the fans and the people were great, I played with some great guys who always made me feel welcome and were real professionals. And I played for some great coaches.

In Pittsburgh the community feels like a part of the team – much more so than when I was with the LA Raiders

Merril Hoge, Steelers Running Back, 1987-1994:

I came from the West – and hunting in the West is very different from the East. I remember going to a bank in a strip mall in North Hills and looking in the woods behind the bank and saying "What the heck – is that hunting orange?" I struggled with that. In the West, there was no civilization where you hunted. You were in the mountains, far away.

To be outside of a strip mall and hunt…I didn't get that. It didn't appeal to me.

Bubby was a big hunter and invited me to go on a commercial hunting trip/show he was doing. He, me, John Elway, and Mike Shanahan all went turkey hunting together. That's the only kind of hunting I'd do when I played.

Dwight Stone, Steelers Wide Receiver/Return Specialist, 1987-1994:

My first year as a Steeler I observed Coach Noll and Mrs. Noll walked out the front door of Three River Stadium after a regular season home game. The crowd of fans circle them like we just won the Super Bowl. Coach asked the huge crowd of fans to step back (in a soft voice). Coach walked his wife to the car and opened the door for her. She got in the car and he closed the door and went to the driver's and opened his door. He started the car and turned on the A/C for his wife to be comfortable. He walked back over to the crazy, but the world's best fans and signed every autograph and smiled for pictures…I knew then what was expected of me as a Steeler on and off the field

Jim Boyle, Steelers Offensive Lineman, 1987-1988:

My best memories with the Steelers are the way they treated people. They treated everyone the same no matter what their role was on the team. And their fans are the best in the world.

I live here in Cincinnati, which most of the City hates the Steelers, but their owner could care less what happens to his players or what even happens with the team. I don't think Mike Brown could care less if the Bengal's do well or not. As long as he makes money he is happy and that's his bottom line.

This city loves their team but hates their owner and that's not a good mix.

Pittsburgh is a great organization in a great city with hardworking people who care about their team and it shows every year with the product they put out there and the seats they fill.

Terry O'Shea, Steelers Tight End, 1989-1990:

Being a local guy was a mixed bag. I grew up in Beechtree and my dad had season tickets to the Steelers. I used to go to the games during the years they were winning all the Super Bowls. He still had the tickets when I made the team. We grew up only ten minutes from the stadium.

Making the team was a blessing. Everything was local – I didn't have the worries of relocating. There was no pressure to make new friends or adjust to a new city. The year I got cut I actually had bought a house nearby beforehand – that worked out well…

On the other side, it did add to the pressure. You go to your usual places and all the people know you and evaluate you every week. After a while you find yourself avoiding places and people. You just don't want to deal with it.

So much is mental. I found myself focusing more on not messing up than on performing at my top level.

My daughter always tells people her dad played for the Steelers. Funny story – I was picking my kids up one day and I ran into

Mel Blount and re-introduced myself to him. He is an impressive guy – the size of him to have been able to play cornerback.

Well, I asked him to say hi to my daughters, and he leaned in and said hi to them. Later on in the car I asked the girls what they thought, and my one daughter said, "Oh my God! I can't wait to tell my friends I met a real Steeler!"

Craig Veasey, Steelers Defensive Lineman, 1990-1992:

One memory sticks in my head. I was at the Giant Eagle grocery shopping. I never thought of myself as anything special – I just played football is all. That people see you and know you was a shock to me.

Well, I'm standing in line talking to the cashier and I asked her if she was going to the game. She asked if I as kidding – the game was sold out and there was no way to get tickets, she said. So, I told her I'd get her two tickets – and it was like she won the lottery. Her reaction to the tickets – you couldn't measure it. It was great.

I didn't realize until then how important the Steelers were to the city.

Richard Shelton, Steelers Cornerback, 1990-1993:

Tell the fans Pittsburgh is a great city. You represent your team – wherever they play you take over the stadium. That's a true sign of great fans.

I would love to work for the Steelers front office. You have the best fans in the world. And the Steelers are a great organization. The Rooneys run it well.

Craig Veasey, Steelers Defensive Lineman, 1990-1992:

Growing up in Houston, the Steelers were my favorite team, believe it or not. The local papers took pictures of me with my Steelers memorabilia when I got drafted. I was happy to be there. Once I left Pittsburgh, I missed it. Nowhere else has fans like Pittsburgh – you kind of take it for granted until you leave.

Levon Kirkland, Steelers Linebacker, 1992-2000

The fans are great. I respect their knowledge of the game. They understood how to approach players – there was no fan I didn't like. They are involved – it's like a religion. It's nice when they recognize you as a good player.

I was blessed to play for a great organization and city. It was not all my doing – I had the support of my family and God. Now, I am giving back to the game I love in a way that is hopefully honest and pure, mentoring and coaching young athletes.

Kendall Gammon, Steelers Long Snapper, 1992-1995:

I remember by first game – in Houston. It was Cowher's first win as a coach. And the AFCC games we lost and won. The highs and lows. And I remember all the people stomping in the stands on game days at Three Rivers. They were feverish fans. It was a pretty cool thing.

Kendall Gammon, Steelers Long Snapper, 1992-1995:

I was just happy to be drafted by anyone! The Steelers were steeped in such tradition. I knew about them of course but you don't realize until you get there what kind of city and people they are. I loved it all – the people and city were awesome. Being in Pittsburgh was one of the best experiences of my life. It was a great organization and I felt fortunate and honored to be there and tried my best to represent it.

I remember staying at the Hilton at the Point. It was a beautiful day and my wife and I went for a walk. Just the beauty of the skyline and the city. It's a great memory for me.

Driving back through the city after practices – the hills and skyline…I loved that. And Western, PA gold courses are some of the best in the country. I'm an avid golfer, I ordered a set of gold clubs within an hour of making the team! I figured that even if they cut me tomorrow, at least I'd get a nice set of clubs out of it!

Going up to Mount Washington with Kevin and Terry Greene and seeing the city is a great memory. There's so much personality in the city that many people don't know. And coming into the city through the Fort Pitt tunnels and seeing the city open up in front of you – wow – it's indescribable.

Tim Jorden, Steelers Tight End, 1992-1993:

I have a great admiration for the Steelers organization and the Rooneys. I have an even bigger admiration for the fans. I have travelled all over the world and I see Steelers signs and jerseys everywhere I go. It is amazing how many Steelers shirts and bumper stickers I see in Arizona…every time I see the Steeler emblem I say "Go Stillers" and I get an approving nod from the Steelers fan.

On occasion I bring up that I played two seasons in The Burgh, but only when I have time for a long conversation!

Chad Brown, Steelers Linebacker, 1993-1996, 2006:

Being a part of Steeler Nation is truly special. The Patriots were special but it's not the same feel and relationship with the city. The Steelers are the city – you can't separate the two. There are kids wearing Steelers diapers, in Steelers sheets in Steelers cribs. These are in real houses – not just on TV.

You can't remove the Steelers from the city. They are one and the same.

Oliver Gibson, Steelers Defensive Lineman, 1995-1998:

You know, I looked forward to playing against Pittsburgh most of all. The players didn't give me grief, but the greatest salutation was the boos I received from fans. They remembered me, which was the greatest honor, instead of them saying "who is that guy?"

Lee Flowers, Steelers Safety, 1995-2003:

It was a great opportunity for me. My last three years of Georgia Tech we didn't win a damn thing - we were terrible. In Pittsburgh I was shell-shocked.

I didn't understand the magnitude of the Steelers and the city when I was drafted – not until I got there. It's all Black and Gold – it was great. The fans would literally die for you.

Tom Myslinski, Steelers Offensive Lineman, 1996-1997, 2000:

Looking back, I should never have left. I loved it there – from the coaches, to my teammates, to the city – and still do.

I'm going to be straight up – moving sucks! And once you throw kids into it, it's terrible. In fact, I'm in the middle of one now. There are only so many great players out there. Life for the average Joe in the NFL is a rough one. A family's love, and a strong independent wife, is the only thing that can survive a move.

Matt Cushing, Steelers Tight End, 1998-2004:

Off the field, Steelers fans are second to none. It was always impressive to travel to places like Seattle, Dallas, and San Francisco and have the Steelers fans taking over the stadium. Seeing 20,000 to 30,000 fans in black and gold at road games was a cool sight.

The support in the community in Pittsburgh was also memorable, including the playoff game that when I drove out of my neighborhood to go downtown the night before the game, most of the houses had balloons and signs wishing us luck. That exemplified the spirit in the community and why I love the city of Pittsburgh so much.

Bobby Shaw, Steelers Wide Receiver, 1998-2001:

The best thing about Pittsburgh – and I know this from being on a few teams – is that it's a football town. From the organization to the fans. It's truly a family affair, that's what sets Pittsburgh apart.

The players all bond together. And I had friends on the team I had known for a long time before. I didn't feel alone due to the atmosphere. They were comedians and all accepting guys

Chris Fuamatu-Ma'afala, Steelers Running Back, 1998-2002:

Pittsburgh is a blue-collar, hard-working smash mouth mentality, and that's how I ran.

I remember pulling up the stadium in camp in my '92 Ultima. I was still on my sixth round rookie salary. It had a dent in the left side…it cost me $2,500 but worked well! I was embarrassed, but the fans didn't care. I was driving with the windows down because the air-conditioning didn't work and I was just trying to keep my head down and not get noticed. But the fans saw me and started yelling "FU!!" They didn't care…I never expected that kind of following.

The fans are so loyal. Back in 2010, I took my wife and kids back to Pittsburgh. They saw pictures but never experienced it. We went through the tunnel and onto the field. There were guys in the stands yelling "FU!" My kids asked my wife why they were booing me! We explained to them what they were saying. My daughter was nine then and she was just star struck.

Troy Edwards, Steelers Wide Receiver, 1999-2001:

The fans had so much knowledge. I remember at a grocery store – Giant Eagle – a woman – she must have been eighty-two years old, she came up to me and said certain things I should have done on a play in some game. Real specific. I was shaking my head at how much this eighty year old knew. The fans were just loyal and smart.

Mike Logan, Steelers Safety, 2001-2006:

Playing for an organization like the Pittsburgh Steelers is indescribable. I was born in Saint Clair Village on the South Side section of Pittsburgh and raised in Whitaker Projects in West Mifflin. I only dreamed that I could make it out and grow up to be a professional football player, let alone for my hometown team the Steelers!

My grandfather was the ultimate Steelers fan and he worked in the steel mills. (He passed away) before my dreams came to fruition, but I always felt his presence on the practice field. The

J&L Steel Mill where my grandfather, Theodore Harber, was one of the first African-American safety managers was demolished and the Steelers practice facility is now housed there.

I was emotional when I signed my contract as my father and I looked out the window at the land where my grandfather had worked. Playing professional football in your hometown is a blessing because your friends and family get to see you up close and personal as you accomplish your dreams, but can quickly become a heavy burden.

Between juggling numerous ticket request, time demands, financial stressors, and everyone pulling at you, you still have to learn your play book & play football! I experienced all of that but I wouldn't have traded it for anything. I truly feel blessed. I was able to come home and spend time with my mother who passed away at the age of fifty-one. She said one of her proudest moments was seeing her son play in the Super Bowl for the Steelers. I'll always have that memory entrenched in my mind.

Jeff Hartings, Steelers Center, 2001-2006:

The Super Bowl parade – I gained a new appreciation and perspective on the Steelers fans after the parade. The Steelers fans can be fanatics and that can be overwhelming. It definitely was for me at first until we won the Super Bowl. Then, I realized they just love the Steelers. They are not obsessed – they are just die-hard fans.

It was a great experience for me.

Rodney Bailey, Steelers Defensive Lineman, 2001-2003, 2006:

I love the city of Pittsburgh, it's one of my favorite places in the United States. The food and enthusiasm...and all of the time, in the offseason and in-season. I'm glad to see the tradition keeping on as new players come in.

I'm proud of my seven-year career. I got the chance to play with great friends and for great coaches. It was a lot of fun. I didn't know what the NFL life would be like but I'm very, very, very happy to have worn the black and gold helmet for four years of my career.

Martin Nance, Steelers Wide Receivers, 2008-2009:

One of my favorite memories was the parade the city had for the team after the Super Bowl. As cold as it was, Steeler Nation was amazing. Everyone came out and showed their love and support for the team. People were hanging out of eighth story windows; they had banners, jerseys, and anything else you could imagine to show their pride. That's a memory all the guys will cherish for a long time.

Jeremy Staat, Steelers Defensive Lineman, 1998-2000:

I never understood the new stadium. The Steelers were worth, what, eight hundred million dollars? But they wanted to raise ticket prices and taxes and put in more luxury boxes. I thought the reason for the stadium and the teams was for the fans!

Being in the military life is about service – service to others and yourself. The owners and players are servants to the fans and I feel like they didn't do true service to the fans. I was taken aback by it. Shouldn't we cut fans a break? These are hard-working people – their houses are painted black and gold, they have Steelers tattoos...I felt they were missing the point!

Team Culture:

While the Rooney family was instrumental in first setting the tone for the family atmosphere of the team, ultimately the coaches and players had to carry that responsibility on the field and in the locker room. And they had to do so while understanding the business side of the game and the fact that winning wasn't optional. It wasn't good enough to be a close-knit team. The Rooneys, and the city itself, demanded a winner.

Early on, mistakes were certainly made. Winning did not come easy at first. In fact, at first, the wins rarely came at all. Why? Art Rooney Sr. was said by some to be "too nice" – bringing in friends as coaches who were less effective, and wheeling and dealing far too often for the quick fix and favored player, rather than patiently building from within and allowing for team continuity. Art Rooney consistently wrestled with the need to maintain that fine but necessary line between friendship and business. It took nearly a decade for the team to find the right balance of close-knit culture and tough-minded business decision-making that often required releasing favored players and coaches for the betterment of the team.

In the end, one of the key moves that enabled the team to take its successful leap into the 70s was Dan Rooney's insertion into a leadership role in the business decision processes of the team. From player and front office personnel accounts, Dan Rooney was better able to make those tough personnel decisions, while still maintaining that family atmosphere his father worked so hard to create.

Looking back, it's easy to understand the Steelers unwavering dedication to building through the draft. It took a decade to undo a legacy of losing by doing the opposite. There is an institutional memory on this team that refuses to let this team repeat those mistakes of the past. And that's to be respected. It's easy to bury a painful history in the past and forget about it. This team reminds itself of those mistakes for the sole purpose of insuring they don't repeat them. And that attitude passed down through the front office and to the team. The front office, players, and coaches recognized they were in the business of winning – while also recognizing you can do so as a family.

Of course, winning seasons also tends to make it easier to bond. Having said all of this, there were still down times and negative moments, especially in those early years. Even the best of families have falling outs and disagreements.

Bill Asbury, Steelers Running Back, 1966-1968:

I was confident that I could learn the plays, but worried about being "tough" enough. A "fight" during a fall practice drill with linebacker Rod Breedlove helped me adjust and gain a measure of confidence, and perhaps respect.

It was part of the rite of passage. Dick Hoak, Roy Jefferson, Brady Keys, John Baker, Ben McGee were among those veterans I got to know as a rookie. They not only were good teammates, but good guys, showing me around Pittsburgh.

Bill Asbury eludes a Cardinal tackler.
Photo courtesy of Bill Asbury

Bill Asbury shows imposing size at running back.
Photo courtesy of Bill Asbury

Ralph Berlin, Steelers Trainer, 1968-1993:

We had a poker game every week at Franco's house. Me, Joe Greene, Moon Mullins, L.C., Bradshaw, who would come, lose a couple-hundred bucks then quit, and Stallworth, who really just came to eat the chicken. We played every week on Monday or Tuesday during the season. It was a nice form of camaraderie you don't have today.

Dick Shiner, Steelers Quarterback, 1968-1969:

We were a young team. The last game of the season we still had tape on our helmets with our names on it. We had eighty-seven guys play that year! I'd look in the huddle and didn't even know our receivers.

The Steelers were a team in transition. Now, that doesn't mean we didn't have good players. There were.

In 1969, we could have won at least five games, but we won one. The Giants beat us by a total of six points in two games. Dallas beat us 10-7; Green Bay 38-34; New Orleans 27-24, and the offense only had the ball eighteen minutes in that game and we ended up losing in the final seconds.

They were young kids. L.C. Greenwood weighted only 210 pounds then, but he had to play because of injuries. Green was a rookie – but even then he was a man among boys. L.C. needed time. Kolb was a rookie and weighed only 230 pounds. Sam Davis, he should have played more. I thought he was one of the best linemen we had, and eventually he became a great player there.

When I was traded to the Giants from the Steelers, I remember talking to Fran Tarkenton. I was eating lunch with him, and he said to me, "I bet you're glad to be here." I said that I really liked the guys here, but not really. I said we could have won five games and we had a lot of good players on that team. It would just take some time. All the guys they drafted weren't the same size they were four years later.

John Rowser, Steelers Cornerback, 1970-1973:

I was there in a growing situation – it was fun to be there. The key was learning not to lose, really. My first couple of years there we would lose games in the last quarter because of mistakes.

I had a talk with Joe Greene about not making excuses, I remember. I told Joe that if Paul Warfield makes the winning catch at the end of the game, that's supposed to happen, but I'm not going to let that happen. If I tip the ball, make a shoe-string tackle, whatever it takes. I wouldn't let it happen – we couldn't make excuses.

The situation got better as we got better players. Fuqua, Pearson, Dave Smith, Ron Shanklin, Hubie Bryant…we got more athletic people – especially from the South. Mixing those guys up with the veteran players gave us lots more talent and less mistakes.

That first year, Bradshaw made a lot of mistakes. But he improved and his wide receivers and line got better, and the defense let up few points.

We were very loose – and that was from the coaches too. Noll played the best people and let them be themselves. The Steelers were the first team to go without team blazers. All the other teams' players had to wear team blazers, but Noll let the team express itself as they wanted. That showed up in play – they let athletes be athletes. They didn't let the system confine you.

Al Young, Steelers Wide Receiver, 1971-1972:

I really enjoyed my time in Pittsburgh. It's a great organization and a great city. The year I got sick, they had no responsibility for me. They could have said "See you later." Instead, they kept me around and paid my contract for the season. They didn't have to do that.

Two years later they called me back to be a scout. I did that for a short while but it just conflicted too much with my coaching job.

I was just a kid from a small school – they didn't have to do all of that for me. It was just wonderful.

Gordon Gravelle, Steelers Offensive Lineman, 1972-1976:

We were a team that had developed a special chemistry of camaraderie and respect for each other, like brothers. We also had the attitude of hard work and confidence that kept everyone focused but loose. It started with Coach Noll who would preach to us to work hard all week in preparation for the next game and then "have fun on Sunday."

J.T. Thomas, Steelers Cornerback, 1973-1982:

We were so synchronized. The team would react in sync but not to the play call. We'd stop the other team and come back to the sidelines and the coach would ask us what we did. Then, that became a play for us.

I think what made it work was that the coaches didn't tell us how to do things as much as they told us what the overall objective was. We didn't play our own brand of football – it was one laser focused brand – to destroy. It was the varied personalities in harmony that was freaky. We had eleven All-Pro starting defensemen in Super Bowl X. The system of play was based on talent and technique more so than theory. That's why when those players retired the playbook became useless.

The coaches would record those plays to learn from them. Dallas tried to implement our defense after we played them. But they couldn't do it – they didn't have the personnel to execute it, they said.

John Banaszak, Steelers Defensive Lineman, 1974-1981:

We were the classic championship football team. That is, you run the football and play great defense. We had nine hall of fame players on those teams. Not one of those great players felt they were any better than the whole of the team.

I can remember a number of years ago when the Steelers lost a playoff game. It was on the anniversary of the Immaculate Reception and Franco had a party to celebrate the anniversary. He invited about twelve to fifteen players and wives. As we were finishing dinner the manager of the restaurant came in our private room and told us that Kordell Stewart was in the next room with his family. We all went over and introduced ourselves and wished him well.

What struck me funny was the fact that he was alone. As a team win or lose we would have had a party or at least guys would of had made dinner plans together.

Lynn Swann, Steelers Wide Receiver, 1974-1982:

The Steelers won six Super Bowls and went to eight. But no matter how many more they win, those guys in '74 can say they laid the foundation. That's a great feeling.

John Banaszak, Steelers Defensive Lineman, 1974-1981:

I never once felt like I wasn't accepted as a valuable member of those great football teams that I played on by my teammates. I knew that I wasn't as talented a football player as Mean Joe Greene or LC Greenwood. I found a way to contribute to the success of those football teams. Knowing that I gained the respect of those great football players is enough satisfaction for me. I never made all pro or played in the Pro Bowl but I've got three Super Bowl World Championship rings and a lot of memories and stories about those teams and players that I wouldn't trade for any other accolade.

Reggie Harrison, Steelers Running Back, 1974-1977:

The older guys I listened to, like Greene – they had been there before and you could see them getting excited. They had been there before the team was good.

We knew it was Chuck's team. Russell and Walden were there the longest. Russell told me that in Chuck's first year he held a team meeting and told the team he knew why the team was losing. "Most of you guys aren't worth a damn," Chuck said, and told them most won't be there for long.

Dick Conn, Steelers Cornerback, 1974:

The whole year was memory after memory but the playoffs and Super Bowl week are still embedded in my mind. After beating the Raiders in Oakland and realizing that we were going to the Super Bowl, wow. I got tickets for my Mom and my girlfriend, now wife, Sharon as well as some of my high school friends. They were only twenty dollars back then.

I remember that I had hurt my elbow the week before and really wasn't supposed to play but Coach Noll made sure I got in the game. I didn't realize what he had done until much later in life. When the game was over everybody ran to pick up Coach Noll after the win but I ran on the field and picked up the game ball. Andy Russell had always stood on a chair after each game and gave the game ball to someone. I had actually intended to give this one to him. I told him it was for him but if I saw him getting ready to stand up on a chair that I was taking it back. Sure enough he was getting ready to get on a chair with that ball and I took it back, put it in my locker. I went back out and got another ball and gave it to Andy. He gave it to Mr. Rooney and I kept the game ball. I got everybody to sign that ball and I still have it.

When it is all over you really get emotional thinking about camp, some of the guys that didn't make the team and my dad who had helped me be the player I was and not being there with mom for the biggest game of my life. I still get real emotional.

Gary Dunn, Steelers Defensive Lineman, 1976-1987:

Ernie Holmes scared the heck out of me. I remember the first day the vets came in and he came out in this rubber suit. You could barely see his eyes through the slits. Halfway through practice he falls down to the ground. The trainers had ice packs on him cooling him down. They told me he does this every year. He was just trying to lose weight!

After practice, we went to the gym then waited an hour for dinner. But I noticed the vets all got in their cars after the gym and came back at dinner. One day I got in my GTO and decided to follow them. I ended up following them to the 19th Hole in Latrobe. I walked in and saw Greene, L.C., and Dwight there. They had iced Rolling Rocks with limes set out for them. They all stopped and looked at me.

They asked me what I was doing there and I said I was getting a beer. They all looked at me and said "Rook, come on over and have a beer." I went every day with them after that.

Neil Graff, Steelers Quarterback, 1976-1977:

When I knew I was going to the Steelers it was a little intimidating because of the great successes that they had accomplished. I will never forget the first night I was in Pittsburgh I was eating at a Pizza Hut and Joe Greene was there with his family and he came over and welcomed me and made me feel very comfortable. That kind of attitude was very indicative of the Steelers. They were like a large family and welcomed me even though I was joining the team in mid-season and had not had a chance to get to know any of the players.

Terry Bradshaw and I were both single, so we spent a lot of time together both on and off the field. It was a great learning experience to play behind Terry and hear how he persevered through some tough times to find success.

Ray Pinney, Steelers Offensive Lineman, 1976-1982, 1985-1987:

It was rare that we practiced in "game" type conditions against our own D-line, thankfully, because they were outstanding as a unit. The thing I remember most was on Friday's we would practice goal line situations. Our offense would practice against our number one defense and "show" them what types of plays the opposing team runs in goal line situations. Most teams run two tight ends on the goal line and I was placed at tight end for blocking purposes on the "show" team. Normally, the opposing team would throw to the tight end and I would have a chance to catch a touchdown pass against the first team defense. Early in the season I caught a couple of passes in this drill and celebrated this event in the end zone.

After a couple more TD catches and celebrations in subsequent weeks, Jack Lambert had seen enough. The next week when I caught another TD pass in the drill, he put a huge hit on me. This first thing I remember is getting up off the ground and trying to find my helmet which was no longer on my head.

Robin Cole, Steelers Linebacker, 1977-1988:

I was expected to learn quickly. Then Toews got hurt in camp so I started every preseason game. I broke my arm though in the first game of the season and that set me back eight games. I played with a cast on my arm when I got back – it was like playing with one-and-a-half arms.

The next year Loren and I shared the position.

It was frustrating at times, but that is professional football.

We learned from one another. We were the best linebacker corps then and I fit in there with my aggressive play. I enjoyed it – I could have easily ended up with a ton of sacks if I was given the opportunity to rush the passer more. But that wasn't needed, we had the Steel Curtain. So I played the run and dropped into coverage. I could cover man-to-man. I didn't carry much weight – I had to cover twenty yards downfield.

Craig Wolfley, Steelers Offensive Lineman, 1980-1989:

As a rookie offensive lineman you run plays as the other team's defense as well as take snaps for your own offense. It was a really hot day, Pinney the starter was hurt so I ran the entire practice from the defensive reps to the starter reps. I was worn out and hot at the end of practice and was slow getting back to the offensive huddle.

Bradshaw calls out to all of us to "hustle up" and I reply that I'm coming but use Webster's nickname for Bradshaw – "Turdshaw."

Well, Bradshaw's on one knee in the huddle, looking down, sweat dripping from his face. Then he looks up at me and glares at me and says "Boy – you ain't earned that right yet."

I remember that – and I'd never say that again.

Jed Hughes, Steelers Linebacker Coach, 1984-1988:

The one memory that stands out was our game against the 49ers in 1987. With the victory, Chuck Noll passed his mentor (and Bill Walsh's mentor) Paul Brown on the NFL's all-time win list. My dad had died suddenly on Thursday before the game. Chuck awarded the game ball to the defense. Mike Merriweather handed me the ball and said the defense had dedicated the game to my father. We won the game 30-17. It was very personal.

Delton Hall, Steelers Cornerback, 1987-1991:

They tried to groom me and guide me, but I had my own ideas. I wanted to chase women and go to parties. Like twenty-two year olds like to do.

I think I hurt my career drinking and staying out late. I didn't get the proper rest I needed. I did all the workouts, don't get me wrong. But the street life wore me down. Coach Noll always said not to burn the candle at both ends. I should have listened to him.

Tim Tyrell, Steelers Running Back, 1989:

I remember once I got into a fight in practice. Delton Hall hit me when I was way out of bounds. It cut my lip...I went crazy on him until the other guys broke us up. I was just on the scout team! Later in practice they ran a sweep to the right and a wide receiver was blocking Hall and I ran right at him and knocked him over. I threw the ball at him and went at him again – I'm glad someone broke us up again. That's the unique thing about it. At the end of the practice you both ask each other if you're ok and you go back to the locker room. I didn't really want to slug it out with those guys – I already was knocked out enough times as a 250 pound fullback flying around the field.

Gary Jones, Steelers Safety, 1990-1994:

Well, we were 4-28 the two years I was there with the Jets. At the time I didn't realize how much I missed Pittsburgh. New

York was so big, and stuff was going on all through the week. We had models and broadcasters on the team. In Pittsburgh, two-thirds of us after practice would go to the Clark Bar and get drinks and shoot pool. In New York, it was like a beehive was disturbed – everyone would go in different directions after practice. You wouldn't see guys until the next day.

It just wasn't close-knit like it was in Pittsburgh. And losing wasn't fun either.

Ernie Mills, Steelers Wide Receiver, 1991-1996:

My teammates are the greatest memories, especially the 1991 draft class. We were so excited and hungry to prove ourselves and had a lot of ups and downs. I wouldn't trade those times for anything. Of course the catch that helped us win the AFC Championship game, had to be the biggest of my lifetime. Fans would be surprised at how focused our team was in 1994 even though the video was getting all of the media attention. That lost hurt equally as bad as Super Bowl XXX, because that '94 team was a great team with so many weapons on both sides of the ball.

Kendall Gammon, Steelers Long Snapper, 1992-1995:

I remember Kevin Greene once as I was coming into practice, using the ball machine to shoot balls at people as they walked through the gate on to the field. But I remember most the guys on Thursdays and Fridays after practice, going to the Clark Bar and playing cribbage, believe it or not. Just having a beer or two – nothing big. There was a lot of camaraderie on the team. It was the closest team I've been on in my career.

You have to give Coach Cowher credit. He weeded out the guys that didn't fit and brought in real leaders, like Kevin Greene. We worked hard and efficiently. We didn't work too long or too short. Coach Cowher was upfront with us that different players got treated differently. I didn't expect to be treated the same as Rod Woodson. He was tougher on me and I appreciate that – it made me a better player and extended my career. I was very impressed with Cowher and the rest of the coaches. I'd mess around with Marv Lewis. This was a team that when I left and saw the people, I'd still talk with them at length. I remember when I made the Pro Bowl when I was playing for Kansas City – the first long-snapper ever selected to the Pro Bowl – Cowher was the AFC coach and I had a good time talking with him and the coaches.

Willie Williams, Steelers Cornerback, 1993-1996, 2004-2005:

It felt great to be a veteran because I knew the younger guys would be watching. I felt I could show through my actions and performance what it took to be a great player. I think Ike Taylor and Bryant McFadden were the guys I mentored. I knew these two guys were going to be great players in the league one day. The main thing they may have learned from me is how to practice. I was a person that was big on the saying "You play like you practice." They saw how I approached the game mentally in the film room as well.

I think it is so successful in Pittsburgh because there's a standard you have to uphold as a Steeler. It goes back to the steel curtain days. Whether you were a backup, you have to be ready to play. Also, I think playing for the Pittsburgh Steelers is a privilege because what was set by the guys back in the 70s. The Steelers are such an oriented, solid and caring organization, it makes you play hard, because you really feel a part of something good.

Cowher was a coach that demanded the best out of his players especially the veterans. He wanted the veterans to lead the way for the rookies because eventually they may have to step up and play their rookie year. The veterans had to set the tone every week. If you couldn't handle it, you had to move on.

Randy Cuthbert, Steelers Running Back, 1993-1994:

I loved the Steelers mindset. Their blueprint for success involves building your team around class people, playing great defense, and controlling the ball on offense with a strong running game. I believe that winning football at any level is predicated on those things. There were so many great coaches in Pittsburgh, but I really enjoyed being around Dick Hoak and Ron Erhardt. They were class people and great coaches.

Tony Parisi (Equipment Manager) and Ralph Berlin (Trainer) were also great to all of us. When I left the Steelers for the World League, they didn't have enough helmets so I called Tony and he sent me my Steeler helmet. What a class outfit!

Jason Gildon, Steelers Linebacker, 1994-2003:

You have to look at it in the context of what it is. It's your job but you are also part of a team and part of a bigger business. The success depends on the team, and guys vying for your job is part of that success and paying it forward. You need to pay it forward – it benefits everyone. You do your part – that's how the organization has been successful and competitive year in and year out. Guys do their part. I've been around a lot of older guys who helped them when they were just starting out. When the new best comes in it's your turn.

You look at the organization as a whole. Being a part of it and calling Pittsburgh home. We're all fortunate. To have an organization like the Steelers and to be able to take part in their success. There's a reason for that. It starts with Mr. Rooney and his approach. It really is a close-knit organization from the top to the equipment managers. You can't see it from the outside but it's a vital part of the success and the reason why the team is continually on the top year in and year out.

I think what contributed most to my success was never being afraid of hard work. If it came down to which guy worked the hardest, I felt I always had a chance. I tried to be the best I could be consistently.

As far as not getting the glory some of those other guys got, I think it just depends on who you ask. I can honestly say I'm proud to have been a part of such a great legacy of Pittsburgh linebackers. It's an honor to have my name in the history books with guys like L.C. Greenwood that graced the team before me. I'm honored to be mentioned in the same sentence as they are.

When I look back on my career, I had a lot of fun. I can't complain. The Steelers organization is one of the best in the country. As for the glory, yeah, it depends on who you ask, really.

Eric Ravotti, Steelers Linebacker, 1994-1996:

My fondest memories at any level I have played were my teammates. The relationships you make when you depend on others and others depend on you are stronger than you can imagine. Unless you have looked across the huddle at a teammate without speaking and you both are thinking the same thing – that is an experience that you cannot put into words.

I could not tell you about the majority of our wins or losses or even my individual statistics, but I could describe with great accuracy the many times where I experienced a moving experience with my teammates, trainers, equipment managers, etc.

Erric Pegram, Steelers Running Back, 1995-1997:

When I was with the Atlanta Falcons I thought that was the NFL, selfish players, no team concept and me, me, me attitude. But when I walked in to Three Rivers Stadium in 1995 and I saw those four Super Bowls trophies encased in glass, I knew right away this was different. Adjustment? It's not that hard to adjust to something special, it was like making the team all over again but this time it feels right.

I'd have to say Coach Hoak inspired me very much, it wasn't what he said but it was what he didn't say, the only time he'd congratulate you was after a win, I never saw him after a loss and he was right, why say what a good job you did after you just got your ass kicked. It made sense to me, like Lombardi said, "Winning isn't everything, it's the only thing," and I dig that.

You ask any player what he misses about the game, as many personal friends as you have on the team, you miss the team, even people you didn't care for as much, they were still part of the trip. We used to vote on a team offensive and defensive MVP which I always thought was silly because this is a team sport and nobody experienced success without the team helping and that's what I wrote in my vote. Coach Cowher read it in front of the team and I was moved that he did that.

Carlos Emmons, Steelers Linebacker, 1996-1999:

The defense relies on you doing your job. It's a machine – a system – and you have to play within the system. You have to buy in to the system – some guys don't buy in and play selfish. If one guy tries to be a hero or misses their gap it gasses the whole defense.

With the Steelers, you can't want a sack every play. Every player wants to pass rush every play. But you have to know that when you drop into coverage you're opening up a chance for someone else. When I played with Jason Gildon, he got probably got three to four times more pass rush chances than I did. I was the better guy in coverage, so that's how they utilized us. To win games, you have to sacrifice some things.

Will Blackwell, Steelers Wide Receiver, 1997-2001:

It was mostly an older team. Kordell kept to himself more then. Charles Johnson trained with me. He picked me up and I showed him San Diego State and he built a training program that we worked out on. Hawkins was a big inspiration and gave me a lot of advice.

Hines was one too – he came in a year after me. We became friends – we both felt the frustration of trying to play. They let both of us play the final game of my second season. Then they let Charles Johnson go and drafted Troy Edwards. We knew it would be the death knell for someone, but it didn't stop me from trying.

Hines and I tried to be the ultimate duo. He did things I couldn't do and I did things he couldn't do – but we both helped the other guy out to sharpen each other's skills. We knew Troy was going to get playing time as a first rounder, unless he insulted someone's mother or something!

Of course we helped Troy. But we were frustrated – we thought we had a nice receiving corps. But there's nothing you can do except try harder. Then, they drafted Plaxico. Now, what do you do? We helped him too. I was still here, fighting for a roster spot. But there were two round one receivers. We had a nice array of talent but still little success.

We were a good group that liked each other. We all played Madden – Hines and Deshea Townsend were the best. Earl Holmes – I remember practicing in the cold at Three Rivers they'd bring the water faucets in to clean them off in the showers. It was like thirty degrees outside and Holmes would get the water hose and start spraying all of us in the shower with that freezing water, We'd run like girls…that water was freezing!

We all had a real brotherhood. We supported each other. When Holmes was close to breaking the tackling record, we all supported him and cheered for him. We all hung out together and had similar interests.

I remember too after the Thanksgiving game where they screwed up the coin toss. I had Thanksgiving at Jerome's house. It was the first time I had Thanksgiving dinner away from home because I couldn't get home.

These kinds of feelings are the ones you have on teams that go. You've got to like each other. It's got to be about "us" – you're all connected – if you're down in the tank, you drag us all down unless we lift you up.

Courtney Hawkins, Steelers Wide Receiver, 1997-2000:

Pittsburgh, for me, going from a place of uncertainty. It was a family atmosphere and the tradition and fans were unbelievable. It was unreal to be accepted by the Steeler Nation. Without question, it was the greatest place to play.

Halfway through my first year there, I stopped in to Cowher's office. I told him "Thanks for bringing me to the NFL." He smiled back at me.

It was what you hear growing up – it was the dream as a boy growing up. Pittsburgh was the dream. This is what I thought it would be. It wasn't like coming to work. It was great and anyone on that team was just fortunate to have played there.

Bobby Shaw, Steelers Wide Receiver, 1998-2001:

We knew how to joke and be professional at the same time. It was a good balance. Bettis was funny – but with his status as a proven vet, he could get away with more than we could.

Cowher was great at allowing some leeway for fun – to take a moment to allow guys to laugh then let players self-police themselves afterwards. That balance allowed us to enjoy the game and being with one another on and off the field.

Chris Fuamatu-Ma'afala, Steelers Running Back, 1998-2002:

I went out there and was just myself. But I think what put me over the top was my one on one with Levon Kirkland in training camp. I got an early jump and hit him and we ended up in a scuffle. I was naive – I didn't know he was the defensive captain! We were pushing and shoving then all the linebackers came in and knocked me over.

I think the coaches saw then I wasn't afraid. But it was a long training camp after that.

They all targeted me after that. You don't touch the captain of the defense. But I didn't back down.

Jerome [Bettis] came in after the scuffle with Levon and pushed some folks back. He and McAfee told me to keep my head on a swivel and told me who to watch out for. We'd watch film after practice and could see who was coming to get me and who to watch out for. It was a long five weeks.

Wayne Gandy, Steelers Offensive Lineman, 1999-2002:

My best memory was probably just how the team hung out. You know if you live in Pittsburgh there's not a lot of places to go. It was different than a lot of teams. It wasn't just three or four guys hanging out. It was ten, twelve, fifteen guys.

If a guy said he was having a charity event, you'd find half the team was there. That was not normal – usually you had two to three good friends, but in Pittsburgh you had a lot of the team support, on and off the field.

The organization, even now, they still send me Christmas cards. Out of all the organizations I played for, they are the only team that has continued to show support and reach out, even with a Christmas card and invite back with free travel to see games and things like that.

Hank Poteat, Steelers Cornerback, 2000-2002:

Earl Holmes was the funniest guy I ever met. He'd watch a lot of movies and knew them word-for-word. Porter was always talking tough and trying to compete with someone on something. Kirkland was a serious leader. And Flowers was funny too.

Pittsburgh was a lot different than New England. All the players hung out together – it was like a big family. All were cool and had fun. The winning, great fans…going out together as a team…I have never been part of anything like it since the Steelers. The families knew each other….I really enjoyed my time there.

Tee Martin, Steelers Quarterback, 2000-2001:

On T.V., you think you learn about the team. But we knew each other's personal lives. We hung out a lot. The older guys had their cliques, so you develop cliques with the guys in your class. Jerome, Kordell, Gildon, Kevin Henry, Dawson, and others – they all hung out with us though.

We all had mutual respect. That was undervalued – we had no egos. We had no fights in practice. All of them were great, professional men.

Antwaan Randle El, Steelers Wide Receiver, 2002-2005, 2010:

When I was drafted, my older brother Curtis came down to Pittsburgh and lived with me. I didn't know which way to go as a young man then. He showed me a lot – our upbringing and belief in God helped me more than anything.

I had to stay away from the clubs and partying. I remember the other players coming in and telling me they should have stayed back with me sometimes! I was never a big party guy anyway. I just didn't want to disappoint my teammates and God.

The best part was that there were no classes – just practice! I thought that was cool! I could practice, be done by around 1:00 then go home and take a nap – no studying to do. During OTAs, I'd practice, do film study, ice up then get back and sleep by 3:00 p.m. I'd wake up at 10:00 p.m. though and couldn't get back to sleep until 3:30 a.m. – then I'd oversleep through my alarm the next morning and be late for practice. I remember Coach Mularkey telling me he was late for practice only one time in his career, but I was late four times already in my rookie season!

After I got married my second season, my wife wouldn't let me oversleep anymore. And when we had kids, there were no naps either!

Travis Kirschke, Steelers Defensive Lineman, 2004-2009:

With the Steelers we had a lot of guys that would loosen things up. Troy (Polamalu) would put together a mix of songs and play them during our stretching. He would have songs from the past to the present so everyone could take part. I think a lot of times our stretching became a dance session. When some of the older songs would play you would even see the coaches taking part. Then on many occasions you could find Hines trying to persuade you to open your mouth so he could throw grass in it. There always seemed to be something going on. Those are the things you miss.

Shaun Nua, Steelers Defensive Lineman, 2005-2007:

Practice squad to me is a great test of how much an individual loves the game. You are at the bottom stage of the development phase for the organization. At every single practice you literally take every single repetition on special teams, offensive scout team, and defensive scout team. This was your opportunity to show that you can play when your name is called due to injuries to those on the active roster.

With all of that, you don't get to travel on game day, you don't suit up on home games, and you even get a much less pay compared to those on active roster. To me, I still loved going to practice every day when on the practice squad. I was on the best organization in football, I basically got a free education from the best coaches, and I was playing football with the best players in the business.

I never really played or contributed significantly on game days for the Steelers, but the lessons I've learned from the best organization in football are invaluable and will help me not only as a football coach but in life. My ways of repaying them back is to take the lessons learned and do well with it and help young players develop. It was very tough not to get to contribute on game days. I was given every opportunity possible to excel in Pittsburgh, but injuries and lack of discipline cost me greatly, and it is my biggest regret. At the same time I am beyond grateful for the lessons learned and I believe that's what is important.

It was by far the hardest thing for me in '07 [to be released]. I felt like I let down a lot of people especially coach Mitchell who I knew believed in me. I didn't take good care of my body and I lost focused on how I got there. Injuries and lack of progression eventually got me cut and got picked up by the Bills.

It was so hard while I was there because I knew I just let a great opportunity slip away with the best organization in football.

The Longest Yard

It's easy as fans to get caught up in the glory that is inherent in the game and its players. The excitement of the game, the larger-than-life characters that play and coach. They all draw us in like moths to flames. And the marketing machine that is the NFL promotes that passion incredibly well.

But what gets missed at times are the real struggles these players faced, to get to the NFL, to overcome rough experiences either before or during their NFL careers, and the physical and emotional cost once their careers ended.

While it's easy to look at the players and feel that they've had lives most would only dream of, almost as fictional characters, most players would see things differently. The struggles they had, and, for some, still go through are ones that they don't often make public. But many have carried heavy burdens of their own and would certainly see their lives as ordinary. Real people with real issues that "happened to have had the opportunity to play in the NFL." After all, they weren't granted these opportunities, they earned them, and many sacrificed a great deal to do so.

Adversity:

Many of these former players have travelled difficult roads to make it to the NFL and struggled to find security after they retired from the game.

Prior to entering the NFL, many dealt with family issues and poor economic backgrounds, racial issues, political and religious persecution, and physical ailments. Because of those difficulties, many found the strength they needed to cope and were prepared for the emotional demands of the game. The game was an escape for some – a way to invest themselves in a sport that didn't require them to think about anything other than the sport itself. And it certainly put the game in perspective– made the stress seem less dire when compared to what they dealt with beforehand.

For most, the NFL meant opportunity: Opportunity to overcome, opportunity for bigger things, an opportunity to realize a dream.

And for many, adversity came during their time in the NFL. At being drafted much lower than expected or struggling at the NFL level due to the higher level of competition or lack of preparedness due to their limited college careers. Fighting daily, just to maintain a spot on the rooster.

And lastly, some experienced adversity after the game. Not just due to the physical toll that the game has on the human body, but due to their difficult adjustment to post-NFL life.

The resiliency these players have shown makes it even more understandable how the Steelers have succeeded as a team. What is stronger than a collective of individuals who have overcome great odds.

Lou Tepe, Steelers Linebacker, 1953-1955:

I was drafted as a center, but I played linebacker too. When they say Chuck Bednarik was the only two-way player in the NFL, that's a lie. I played two ways too. I played center, but when we were playing my rookie year, we couldn't find a linebacker. We were playing a game and down 35-7 – the tight end caught seven passes in the first half. I told the coach that if I couldn't do a better job than the guy out there, I would save him the trouble and quit. He said "Ok, loudmouth." So I went out there – and in the 5-2 we lined up in – lined up over the tight end. I said to the guy, "You're not getting off the line again, you SOB." I knew he would try to do one of three things – block me, block the tackle, or go out for a pass. He didn't get off the line the entire second half!

Art Michalik, Steelers Linebacker, 1955-1956:

We played the Rams in L.A. and flew back to San Francisco afterwards. My two teeth were knocked back, so they pulled them both out Monday. On Wednesday we flew to Cleveland and they hemorrhaged on the plane. They rushed me to the hospital and I got out that Saturday, just in time for the walk-through, and I played on Sunday. That game, I hit Otto Graham across the face and he had to have eleven stitches – he was sewed up at halftime. He was allergic to Novacain so he did it without any help. But the next game, he needed a facemask I guess and that's how the facemask got started.

Dick Haley, Steelers Cornerback, 1961-1964, Steelers Director of Player Personnel, 1971-1990:

I was okay in high school and at Pitt – I had no issues there and played both ways in college. I always wanted to play offense in the NFL but the Redskins had me play defense at the time until their doctors said I should stop playing and they put me on the expansion list. Minnesota picked me up and I talked to Coach Van Brocklin about playing offense. I got to play some early, but then they put me on waivers. I guess I wasn't doing was well as I thought.

The Steelers claimed me. Supposedly they were going to draft me – they called me during the draft actually – so when I was waived they decided to claim me then. There, I went back to playing safety.

Riley Gunnels, Steelers Defensive Lineman, 1965-1966:

I was drafted by the Steelers in '59 and ended up playing for the Eagles. You are right, when the Steelers drafted me out of Georgia, I was known more for my play in college as an offensive left tackle and not as a defensive lineman. I enjoyed playing defensive line though and when the Steelers designated me on defense, I did not object.

I was aware at the time however, that I needed playing time to develop myself for the defensive line. Unfortunately, there was not enough time. Although I was able to learn and condition myself to play on the other side of the line, the coaching staff decided to waive me at the end of training camp.

Til' this day, I do not know if the Steeler staff knew that I was a more experienced offensive lineman when drafted. Anyway, although I was devastated at being waived, it was a blessing in disguise.

During the short time I spent at Steelers camp, I was able to learn a tremendous amount of defensive line play by watching probably the best ever, Ernie Stautner. I was claimed off waivers by the Eagles, a team destined to win the Championship in '60. I was ecstatic playing defense, was Eagles Defensive MVP in '62 and picked up the ring. We beat Coach Lombardi's Packers in Franklin Field.

Lee Folkins, Steelers Tight End, 1965:

It was a real downer to join the Steelers who had just fired their head coach. When I got to Pittsburgh, I enjoyed my colleagues, as football is football wherever it is played. Football players share much to have reached that place in the NFL. I really enjoyed Pittsburgh and the people; just a great place.

On the down side, we practiced at the Alleghany County Fairgrounds with facilities that were less than exemplar! The shower room had maybe sixteen shower heads but only four or five worked, and if you weren't one of the first into the shower the hot water ran out.

I also recall waking up early one morning to see a beautiful blanket of white snow. However, as the day went on the snow was dusted with black. That would have been before the EPA!

At the risk of attempting to make a complex problem simple, football is a team sport. It is pretty hard to start the first game of the season with the head coach being fired, with an assistant coach trying to make it as a head coach and the players trying to make the best of it. We were a great bunch of guys but we weren't a "team."

Tight end Lee Folkins goes over technique with coaches.
Photo courtesy of Lee Folkins

Larry Gagner, Steelers Offensive Lineman, 1966-1969:

I didn't realize at the time that a broken and dislocated left hip suffered in an off-season automobile accident in '69 would be the beginning of the end of a promising career for me. I believe that after the Steelers figured out I was soon to be history (medically speaking) other teams I got traded to followed suit accordingly. Except for the KC Chiefs two years removed. Coach Hank Stram invited me to training camp in 1971, and I made the team as a fourth guard when most other teams only carry three.

I felt lucky and fortunate to get in my five years. Yeah, I didn't get in my ten expected years most decent offensive linemen strive for, but I've got two perfectly good knees to show for it. Any ten year plus linemen out there want to trade? I didn't think so.

Bill Asbury, Steelers Running Back, 1966-1968:

I never expected to be playing professional football (or any sport) after acute renal failure during the timed mile run to start fall of 1964 practice at Kent State. It was a miracle recovery, having lost fifty-eight pounds while in Akron General for five weeks.

I had a great fifth year at Kent State in 1965, including a game we lost to Penn State. That outstanding year happened in part because of an untimely injury to my replacement, Don Fitzgerald. I was able to garner honorable mention academic and AP All-America Honors under Coach Leo Strang. The system he ran, unbalanced winged-T, and great teammates, like Jon Brooks, Al Tate, John Michelak, and others allowed me to play tailback at 230 pounds.

This, unknowingly prepared me to play for the Steelers, after the new Atlanta Falcons team cut me. Art Rooney Jr. was the Steelers scout who approached me several times before the draft during my senior season and told me I had potential. So, going to any team at all, was a true blessing, having been so close to death only two years earlier.

I relished knowing Art Rooney, Dan Rooney, Artie, and "Skins" during my brief time there. Losing built character!

Bob Adams, Steelers Tight End, 1969-1971:

Chuck taught me humility and compassion. Going in to my second year of camp was very tough and stressful. The players union convinced us to go on strike and, of course, I came to camp with four hundred dollars to my name. We were locked out of camp and the Steelers brought in busloads of "scabs" to try and scare the vets back to camp. It worked, especially on the young guys. We were convinced it was a form of terrorism, at least for the free agents and guys who were broke such as me.

When we returned with our shortened tails between our legs, there were a few dozen of the scabs on the practice squad. One was a tight end named Dennis Hughes. He was my nemesis and I was sure he was the devil incarnate. To make matters worse, he amused Chuck and our new first round draft choice, Golden Boy himself, Terry Bradshaw. They were already pals.

I suffered through four pre-season games with Dennis. And he won the starting job. I was very depressed. Dennis seemed to not take anything seriously and he was happy go lucky. At the time, I was a complete opposite and anxious about keeping my job. Camp could bring on the most extreme emotional stress. I felt if our bodies were not young and strong the leading cause of injury or death would be heart attacks.

Eventually, Dennis and I would become good friends. Positions are dearly won in sports, perhaps the most desperate of sorts, with inner hostile thoughts about your competition held within and suppressed

The final pre-season game in '70 was in Oakland. I asked Chuck if it would be okay if my wife could ride home on the plane with us, which was pretty brazen of me for the time of year. It was a way to get a sneak preview if I would be cut or not. If he let her on, I may have made the team. There was a gamble that he would cut me anyway, but I took the risk. He said it was ok. I was elated, yet weary. Little did I know what was being planned for my future.

We arrived in Oakland and my wife met me at the hotel. She was not feeling well. She had lost a lot of weight while I was in camp. She was depressed. The following night we played Oakland and headed home to Pittsburgh, the only wife on the plane. The following day, she went to the hospital to get a check-up. She was diagnosed with a mental disorder and was to stay in the hospital. I was now quite unsettled. What if I don't make the team, my wife is in the hospital, and questions ran around my head. I had no health insurance; we are now in Pittsburgh with only $250 left and no place to live. At least I had a car.

On Tuesday, I was very nervous sitting on my locker stool. Our equipment manager Tony Paresis approached me; he told me to go see "the Coach." I broke into a sweat while my heart fell like a base drum in my chest. I entered Chuck's office trying to look poised and as bright as I could. He had his hands folded on his desk. He looked up at me and said, "We waived you this morning," which means you're cut from the team.

It felt like a thousand bricks caved in on me. Tears welled up and I began to cry. As hard as I tried, I could not hold them back and the dam broke. All the stresses hit me at once. He sat patiently until I had it under control then asked what is happening? I told him about my wife, that she was in the hospital suffering from some kind of mental stress, which was being diagnosed. (Actually, she was simply suffering from malnutrition and dehydration from a no-protein fad diet she was on for over two months). She became depressed as a result. I took for granted the diagnosis was correct at the time and it was quite frightening.

After explaining this, Chuck acknowledged me softly. He then said something, which he did not have to say, but he did. He told me that at one time in his life something similar had happened and he understood what I was feeling, and that everything would work out, he assured me. I felt I was beginning to rise from the dead. He then added, "By the way, you cleared waivers, and we are keeping you on the team. We could not put Terry Hanratty (our back up QB) on waivers or we would probably lose him. We thought because you are not a known commodity we slipped you through waivers the way we hoped it would work out. So, go get suited up for practice."

I thanked him and walked down the hall towards the locker room. I began to choke up again as it hit me, I made the team. I opened a door into a storage room filled with blocking dummies, closed the door, and buried my head into the foam rubber and cried very hard for several minutes until I had exhausted the grief from the relief knowing that I was still on the Steelers and would play on Sunday. I had narrowly escaped the bullet. And I still had to find an apartment to rent and a wife to get out of the hospital. I would have a game check next week; we would not have to sleep in the car after all.

Hubie Bryant, Steelers Wide Receiver, 1970-1971:

I got my report to camp letter and saw Tony Parisi for my equipment. He told me the rookies are in the back of the locker room so I went and looked but didn't see my name. I couldn't find it.

I went back and he asked if I was supposed to be there – he looked at my report to camp letter again and told me to go to lunch and he'll take care of it.

When I come back I look for my locker and it's still not there. Then I see it – he put a chair by the door and tape above it with my name on it. Above the chair was a nail with my helmet hanging on it. On the chair were my pads.

I said to myself, they don't think I'll make it. I told myself they may not know my name now but they'll know my name before I leave. And I prayed for the strength to make the team!

Al Young, Steelers Wide Receiver, 1971-1972:

Yeah – I didn't know what to expect. In college, we ran the Wing-T. We didn't pass much. I played tight end and we only had little middle routes – nothing deep. That was a big issue for me. Learning to play wide and reading defenses.

My biggest struggle was dealing with bump and run coverage. They could bump you all the way down the field then – I never had to deal with that in college either.

Another big issue was that I had no weight training in college. I always felt I was naturally strong, but not like when you lift weights. I thought that was a big disadvantage for me.

After my '71 season, I was called in that December to take a physical for the military draft. My blood pressure was high – 4F – so I didn't qualify. My next year, in '72, I had some issues with my heart and blood pressure in camp. They kept me out of camp for three days while they ran tests, then they let me play.

In '73, my second day in camp I passed out. They took me to the hospital for eight days while they ran tests. They couldn't allow me to play after that and told me I should retire.

My whole world fell apart. I thought I was really understanding what it took to play in the NFL.

I was shocked that they didn't want me to play. I suffered since I was seventeen from high blood pressure but I could still play. I passed out for a short period of time. They just couldn't find a reason for it and couldn't have that responsibility. As you play, the excitement causes your blood pressure to raise.

J.T. Thomas, Steelers Cornerback, 1973-1982:

I was the first Black player at Florida State to play and graduate. I was breaking the color barrier really since junior high school – I was in desegregation mode even then. I grew up on the back of the bus and ate at the back of Burger King.

Even though the Bill of Rights was passed in '65, there was no enforcement. In my junior year I had no idea where I was going to go to college – most weren't taking Black athletes.

So, no – I didn't really feel that pressure after all of that, and the fact Pittsburgh hadn't really won in forty years.

John Banaszak, Steelers Defensive Lineman, 1974-1981:

I made a very young defending Super Bowl championship team as an undrafted rookie free agent. Not a whole lot of people gave me a chance to make that team. I remember the first day of training camp when George Perles told us that we could forget about beating out LC Greenwood, Joe Greene, Ernie Holmes, or Dwight White. The only way we were going to make that team was by playing on the special teams.

That is what I needed to hear, a way to make the team. I worked hard and played well on special teams in the pre-season and was one of only three rookies to make that team.

George took me aside and explained my role on that team. I was to be the entire scout team for the offensive and defensive lines. My job was to get them ready to play on Sunday. He told me I could forget about playing and concentrate on getting everyone else ready to play and also to play well on the special teams. He didn't lie to me. Other than a couple of mop up opportunities at the end of a game I didn't get any serious playing time until early November against the Houston Oilers.

Dwight was going to miss the game because of an ankle, Steve Furness would replace him. That left me as the only available substitute defensive lineman on the sidelines. Sure enough in the middle of the second quarter LC got his leg caught in a pile and twisted his leg. While the medical staff was administering to LC on the field a frantic George Perles was administering to me. He said, "You can't get hooked, you can't get cut, OMG isn't there anyone else I can put in the game." I of course nodded and told him that I was the only one left. He repeated his obviously panicked words and as I was leaving he pulled me back and said "don't blow it." With that motivational message ringing in my helmet I ran onto the field.

As I approached the huddle I realized that George was right. This was my chance to prove to the twenty-seven other teams in the league that I belong, that I can play in the NFL and if I don't blow it, I win.

It certainly was calming when I got to the huddle and I looked to my right and there was Mean Joe. I looked to my left and there was Jack Ham. In front of me getting ready to call the defense was a toothless Jack Lambert. I immediately was at ease. I was surrounded by three future hall of fame teammates, how bad could I blow it.

Then I realized that the Oilers were going to test me right away. They had no success running the ball at Steve or Ernie or Joe, they would try and run at me. Sure enough, they ran a power right at me and we stuffed it. It was now third and long and an obvious passing situation. I was excited about the situation and I was going to use my best pass rush move and it worked.

On the first two significant plays in my NFL career I had a solo tackle and a sack. I was so excited that I raised both arms in the air and ran off the field becoming the first player in the history of the NFL to celebrate a sack. What made that day more memorable however, was that my teammates gave me the highest honor that a player can get and that is a game ball. I'll never forget how special that moment was.

Gary Dunn, Steelers Defensive Lineman, 1976-1987:

Well, the draft was all messed up that year due to the union thing at the time. The Steelers called me at eight at night – I waited around and no one called me. Then they finally called and said they were going to draft me in the sixth round. I said "Great!" Then I thought "Didn't I just see them in the Super Bowl? Isn't that the team with the Steel Curtain defense? Isn't that the spot I'm supposed to be playing?"

When they called they actually asked me if I would be interested in trying to play on the offensive line and I said "Yeah, I'll try anything." I was apprehensive though…people were actually asking me if I was going to beat out Joe Greene!

I worked out like a maniac that year. People think you go to the NFL trying to be a star. That wasn't true though. I thought I was going to be cut and would have to find work on another team. They actually kept an extra defensive lineman that year just to keep me.

They had six preseason games then – plus the College All-Star game. We made $120 a week as rookies then. I was just thinking that if I could make it to the College All-Star game, I'd make seven hundred dollars. That's more money than I had ever made. My goal was to make that seven hundred dollars and play in the All-Star game.

The vets came in two weeks after camp started. I remember seeing all of the Lincolns and Mercedes pulling up. Then one pulled up with people running alongside of it. The door opened a big guy with a beard stepped out – it was Joe Greene. Two kids opened up the trunk and pulled out his shoulder pads.

I realized then the adjustment to the caliber of football I had.

Sydney Thornton, Steelers Running Back, 1977-1982:

I suffered a massive stroke about five years ago yes. Since then I have been on a steady course of rehabilitation and am keeping the faith. I'm trying to stay up and positive.

One former teammate was at my side and helped me to learn how to go about things when I had no idea. Rocky [Bleier] stood by me and relieved me of the problems I had worrying about money and making sure bills got paid. He was down here at the time for a speaking engagement. He fulfilled that obligation then, without asking me, came to the hospital and was there for me like a knight in shining armor.

Brad Cousino, Steelers Linebacker, 1977-1978:

Not only was I not drafted, but I was a "walk-on" in college like the popular movie "Rudy". As background, I grew up in Toledo, OH and my dad worked in a glass factory. As a factory worker pay scale, there was no money for college and I needed a football scholarship if I wanted to attend college. I was less than six feet and weighed 185 pounds in high school. I wrote letters to football coaches begging for a scholarship.

I was turned down from over twenty-five colleges for a football scholarship...including Division II and Division III colleges. However, one letter was sent to Miami (OH) University head coach Bill Mallory and was told that they didn't have a scholarship available, but they did have an alumni in the Toledo area that thought he could get me a decent paying job – if I was willing to do some very tough work. I agreed and that summer I worked twenty feet underground cleaning out storm sewers of the "sludge," mud, and debris that inevitably clog up storm sewers along the I-75 & I-475 interstates. It was grueling work. But it was a real wake-up lesson about life. I earned $5.25 per hour, but that did pay for my first quarter of school.

I was invited to Miami's summer football camp as a non-scholarship walk-on in 1971...the last year of freshman ineligibility. I was initially an inside linebacker...but due to a series of circumstances ended up playing middle guard (nose tackle) a down defensive lineman who weighed in at less than 197 lbs. I ended up starting as a sophomore and played every game from my sophomore year through the end of college.

Dennis "Dirt" Winston, Steelers Linebacker, 1977-1981, 1985-1986:

Coming in as a rookie, I had problems at home. My dad was sick – dying of cancer and could go at any time. I knew I was going to make the team if I had to knock everyone out to do it – I wasn't coming home.

Being a fifth round pick you have to fight to get what you want.

Fortunately, Jack came in to camp late that year. That gave me the chance to play more and be seen. When he came in he took me under his wing.

Me, Robin, Jack – we played everything. Chuck didn't care who you were – you played special teams. Even Blount and Shell did.

We used to have fun on kick-offs, all of us screaming and hollering at the other team as we ran down the field looking for people to hit.

Tom Beasley, Steelers Defensive Lineman, 1978-1983:

I was the classic example of being the big fish in a small pond in college to being the small fish in a very large ocean in Pittsburgh.

I was undersized at the time I graduated. I weighed 235 pounds in college. I got married right after I graduated and after that, over the next three and a half months, through a good weight program and home cooking, I gained twenty pounds. My agent sent out a letter telling teams I was now 255 pounds. Three teams flew me in to weigh me then sent me back home. It was a couple of weeks before the draft, I guess they didn't have time to send scouts to verify my weight.

I was told when I was drafted that I was brought in to replace Joe Greene. Banaszak was there to replace Dwight White.

Randy Reutershan, Steelers Wide Receiver, 1978:

My health is great now after my car accident in my rookie season [and that ended the NFL career]. I remain very active athletically. Occasional memory problems exist but I deal with it.

The Steelers were very cooperative and made sure I received outstanding medical attention and took care of my parents during the very serious period.

After my accident, members of the team and coaches were often at the hospital and while being cared for in Philadelphia for five months I spoke with them over the phone once I was able to.

Greg Hawthorne, Steelers Running Back/Receiver, 1979-1983:

I didn't realize how special it was then in Pittsburgh. They were moving me from running back to wide receiver. I wanted to play running back. I was having a bad camp and they were moving me to receiver. If it were Swann or Stallworth, Chuck would make sure Bradshaw got them the ball if they were open, but when I was open I never got the ball. I got tired of that and thought it would be better somewhere else. They also drafted Louis Lipps in the first round, and I saw the writing on the wall. Chuck always said if you want to leave the team to just see him in his office. So I did and asked for a trade.

New England was just being back in college. The Sullivans were not a football family like the Rooneys were then.

Matt Bahr, Steelers Kicker, 1979-1980:

If the worst thing that happens in life is getting fired by a professional football team then it's a pretty good life. You can't be overly upset. To play a professional sport is neat, whether it's for one year or ten. If the worst thing that happens is you get fired then you've done pretty well.

I will say I never gave their playbook back. I have all of them. What are they going to do, fire me? There wasn't much in it anyway. Kick it this way, through those things...

Tunch Ilkin, Steelers Offensive Lineman, 1980-1992:

I actually got cut my rookie season – I was released in training camp. I was called into Chuck Noll's office and I knew that wasn't good. Back then there were no taxi squads or practice squads. If a team wanted to keep you – they'd say you were hurt. "I tweaked my hammy" or something. They did that for a couple other guys that rookie year and I was hoping they'd do that for me as well.

But I let up a pressure in my first preseason game and had a holding penalty too. I got pulled from the game. Practice that Monday, I got called in and Chuck said he put me on waivers that morning. I didn't know what that meant – then it dawned on me that he was cutting me.

He told me to stay in shape – that if someone got hurt they'd call me. I thought it was just something he said to make me not cry. But I did anyway...

I went back to Chicago where I grew up. My parents moved to San Francisco so I stayed with a buddy, He didn't have a spare room but he had an enclosed porch with a cot. I slept there and worked at a health club, vacuuming and cleaning mirrors and stuff like that. But I got to work out and ran during lunchtime.

I also played in a touch football league, and I am proud to say I led the league in sacks. I took all of the moves Joe Greene and Dwight White beat me with in camp and used them!

Then Steve Courson hurt his foot. Chuck called and asked me if I was in shape and I said yes! He asked me to get on the next flight, which was in forty-five minutes. I had no extra clothes with me. I went in my gym clothes, I looked like an immigrant for the second time in my life!

Keith Willis, Steelers Defensive Lineman, 1982-1991:

You have to go back to where I grew up in Norfolk, New Jersey. I didn't come from a lot. I had no desire to play football early in my career. I played one year in high school and that was it. No Pop Warner.

I knew I couldn't live like that – I knew what I had to do. I went to Northeastern and took advantage of my time there.

We were playing New Hampshire at Northeastern. The scouts came to see a linebacker that played for New Hampshire and I had a good game. Bill Nunn was there and saw me and took my number and told me to keep in touch with him. A couple of weeks later he invited me to go to Boston College to run the forty with the Boston College players.

Gabe Rivera, Steelers Defensive Lineman, 1983:

[After being paralyzed in a car accident] They knew how things were going to be for me and just knowing that the other players were supportive of my recovery was helpful. The whole Steelers family treated me and my family with great support. I remember that my mom would go to Church with the Chief most mornings. The Steelers took very good care of my family during those difficult times.

After my rehab was over I would go to the locker room and visit the players. I also started doing some exercise there by going up the ramps. I went to most of the home games and visited the locker room after the game. It was a good feeling. Then when I moved back home to San Antonio I had the opportunity to see games in Houston and sometimes in Dallas.

It is a very hard thing to explain at first [when helping other paralyzed former players], but when we meet each other it is a bit more easy to talk about since we have gone through the same difficulties and feelings during those early stages. Both were difficult but the psychological part is most difficult to overcome. There are things you want to do but you are limited in those areas. I try to have a good and happy feeling when I start my day off and keep throughout the day.

The hard thing that I tell them is that you will know who your friends are by the ones that stay with you during these difficult times.

Pete Rostosky, Steelers Offensive Lineman, 1983-1986:

Being shot in the head my senior year in high school was a life-changing experience. What most people would consider to be the worst day of my life, wound up actually being a huge blessing for me. After being shot, I was told I would never play contact sports again as I still had twenty-three shotgun pellets remaining in my skull after they operated and removed fifty-seven. These were left behind as they were too risky to remove, and the fear was there would be too high a risk of further injury to my eye and brain. This was at the end of a great season for Elizabeth Forward High School and the first time our school ever made it to the WPIAL playoffs in our school's history. I just wanted to play what I thought would be the last game of my career.

After a fruitless search all week for a doctor to give me the magic 'pink-slip' release to allow me to play with my head loaded with stitches, pellets, and still in bandages, I refused to give up hope. Finally, the day before the game, my mom drove me way out in the country to an obscure doctor's office. He poked around, grunted a few times and gave me the OK. I was so psyched to get that slip in my hands and couldn't wait to get out of his office before he changed his mind. It wasn't until later I learned that he was actually our farm veterinarian!

I guess when the dream is big enough, the facts simply don't count. Because I thought it was my last game ever, my last chance to ever hit someone without getting arrested, I played my heart out. I was hitting anything that moved, including my own teammates. There happened to be scouts at this game to see some other players on my team, and one scout from University of Connecticut offered me a full scholarship.

Funny how things work out.

Eric Williams, Steelers Safety, 1983-1986:

How do you deal with the stress of making the team? You get an ulcer! Then you take medicine for the ulcer. But other than that you just have to deal with it. There's no job security – one day you have a job and the next you don't. In college, I had a scholarship and I was safe. In the NFL, your scholarship last twenty-four hours.

Rich Erenberg, Steelers Running Back, 1984-1986:

The biggest adjustment by far was grasping the speed of the game. I just couldn't believe how big, fast, strong and athletic the linebackers were. It seemed almost unfair to me that guys at 230 to 250 pounds would run 4.5 to 4.6 40s. I figured out early on that I wasn't going to beat out Abercrombie or Pollard for a starting roster spot. They were just bigger, faster, and quite honestly better football players than I was.

I knew my only chance was to make the team as a situational or special teams player. I had good hands and I ran pretty good pass routes so the coaches began working me into the passing game. I became the third down specialist and returned kick-offs. I was just glad to have a job.

You have to block out the negative and you need a little luck along the way for things to fall in place for you. Sometimes, a decision is made ahead of time and there is nothing you can do about it. My last preseason game for Atlanta I was 7-10 with a touchdown and played well. I also got cut a few days later. In Pittsburgh I just won a fan vote in the paper for the starting quarterback job. I got cut the next week. Such is life in the NFL.

Scott Campbell, Steelers Quarterback, 1984-1986:

I had to fight like crazy each of my seven NFL years to make the roster in Pittsburgh and Atlanta. I always had to overcome questions about my size (6 foot).

I carried a bit of a chip on my shoulder because of that and I think that helped me mentally. I think the coaches could see

I was confident and I could pick up the offense rather quickly. I credit this to the fact that I was raised by a coach who taught me football since I was very young and because I played in an open, pro-style offense at Purdue.

Preston Gothard, Steelers Tight End, 1985-1988:

I was a walk-on in college at Alabama. I was used to having to work from the bottom up. My high school had thirty kids in its graduating class – it was a real small school so no one knew who I was. Alabama just came off back-to-back championships under Coach Bryant, so I already knew about working my way up. The pressure didn't bother me. I was used to it I guess.

Dan Reeder, Steelers Running Back, 1986-1987:

I played with some great guys. My frustration was staying healthy. Success is when preparation meets opportunity and in 1986 Frank Pollard went down with cartilage issue with his knee. I had a great opportunity. Literally, the game I had my chance, I had a high ankle sprain/torn ligament in my ankle and had to go on IR for four games. In the meantime, they bring in Ernest Jackson and in my first game back Ernest and I split time…neither one of us did anything spectacular and the next game Ernest had 150 yards. We were both the kind of guys that had to get into the flow of the game he did and he went on to be All-Pro that year.

I lost a step with my ankle injury and I saw my role become one of a blocker for pass protection and lead blocker for either Ernest or Walter in the run game. I also played on special teams. Like in life, there is a fine line between success and failure and unfortunately you need to stay healthy to take advantages of opportunities.

Sometimes things happen for a reason. My experience has made me a better man and better competitor so it was worthwhile and I have no regrets. I am in the kind of business where you are as good as your last deal and you have to love to compete. In football you are as good as your last play and like football it has many ups and downs, so work effort and focus are keys to succeed. Like Coach Noll and Coach Raymond, the longer I am in business the wiser and more experienced I get, so although I'm older and grayer I don't have to worry about my body failing me – so I become more valuable.

The journey to get to the NFL was as much fun as actually playing so in life enjoy the journey.

Chuck Sanders, Steelers Running Back, 1986-1987:

I was the Bus before the Bus. I was before my time! I was a big running back but they put me at fullback. That's what they did then – the NFL wanted smaller, faster guys like Tony Dorsett and put the bigger guys at fullback. My style was as a running back though – that was before guys like Bettis and Eddie George were in vogue.

It was very frustrating – but I had no choice. I was an eleventh round pick out of Slippery Rock. You just shut your mouth and do what you're told.

Plus – the strike in '87 also hurt me as a player.

No excuses….I finished strong in '86 and started seeing some playing time. Then in '87 I crossed over when the strike came, and when it was over a number of the guys were angry – the locker room was divided at first.

Some big names crossed over. But the average Joes that crossed the line never made it. Pittsburgh was a strong union town – you could see it in the articles that were written. I knew I wasn't in the inner circle after the strike – especially as a younger player.

Lupe Sanchez, Steelers Safety, 1986-1988:

I grew up pretty sheltered, due to the fact my parents were immigrants from Mexico. My dad passed away when I was only four and therefore my mother was Mom and Dad as I grew up. She raised us on her own and she is the reason I came back.

I did have a brother fourteen years older than me and he was great to me.

But my point is that I had never really been much outside the town of Visalia, where I grew up and where I now currently live. So when I got to Pittsburgh I had no idea what to expect. After getting there and getting to know the people there, I was so pleasantly surprised at how genuine and down to earth people were. The friends I made and still keep in touch with to this day made it such an incredible experience. So thank you Pittsburgh for making my dream come true! And boy do I miss Primanti Bros to this day!

Rodney Carter, Steelers Running Back, 1987-1989:

The first two games, they tried to use Merril as the third-down back, and I don't think it went as well as they hoped. Then the strike started, and Cleveland called me. They were surprised I was let go – they knew I played on third downs from my play during preseason and wanted to bring people in after the strike happened. The Colts called too. I thought through the process though and called the Steelers to see if they'd sign me back because of the strike. I figured that I knew the offense and would start then – and if I could play during the strike and do well, that other teams would see me. I wanted to play, and in Cleveland and Indy, I'd just be one of the guys.

So I played versus the Falcons and the Rams, and the third game I didn't play because I had a hip pointer. Pollard came back by then, and my good friend Chuck Sanders got to play a lot. As the starters started to come back, I was like, uh oh. I told Chuck Sanders, that if it was between him and me, I knew I could do things he couldn't do – like catching the ball. They kept me, and moved me into the third down back role like it was nothing. The next week I caught two touchdowns. And in typical Chuck Noll fashion, a reporter told Chuck that I didn't even know I'd be there. Chuck just said "Well, that's not a bad thing."

Jerrol Williams, Steelers Linebacker, 1989-1992

The road I traveled to get drafted was difficult. I left college after my senior season and got into a bad car accident with a buddy of mine. I couldn't work out at the combine – I just took the physical. By the time I got better I could really only work out for a couple of teams – it was close to the draft by then.

It was a shock to get drafted. A blessing. There was no pressure for me because I didn't think I'd even get drafted.

Tim Worley, Steelers Running Back, 1989-1993:

First of all, coming into the Steelers as a first-round pick, I felt a lot of pressure to be somewhat of a 'savior' and turn the program around.

I missed most of training camp my rookie year, so I was behind and had to play catch-up by the time I came in. Early on in the 1989 season I made a lot of mistakes because I was playing catch-up.

Once I got my feet under me that first year, it gave me some confidence and I was able to adapt on the field to the speed of the game and make that transition from college to NFL football.

If you notice, I said that I was able to adapt to the speed in the NFL, but coming into that second season my challenges on the field were directly related to my failure to adjust to life off the field. I made many mistakes off the field which led to underperformance on the field.

They are directly related.

Rick Strom, Steelers Quarterback, 1989-1993:

It was very disappointing. I also broke my leg as a senior at Fox Chapel and missed the entire season. Missing the playing time in the last five games of my college career hurt the most because I needed the playing experience. I did make it back for the Blue Grey All Star game and played fairly well.

When I was visiting with the Steelers after the draft, Myron Cope stopped in QB Coach Tom Moore's office to tell me that after he saw me play in that All-Star game, he "told the Steelers brass they should look at you." I was thrilled to have the opportunity to play for the Steelers. There were many wonderful blessings that happened because of the injuries. I have to admit, however, there is still a part of me that wishes I could have gotten out-of-the-way of the hits and played for the entirety of both of my senior years.

Barry Foster, Steelers Running Back, 1990-1994:

I didn't see the Steelers drafting me – I thought it was going to be the Browns. They called me during the draft and said they were going to take me in round two – that was their first pick of the draft then – they didn't have a first round pick that year. When they got up to the podium, they said fullback and I thought, there I was. But they selected Leroy Hoard from Michigan instead. I was shocked – they just told me they were going to take me. I was disappointed and left my dorm room. Three rounds later the Steelers called and took me. I didn't know anything about who was on the roster – I just wanted to make the team.

Dan Stryzinski, Steelers Punter, 1990-1991:

I moved from many teams to start with before landing in Pittsburgh. There are so many players with ability. It's how it wears on you mentally when you miss a kick or make mistakes. About eighty percent of the game is mental for us, in my opinion.

You have to have confidence. You only have three or four plays a game as a kicker. If you don't do well on one play you feel like it's a bad game because it's such a big percentage of your plays. Other guys may play seventy plays – one bad play for them is a much smaller percentage. You just have to know the coaches have confidence in you and do your best.

Sammy Walker, Steelers Cornerback, 1991-1992:

I was working for my grandma and was hit in the eye. It was worse than being blinded in the eye – I had 20/2,600 vision. All I could see was colors – like when you have too much chlorine in your eyes. It was hard to judge catching the ball. When I was with the Steelers, LeBeau said I couldn't catch AIDS if I had sex with the virus! He asked if I would go have eye surgery and I said sure. They gave me a lens implant and corrected it

Leon Searcy, Steelers Offensive Lineman, 1992-1995:

I had bad relationships with people around me. The women, agents, advisors – they had their own agendas. I wasn't grounded. I was partying, drinking, clubbing, and had those people around me all the time. I had no sense of humility about me then and couldn't see them for what they were. They all had agendas and I'm a very giving person and wasn't able to say no. I should have just said no to them but I felt I owed all of my success to my family – that I owed them for my success. It came to the point though that I was actually their sole source of income. It was troubling to me – I was around them the majority of my life and they had always worked. To see them say they can't make it now without me was troubling.

So I tell kids now to play like each game is your last game. When you're young you think you're invincible. That money is always coming in. When it all ends though you're left scrambling for help and there's no one there to help you. I had eleven years of partying. I mean, I played some good football, but I never settled own. I played eight years of injury-free football. Then bang bang bang I was hurt in Jacksonville, Baltimore, and Miami and was out of the league.

Levon Kirkland, Steelers Linebacker, 1992-2000:

I was nervous about it but was open to playing linebacker. To help my draft status I was willing to do it. The coaches in the Senior Bowl and All-Star games put me inside a lot. I guess they saw something I didn't see.

Funny story – one of my college coaches that recruited me was an inside linebackers coach. He said I'd be a good inside linebacker too. I guess it all worked out.

When you look at my size then it was a unique thing. When I started I was 240 pounds. I didn't realize in the 3-4 that the offensive guards get on you free – there's lots of banging on you as an inside linebacker in the 3-4. In the 4-3 you could run around, but in the 3-4 the inside linebackers have to be more athletic in the run and pass game.

I wasn't as strong as I needed to be to take that pounding at first. That size and weight was an advantage for me in the end. I worked out – most don't realize – I worked out twice a day before most were doing that and had a boxing coach too. Some looked at me as too big but I had quick feet and was aggressive. In coverage I was patient and understood what I could and couldn't do. With God blessing me and hard work I was able to learn.

Alan Haller, Steelers Cornerback, 1992, 1993

It was very interesting, it was a Wednesday practice. I had a great practice – intercepted a pass and had a fun time running it back...I was on the active roster then. I went home – I was staying across the street and was cooking spaghetti for dinner – I remember that – when I got a call from the Director of Player Personnel telling me that Coach Cowher wanted to speak with me. I thought after that great practice he wanted to elevate me to the dime or nickel. So I ran over there – I was excited. I went to his office and he said that I had an incredible practice, but that tight end Craig Keith got hurt in practice and they weren't going to put him on injured reserve. They needed another tight end, so that meant they were going to release me and put me on the practice squad. So it just meant I wouldn't be on the active roster. I was like "Ok, cool..." and went home to my apartment to finish making my spaghetti.

The phone rang again, and this time it was the Cleveland Browns. They told me they picked me up from the waiver wire. I just said "huh?" I had no idea what they were talking about.

I didn't know anything about the waiver wire. I could tell he felt my disappointment in my voice...he told me they were excited to have me and they knew I was disappointed, but they needed me to go there that night. So that night I got rid of the spaghetti, drove from Pittsburgh to Cleveland and practiced with them the next day.

Chad Brown, Steelers Linebacker, 1993-1996, 2006:

In hindsight I didn't handle the pressure too well. I quickly established myself as a third-down pass rusher. But I didn't dedicate myself to the second-down aspect of the game. Jerry Olsavsky was in front of me and I thought it was his job, so I didn't pay attention in the film room and wasn't prepared. I conceded the job to Jerry.

Well, Jerry O, tore up his knee and I was ready to go in but they put undrafted free agent Reggie Barnes ahead of me. He was hungrier – as an undrafted free agent he had to earn his spot.

That Monday I marched into Marvin Lewis' office. As he tells it, I pounded on the table with my fists and demanded the job. I'm not sure it happened quite that way! But I did tell him I made a mistake – I would never be unprepared again.

Kevin Henry, Steelers Defensive Lineman, 1993-2000:

You see, failure wasn't an option for me. I had kids at an early age, no job, bad grades, was on academic probation, and to make things worse I added a wife in college to my situation. I want people of all ages to know that you can achieve anything you want if you keep going through the fires of life. Anything is possible if faith is present.

Jim Miller, Steelers Quarterback, 1994-1996:

Three way quarterback battles do not work! Bill Cowher will even tell you that in hindsight.

I wish I had more than a half to prove myself in Jacksonville in my first NFL start. We did score three out my five first half drives. But I needed to hit Andre Hastings with a touchdown pass. I threw it low. Bill explained to me why he was going to change to the veteran, Mike Tomczak.

I wish I had more of an opportunity to prove I was the Steelers guy at quarterback. You play with the cards your dealt. Ultimately, it was good for me. It made me mentally tougher and when my opportunity arose in Chicago, I was pretty much bullet proof mentally. I actually got my opportunity in Chicago because of Bill Cowher. Bill recommended me to the late Mark Hatley who was the GM of the Bears. Playing in Pittsburgh was very special, it is a special place for football.

Eric Ravotti, Steelers Linebacker, 1994-1996:

During my senior year near the end of the season I had an illness that caused me to collapse and go into convulsions on the sideline during a game. When I awoke I felt as if I had been hit by a truck. I missed the next two games and then came back for my last regular season game against Michigan State. There were no after effects from this, but it became an event that affected my draft status.

The unknown was enough for me to slide down the draft board. I was excited just to be taken considering this and when it was the Pittsburgh Steelers who selected me, I was overjoyed. When I went into camp I was faced with competing with the likes of Kevin Greene, Greg Lloyd, Chad Brown, Levon Kirkland, and Jason Gildon to name a few.

The reason why I think I made the team facing these long shot odds was that I understood the defense better than most and could play all four linebacker positions instead of only one or two. This versatility and special teams play are what helped me make the team and stick around for a while.

Kordell Stewart, Steelers Quarterback, 1995-2002:

I think because I played receiver, people saw me playing quarterback as just an "experiment". But you don't go to an AFC Championship game twice as an experiment. Vick never went to one.

I guess it also depends on where you are. Vick was embraced. African Americans loved his style of play – they all played the same way in their neighborhoods in Atlanta. He wasn't accepted in Green Bay or Indianapolis. But he got his chance in Atlanta. And in Philadelphia, he followed McNabb, so he was accepted there too.

In Pittsburgh, they thought that because I was that athletic, I should have been a receiver. They didn't accept that kind of talent at quarterback. It just wasn't what they were used to. In part it was because they were more traditional than in the South. They didn't like a different style.

I was like a dagger when Maddox came in. I went from team MVP to being benched. I didn't understand it. It was crazy to me.

I'm not going to discuss too much of what was said – my conversation with Coach Cowher. It was the end for all of us. It just was enough. When Graham came in the got hurt, I went in and played well, then I was benched again. I just didn't understand it – few quarterbacks get to the championship game then get benched.

As for Cowher....he just wanted to move on, he said. He thought it would work better with those other guys, But it didn't. I had a cool relationship with him in general. He had his moments. I guess you could say it ran hot and cold.

Barron Miles, Steelers Cornerback, 1995:

I didn't say anything to anybody with the team and I went into my first preseason game knowing my wife is bleeding to death and my child is coming into this world four months to soon. Doctors giving her less than five percent chance of survival. I walk into the stadium and the rest of the defensive backs are saying "play like you've been playing all camp." I'm thinking okay that's kind of strange. Coach walks over and says "you're the corner on one dime," which is a big deal. Now think about what I've been going through back home with my wife, and I'm on the field with Jim Kelly, Thurman Thomas, and André Reed. Let alone the all-stars that where on defense.

The defense was on the field for the first time. I was lined up against André Reed. Thurman Thomas was the running back. Jim Kelly was under center. The ball was snapped. It was a screen to my side. I needed to force the play. I feel like I'm in super slow motion. Kevin Green tips the ball, catches it and we score a defensive touchdown. Life is great. On the next kickoff they fumbled and I went to scoop the ball up. During the play I tore my ACL and MCL. In a split second it went from playing with all-stars to a possible career ending injury.

Henry Bailey, Steelers Wide Receiver, 1995-1996:

The biggest adjustment for me was the fact that I was a running back in high school and about forty percent of the plays I ran in my senior year at UNLV were plays from the slot in which I took a lot of handoffs and caught a lot of short passes.

Upon arriving at my first mini-camp I focused on the realization that I was now required to run precise routes from the X or Z position and catch passes from NFL quarterbacks with my hands. It took approximately half a season to really feel comfortable using my hands to catch passes and run crisp routes. It primarily came down to me rationalizing with myself on a daily basis. The impact of running routes against Rod Woodson, Carnell Lake, Deon Figures, etc. was making me an NFL receiver and one day it happened.

Jahine Arnold, Steelers Wide Receiver, 1996-1998:

In 2007 there was a new challenge, Primary Sclerosing Cholangitis (PSC), a.k.a. Walter Payton's Disease. PSC is a condition of the bile ducts, they basically close off so that the bile cannot enter the stomach for digestion. It has changed my life, it has changed my thinking about life. Walter Payton announced his illness in April of 1999, and passed away from complications in November of the same year. I am doing what I can do to stay in the best health possible.

Walter's story really had me think I would already be gone. I face everyday issues with PSC, itching, fatigue, I am irritable, I cannot maintain a consistent weight, I feel that my body cannot follow my mind, forgetfulness, and sleep problems. That is a short list of things I feel from PSC, there are more that would require additional explanation.

Right now I sit in a position where I don't know how this will end. I don't have insurance and I am without a deposit for the transplant list. I have had some great assistance though. I have worked with P.A.S.T., an organization that assists former players with medical procedures that are otherwise unattainable. I do not know where I would be if it were not for them.

I did not receive any assistance from the Steelers directly, but I also did not ask them for assistance. I didn't think asking them for help would have led to anything, it just didn't seem like that was the correct route to take. I did find other organizations to help…The Player Care Foundation, Dire Needs, Players Trust Fund (which are NFL related), Gridiron Greats, and as mentioned before P.A.S.T.

It isn't easy to go from a world class athlete to being in a situation like this. Not being able to compete in sports, or exercise as I feel I want to do is very frustrating. And it also isn't easy asking for help when you aren't accustomed to doing that. If I think back and try to determine if it affected me during my football career, I am not sure. I do you know that during my entire career I was unable to gain weight. This is the only symptom I can tie to those days.

Carlos Emmons, Steelers Linebacker, 1996-1999:

The lower picks were really treated as second-class citizens by the coaches. The higher-round picks get all the money and attention – the coaches and people who draft the higher round players have to keep their jobs. So early on you realize the politics of the game.

I was left out of a lot of the individual drills – I had to take advantage of every chance to shine. Greg Lloyd, Kirkland, Gildon, Brown…they knew I wasn't getting many chances and told me I had to prove myself on special teams. Problem was I was like fifth on the depth chart even for special teams.

Earl and Steve in preseason games were given a chance to play special teams in the third quarter of a game – the coaches decided to give me chance too for some reason. That game I had like seven or eight tackles and a sack in a quarter and a half. From then on I got treated like the higher picks. Then I got the chances too.

I told some of the other players – they don't know what it's like being a low-round pick. You go through so much more.

Pete Gonzalez, Steelers Quarterback, 1997-1998:

I was a football player. Not a football model. You know the football models, six foot, four inches, can throw the ball a mile, cocky, entitled because they got a couple of awards in college! That's not what you get with me!

I believe that when you look at my body of work – it says one thing – football player! Mentally strong and willing do whatever it takes to not let his teammates and coaches down. Walt Harris and Tom Donahoe can vouch for that! Oh, smart as well! Play the game!

Kevin Gilbride really liked Anthony Wright. That was his guy. I was a Ray Sherman and Tom Donahoe's guy! Anthony was a Bill Cower and Kevin Gilbride's guy. Need I say more?

However, Anthony had talent and he was great guy. I'm glad he had a good run and lived out a part of his dream.

George Jones, Steelers Running Back, 1997:

I had to alter my game in that scheme. If I played in a system with a guy like Brady or Manning with one back and a spread offense – that's what I was built for. It was difficult for me in a two tight end offense like Pittsburgh's. It was a power offense and they wanted you to run downhill. They didn't want you to dance and reverse field – they wanted you to get positive yards and keep the chains moving. But I was drafted where I was drafted. I stayed positive and did what I could do.

Hines Ward, Steelers Wide Receiver, 1998-2011:

I knew that there were receivers a lot faster, bigger, and stronger than me. No one really saw me as a receiving threat and early on the Steelers didn't seem to be confident enough in me to be a #1 as they drafted Plaxico Burress and Troy Edwards in the first rounds of consecutive year drafts. So I knew I had to do something to separate myself from the others.

I decided that the best way for me to help my team and protect myself was to hit rather than be hit. So I decided I was gonna hit you before you hit me. In our style of offense back then we were predominantly a run-oriented team. We didn't pass much. So as a receiver, you either had to block or be cut. I decided that I was gonna take my fate in my own hands by being the best blocking receiver that I could be. Most receivers back then didn't do that. So I just started knocking people's heads off and hitting anyone and everyone in my way.

Bobby Shaw, Steelers Wide Receiver, 1998-2001:

You know, I was projected to go much higher in the draft, even as a junior in college. You never know how things are going to go on draft day. What team needs what.

I was definitely disappointed but I never felt that my draft status would define me. It just increased my desire to succeed and passion to prove people wrong. I did that all through my career. There were many people who didn't think I'd be nearly as successful as I was in college at California and even more people with those same kind of thoughts about me in the NFL.

I worked harder at the little things – routes, catching the ball, making people miss drove me more. And I'm sure I'm not the only player to ever be disappointed on draft day. You just have to make the best of it and don't let it define you. You just have to improve you self and make yourself better, regardless of where you were drafted.

Matt Cushing, Steelers Tight End, 1998-2004:

It was very difficult to make the team. There are a lot of guys directly competing for your spot and a lot more that would take it in an instant if offered. I did not make the roster to start the season until my forth training camp. Ultimately, it was my ability to play fullback that helped me get on the roster.

Being able to play multiple positions and doing it consistently is how I proved myself to Coach Cowher.

It was difficult. Living life on the bubble was stressful at times. Not knowing if you'll be employed from week to week or day to day can get to you but I learned to live with it and the constant evaluation that goes on in the NFL. It made me a better player because I felt like I had to prove myself in every drill, every practice, and every game. Ultimately, it made be a stronger person.

Jeremy Staat, Steelers Defensive Lineman, 1998-2000:

Well, I left on bad terms. I was a Donohoe draft pick and was caught up in the politics between he and Cowher, Those guys hated each other's guts. When Donohoe was fired I was done. All of Donohoe's picks were weeded out after two or three seasons.

It wasn't a good scheme for me. I was more of a heads-up, 4-3 defensive lineman, not a 3-4 end. Then they shoved me inside when Aaron Smith was there and they brought in Kimo.

It was unfortunate. I was passionate about the game and worked my butt off every play. It was the first time a team ever turned its back on me. I busted my hump and it made no sense for Cowher to turn his back on me because of Donohoe.

Shar Pourdanesh, Steelers Offensive Lineman, 1999-2000:

Having fled Iran during the '79 revolution as a nine year old with my family, I understand how it feels to face struggles at a young age. My early teens were a psychological nightmare for me. I was harassed, attacked and hated when I came here, and I get what it feels like to have obstacles in your life. My son has autism, the ultimate obstacle in his life, and now I must help him and other children like him, in their struggle.

The worst injuries that I ever suffered came from a car accident. I drove off a cliff and fell 150 feet below, and by the grace of God I survived. I destroyed my pelvis, and tore several tendons and muscles in my left arm. But thanks to some great doctors and therapists, I'm back and able to do most things that I enjoy.

Troy Edwards, Steelers Wide Receiver, 1999-2001:

I was dedicated to the game in college. The NFL was just so different. I blame myself for my career. I was just a simple guy – liked the simple stuff like fishing. The Steelers are a great organization – it was just all so big. I didn't want the attention – the autographs and pictures. I just wanted to play and I just went into a Ricky Williams kind of shell.

It was a totally different system from college. The Steelers were a tough, hard-nosed organization. I was just freestyling in college. I didn't know how to play the wide receiver in the NFL until I got to St. Louis. It's so hard to play wide receiver in the NFL. I think it's the second-hardest position besides quarterback. There's so much stuff you need to know and I had no clue.

They tried to teach me. I was just too rebellious. Hines wanted to help me but I just wanted to freestyle. I just felt like I knew it all. The team gave me great information. I just didn't want to listen. I had the greatest receiver in Hines. I just wouldn't listen. I was too stubborn.

Hank Poteat, Steelers Cornerback, 2000-2002:

I was cut three times in two years. Billichick challenges players to understand the bigger picture. He's a situational coach and every day in practice he runs a different situation to help you see the bigger picture – so when it happened in the games you were used to it. I try to use that now.

In Pittsburgh I was successful due to my athletic ability. I wasn't a student of the game. I got drafted by the same city I played for in college – that helped create a lot of distractions. I can't remember studying film – I wasn't used to it.

I became content in the NFL and didn't take advantage of my opportunity.

I had success as a punt returner my rookie year. It fed that mentality that I could do it on my athletic ability alone. But it caught up to me. As a defensive back I didn't know what I was doing. I could play man coverage but not zone. At Pitt I was a running back at first – I didn't play defensive back in high school, but Johnny Majors moved me to defensive back – I wasn't really excited about it.

Then Walt Harris came in and moved me back to running back. I went to him and asked him to do it. I played running back for a couple of games and then changed my mind and asked him to move me back again. I played corner on athletic ability and was in the top three in the nation in interceptions my junior year. My senior year no one threw on me.

In college, the coaches let me play any way I wanted. I was good at press man so I always played press even if the defense was playing zone. In the NFL you don't have that freedom. As a rookie you do what the coaches want you to do. I got frustrated and didn't learn the off-man coverages. I struggled with that. I ended up getting cut a couple of times, it gives you time to think – to see that you need to do it differently next time.

Tee Martin, Steelers Quarterback, 2000-2001:

We were a tight group. You know the higher paid guys will start unless there is an injury. Then, do you play a rookie or the veteran backup? I knew I wouldn't play – it was a delicate situation. You understand it and just do your best to get better for the next team and opportunity.

As a competitor it's frustrating, yeah. In college it's different. The NFL is a day-to-day job. You could never get comfortable like you could in college. Every day was a blessing just to be on the team.

It wasn't harder even with the success in Tennessee. When you are drafted in the fifth round you understand. If there was no injury to Bledsoe you don't hear about Tom Brady. I never had that situation happen for me. I never had a coach leave and take me with them. It's frustrating but you just have to work to put yourself in the best position for the next job.

Tommy Maddox, Steelers Quarterback, 2001-2005:

Health-wise it was frustrating. I think I came back too early from the arm injury. To this day I can feel the nerves shoot down my arm every time I throw a football. It doesn't hurt, but I can always feel it. Funny because I don't feel it when I throw a baseball, but just a football.

Also, I think the offense took on a different tempo and style under Ben. The timing was just different. I still wanted everything to be on my timing, but it wasn't. Trying to run plays and throw balls off the timing that I remembered was hard because the timing had changed. It was Ben's offense and was different from all the memories I had of running the same plays for three years. It just wasn't the same and it was just as frustrating for me as it was for everyone else. I truly believe that the thing that helped me the most, playing in the Arena and XFL, also started to take its toll. I played a lot of games in a short period of time and as I started getting older and not having all the reps, my body would not respond the way I wanted it to.

I am so thankful for being able to play as long as I did, but it is not always easy. Especially once you have a family. Moving them around from town to town and not knowing what is next is tough. A lot of time and effort goes into playing this game. Most fans think and see Sunday, but the off season and during a game week is very intense.

After the XFL, I contacted every team in the NFL and ask them to just give me a chance to go to camp. I knew that if I could get into a camp somewhere I could make the team. Getting into camp was the hardest part after being away from the league for so long. Pittsburgh invited me to come to town. I was able to meet with Coach Cowher and work out with Mike Mularky and Tom Clements. I think it was a good fit for everyone. I told them all I wanted to do is go to camp. If it didn't work out they were out nothing. I guess it worked out.

Mathias Nkwenti, Steelers Offensive Lineman, 2001-2003:

I never planned on being drafted. It was like a tornado came and twisted my life around. It was the craziest year. I switched positions the year before – from defensive line to offensive tackle. The scouts, they come see us as juniors in college and I was this big 285 pound guy that ran a 4.7 forty. That opened a lot of eyes. I just wished I switched earlier – I would have been a first-round pick! Temple wasn't a big school known for players either, so that may have held me back too.

I was mature beyond my years. My parents lived in Africa so I was used to taking care of myself. I worked while in school and had some family friends to help me, but I was really on my own. I had to grow up quick – and I loved to travel. So, it wasn't difficult adjusting. I just was glad I wasn't drafted by a team in the sticks – like Green Bay. A lot of players in college talk about that sort of stuff and I remember I was happy not to go there.

Verron Haynes, Steelers Running Back, 2002-2007:

My father instilled in me that nothing comes easy. I was always taught that you have to work harder than the next man, work while others sleep. I saw the effort he put into his work and it stuck with me from a young age.

Buggy also was very straight forward with me that pro careers, especially football, are short so a backup plan and education is important. I try to invoke the same drive, compassion, and emphasis when giving back when I talk to the youth or even rookies. In Trinidad, something as simple to an American as hot water is considered a luxury. When you grow up in lower class and less fortunate setting, it is a humbling upbringing that makes you want to help others achieve their dreams.

I want the youth to aspire for more than monetary gain, a degree and a meaningful career is more fulfilling than any check.

The bottom line about my off the field incidents is that I was in the wrong place at the wrong time twice. Was I guilty of the accusations? Not necessarily, did I get punished? Yes I did. People that really know me know what I have to offer to society and others.

Jeff Reed, Steelers Kicker, 2002-2010:

On the field does not describe the true character of a person; however, it can bring out some great things and not so great things in an individual. Football is a game though, life seems to be, but in general it is what you make of it. We can control a lot, not everything...

I have so much to offer as a person and learned from those mistakes...hitting a paper towel dispenser with the side of my fist which led to a plastic piece falling off is not national news. However, if you are a Pittsburgh Steeler with crazy hair and a "fun" personality, it can turn in to that...coming to the aid of a teammate in a nonviolent manner is also not national news, however, that was the second time my name was in the picture, so it made it that way.

My parents were with me in both instances: Obviously the time to act like a complete fool and get involved in shenanigans is not with mom and dad around. I learned from it, I'm guilty of being in the wrong place at the wrong time. My coaches and front office preached that to us numerous times in meetings – I was a victim.

Kendall Simmons, Steelers Offensive Lineman, 2002-2008:

When I was diagnosed with diabetes in 2003 I did not know what was going on with me physically and if I would ever play again. I owe Mr. Dan Rooney, the owner of the Steelers at the time, special thanks. I really appreciate how he checked on me every time I saw him downstairs. I also owe the training staff John Norwig and Ryan Grove huge credit for going to all my doctors' appointments at Faulk Clinic with me. They also did a great job with all my needs on the field.

I did not realize at first how hard it would be to feel normal again. It was very hard to get back to the level of performance needed to play in the NFL. I had to constantly check my blood glucose levels. I would test five to six times on practice days and on game days it went to about eight times. The only way I could feel well enough to play was when I kept my blood sugars below 180. That was extremely hard because adrenaline causes your blood sugar levels to rise.

My target numbers were 120 and 170. If I dropped below eighty or were higher than 180, it affected my performance.

Chidi Iwuoma, Steelers Cornerback, 2002-2006, 2006:

I really battled in training camp in order to have a more significant role on the Defense however after having a discussion with Coach Cowher, he explained the importance of special teams and how by playing them I could have a major impact on the team.

I always took pride in getting double and triple teamed and also having players from the other team pointing in my direction as a threat.

2006 was a crazy year for me. Honestly because of lack of job security, you never get too comfortable. That was hard for me to do because the city of Pittsburgh and the fans are so great.

Basically, every training camp you expect the unexpected and have faith that your resume speaks for itself in the opinion of other teams.

Chris Doering, Steelers Wide Receiver, 2003-2004:

Going back and looking at the preseason – I probably lead the NFL in preseason catches and touchdowns. It was stressful because I always had to play and prove myself. I moved twenty-two times over my time in the NFL and got cut ten times. Many would have given up, but for some reason I persevered. That's what I would love fans to know. For every Plaxico, there are guys like me on the cusp – not making a million bucks.

It was fitting for me – I walked on at the University of Florida and still hold the record for the most TDs in the SEC. Yet I was drafted in the sixth round – I always had to prove myself. I wish people would relate to how touch and cutthroat this business is.

I remember playing the Eagles in preseason as a Steeler. It was the fourth quarter – guys my age are not usually playing but there I am on the kickoff team. I was thinking – I gotta block L3. That means the third guy in, who was a linebacker, who probably was 240 pounds and ran a 4.3. When they see me, I know he's going to try to run right through my face. I'm thinking, this sucks. There's gotta be a better job for me. The ball is snapped, and the guy runs right through my face. Looking back on it, I would gladly do it again for a chance to play.

I guess there's stress in whatever you do. What I thought was a tough life – now I'm in the mortgage industry during some of the toughest economic times since the depression.

Brian St. Pierre, Steelers Quarterback, 2003-2004, 2006-2007:

When the Steelers cut me in 2005 I was angry. I felt I had earned the right to make that team and was actually told I did two days prior to being cut. I still, to this day, don't know what happened, but when Coach Whipple asked Bill if he was going to put me in for the fourth quarter versus Carolina (fourth preseason game) and the answer was no, I knew my fate was sealed.

Baltimore picked me up and I was ready to move on. When Ben got injured mid-season vs. San Diego, Kevin Colbert called to try and sign me off of Baltimore's practice squad, but I declined because I wanted to play and Baltimore said they would pull me up to the roster and they did. I wanted to be in a situation where I at least may have a chance to play. I knew that wasn't going to happen in Pittsburgh. I still had dreams and aspirations. I wasn't one of those guys just happy to be there. I played with a lot of those guys and it always rubbed me the wrong way, still does.

Travis Kirschke, Steelers Defensive Lineman, 2004-2009:

Being a backup definitely had its challenges. Not only are your game reps limited but your practice reps too. Starters obviously get the majority of reps so you may never get the opportunity to practice against a certain look and despite your limited reps the expectations for your play don't change.

Also, it was difficult getting into the flow of a game. Many times you are only in for a play or two then have to what forty-five minutes before getting more plays. You would feel like you needed to get warmed up all over again.

I tell you what, it is a tough road to travel in order to make a roster. Being undrafted you didn't get many opportunities to prove yourself so when you did they better of been good. You always felt that you were just a body to fill in, so they would have enough to get through camp. However, I think it helped me because I never allowed myself to become complacent. I really embraced the notion that NFL stood for not for long.

Max Starks, Steelers Offensive Lineman, 2004-2012:

I was excited to be drafted. My dream was always to further my career. Could I make a living doing this? It was special, the anticipation was difficult but I was blessed at least that then the first three rounds were on the same day. I was disappointed though as the third round was winding down and I wasn't picked yet. I was actually on the way out – was leaving – done for the day. But as soon as I was about to go I got a call from a 412 area code. I didn't know where that was from. My friend Josh was there and he was from Pittsburgh so he knew and he told me. When I picked it up I was placed on hold. Then Omar Khan – who was in charge of negotiations then – got on the phone and started asking me some questions. "Did I like cold weather," stuff like that. Then Bill Cowher got on the phone and asked me two questions – "Did I like cold weather and did I like to run the ball?" I said "Yes!" He said, "Congratulations. You're a Steeler!"

Shaun Nua, Steelers Defensive Lineman, 2005-2007:

I had to gain some weight to play this style of defense and I don't think I gained it the proper way so that was different but not too bad. This defense is not designed for defensive linemen to stack up the stat sheet. You must be a selfless player to play in this system. I came in with the mentality that making plays was the only way to survive. This was the hardest thing for me to comprehend in my first year, but after learning more about this system I fell in love with it.

It is a very interesting concept; the defensive line gets the least publicity but at the same time the entire defense starts with them. I love it and to me, personally it's the best system out there. But like Lebeau always says, there is no perfect scheme out there but this is the one we believe in.

Andre Frazier, Steelers Linebacker, 2005, 2007-2010:

I was cut before the first game, but then Matt Kranchik got hurt and they called me while I was driving home and told me they wanted to put me up to the active roster. It was amazing. All my dreams had come to fruition. I was ecstatic.

It's funny because on that same day when I was driving home I got into a car accident – I was rear-ended badly on the highway. My back was hurting. When the training staff asked if I would be ok, you know what I told them – "Yes!" I even got a sack that game against Steve McNair when we were up by like forty.

Fast-forward- I got hurt in the AFC Championship game and couldn't play in the Super Bowl.

Trai Essex, Steelers Offensive Lineman, 2005-2011:

I was the starter going into camp. I had a really good OTA – my best as a professional. But I had a scope done afterwards and I never really recovered from it in time for training camp. I struggled mightily. Then Beachum came in and had a good camp. They brought Marcus Gilbert in and Max was brought back. I saw the writing on the wall.

I cried when Kevin Colbert called to tell me I was going to be released, don't get me wrong. But I knew I had tape out there – I played in Super Bowls and could play multiple positions – I knew I would had value for some team, but I knew it wouldn't be until after week one, when contracts weren't guaranteed any more. That worked out well for me.

Jacksonville and Indianapolis called. Me being from Indianapolis – it was an easy decision. My parents so they could easily see me play – and it was like a homecoming. We actually thought about moving to Indianapolis the year before to be closer to my parents – free babysitting!

Also, Bruce Arians and Goodwin were in Indianapolis too. It made the transition easy. I knew everything – just the terminology was a bit different. It was the easiest decision to make.

Anthony Smith, Steelers Safety, 2006-2008

I was one of the better defensive backs there – you can ask the coaches. It was just a conflict thing. Troy and I were the same style of player. And how the defense was designed, I was too aggressive as a free safety for Dick LeBeau. It was a successful defense, but he wanted a stay at home guy. In my second year when the job was up for battle, I was making plays all through camp – I think I led the team in interceptions in camp. But patience was the issue. I couldn't stay back. I was a ballhhawk in college – and you're the player they draft. I can't try not to make plays. That hindered my play in Pittsburgh.

Jason Capizzi, Steelers Offensive Lineman, 2007-2008:

The offensive line was very difficult to make any headway with the Steelers. There is a ton of seniority and coming out of a D2 school no one really expects you to do much. I was not given as much playing time as I would've liked but all I know is every day in practice and in preseason games I gave it my all and tried to get better each day. In the end I am not mad at all because I left it all on the field. What happens in the coaches office for playing time is out of our hands and we can only control what is done when we are in there playing.

Your teammates are helpful to a certain extent but in the long run everyone is fighting to make the team themselves and it is tough to trust what someone else is telling you because you never know if they are giving you false information to make you look bad.

Jared Retkofsky, Steelers Long Snapper, 2007-2009:

It was tough to try and live this dream. The hardest part was knowing that you could be released at any second for any reason. I struggled to live the "normal" life because we never knew where we would be. People have said it's really tough to make it to the NFL. I would argue that it's even harder to keep it. While playing, I was always looking over my shoulder knowing there are people waiting for me to screw up. It was difficult dealing with the stress of knowing if I have a job tomorrow or not. I overheard a veteran player tell a younger guy, "It doesn't matter how good you are, the day they signed you, they started looking for your replacement." That statement was very true. This is a big business, and the best player is going to play.

Dallas Baker, Steelers Wide Receiver, 2007-2009:

I didn't gel well with Pittsburgh, the opportunities were slim for me. Especially for a guy like me with confidence issues, to beat out a guy but not start was difficult. Other guys who made more money who were older, they were given more than one shot. With me I just felt like what was the point, I had such low confidence.

The team was very family-oriented, they would take care of their players. I tried to quit a few times when it would all get at me. I couldn't deal with the pressure all on my shoulders. I felt like it was all against me. It wasn't that I wasn't good enough – I wasn't bigger, stronger, or faster than other players, but I was smarter. I knew all the positions. My one kryptonite was my confidence – it was the one thing that stopped me. But Coach Tomlin wouldn't let me quit.

I walked away a few times in training camp, I told him I wanted to be a coach. He told me I had the ability and the only reason why I fell in the draft was because of my forty time. He said my forty time hurt me, but they knew I was a top wide receiver in my class and thought I was a steal. They wanted me to stay. He wouldn't let me leave, he told me he believed in me.

Tyler Grisham, Steelers Wide Receiver, 2009-2011:

I missed some practices my rookie training camp due to some hamstring injuries ("you can't make the club in the tub") and I even had a level three AC shoulder separation my last pre-season game, but I showed just enough to intrigue the coaches to keep me around for the practice squad.

I was a newlywed and I was on cloud-nine and in shock that the Pittsburgh Steelers saw my abilities worthy enough to play (or at least practice) for them. With a separated shoulder and pain-killers running through my bloodstream, all they wanted me to do was run routes for the defense. For a number of weeks I could only use my left hand to catch passes if they were thrown my direction. I normally was placed in the slot to mimic the starting slot for the opposing team's offense every week.

John Malecki, Steelers Offensive Lineman, 2011-2013:

No one likes being told they aren't good enough. No one enjoys getting cut. Being an undrafted free agent you learn very quickly that that is how the league works. For me it took a lot of self-reflection and good agent to make it to where I did. There are hundreds of players every year trying to get into the NFL who are great players. I knew what I was up against. My body type and size weren't what the NFL was looking for, and neither was my lack of game time experience playing center. I couldn't control any of that; all I could control was my effort and my attitude. How an individual approaches a situation is a choice.

The fact that I was short and not too fast and not a center were out of my hands. But my mentality was all mine. So I chose to not let what I couldn't control affect me. And I still keep the same mentality to this day. If you walk through life and let everyone else dictate how you feel I promise you will be miserable most of the time.

Baron Batch, Steelers Running Back, 2011-2012:

My dyslexia forced me to work harder than everyone else and my ADHD is the engine that runs my creativity. In my eyes neither is bad. Honestly they are kind of like superpowers if they are truly embraced and used correctly.

I definitely think that I kind of broke the mold of the average football player, and I find that disconcerting for two reasons. The first reason is that there are plenty of athletes that are interesting people and passionate about different things. Unfortunately, those don't get as much attention as when someone gets arrested or something like that. I do think that the fanbase embraces that I was the underdog and an interesting one at that, but at the end of the day being interesting doesn't win football games so things like that disappear as quickly as they appear.

Because I tore my ACL I began to paint and found a career that will last me way longer than football ever could. If I could go back and not tear my ACL and end up making five pro bowls or win a Super Bowl, I wouldn't go back and change a thing. I wouldn't want to be doing anything other than what I get to do at this moment in time. No amount of money or fame is worth more to me than being able to have the ability to live out my passion and do that on my own terms.

John Norwig, Head Trainer, Steelers:

The length of the season is the biggest issue for rookies not to burn out by December 1.

In college, players have academic responsibility only – some embrace it and some do not, but the mental toll on NFL athletes is much greater.

In the pros, players will be in the classroom for a good few hours before practice even begins and they have to embrace that to succeed. That's something most fans aren't aware of or appreciate. They have huge classroom responsibilities – it's a big part of their job.

Physical Impact of the Game:

The most difficult conversations I've had with these players involved their long-term health issues. Many of these players are not in good physical condition due to the toll the game had on them. That's not a great surprise. But it's a different thing to read of the issues suffered by players in general, than to hear it directly from those you followed as a fan as they describe in detail the problems they are now facing and how those problems affect their day-to-day lives.

The problems range from difficulties walking and suffering through multiple operations, to concussion symptoms that have devastating effects of memory loss and lack of emotional control (often bouts of rage), to more emotional-based issues like depression.

Some of these ended careers. Perhaps worse, some impeded but didn't end careers – enabled players to compete at just a high enough level to cause more severe health concerns as they got older. And of course, many manifest themselves years later, well past retirement, when they are less able to deal with them effectively.

Many have sought support – both financial and emotional – through NFL programs. Despite what some say, the NFL has helped many of these ex-players, some substantially. Many others though have not been helped – at least not enough. Especially for many of these older NFL veterans who earned less and who suffered for the need of better equipment, better field conditions, and the medical advancements and care that today's players benefit from.

In the end, many players have avoided these physical issues. Many are suffering through them now. And in some of the more disturbing conversations, there is an entire class of players who simply won't know what the future holds in store for them. The newly retired, who express fear for themselves and their families as they live in the unknown. Hoping they don't suffer from the same issues as many of their mentors and friends.

Bill Kisher, Steelers Offensive Lineman, 1958-1959:

In '58, I had my head split open by teammate Mike Sandusky, in practice. We didn't practice with helmets on in those days. Earl Morrall called the play, and Mike and I both pulled. One of us in the wrong direction – we argued about that for years and still haven't resolved who was wrong! Well, we collided into one another and my head was split open. We had the same doctor then who used to sew up the NHL guys when they were still on the ice. I couldn't get my helmet on after that, my head was so swollen.

Theron Sapp, Steelers Fullback, 1963-1965:

In '63 we were playing a home game versus Pittsburgh. Their linebacker, John Reger, tackled me and my knee hit him. He swallowed his tongue and they had to perform emergency surgery on him on the field. The whole stadium was quiet.

Well, a couple of days later I was watching TV at the hotel and I saw on the news that I was traded to Pittsburgh. I called Vince McNally and he told me I had to be in Pittsburgh by 6:00 a.m. Tuesday. So, I loaded up my car and drove to Pittsburgh.

I met with [Steelers coach] Buddy Parker – he told me I'd be playing a lot on Sunday. And I did – I played a lot in the ballgame on Sunday. I was happier because I had gotten to play a lot more in Pittsburgh. The only thing that bothered me was that Green Bay never called me to tell me I was traded.

Bob Sherman, Steelers Cornerback, 1964-1965:

I would like to see the problems with concussions addressed more. I don't want to get on my soapbox. I already got four or five solicitations from lawyers suing the NFL. It's going to get a lot worse down the way.

At Iowa, I played with Wally Hilgenberg who played fifteen years in the NFL. He died of MS. Mike Bradley played for Chicago for five years and he has dementia and Alzheimer's. It's scary – and we're probably just discovering how extensive this all is.

The helmet today is a lot better. The NFL is doing as much as they can now, I think. They are very aware, but probably should have started years ago to take care of the players that had problems earlier.

I hated to see John Henry Johnson destitute. It made me sick. A guy like that, after all he did for the NFL. It just makes you sick.

I don't have all the answers. It's a tough, violent game.

Gene Breen, Steelers Defensive Lineman, 1965-1966:

It started in early 2004. I starting losing control of myself – anger issues and I was unable to sleep or focus. I didn't know myself anymore. I lost a lot of self-respect and was out of control.

I got into some trouble and was put into a hospital. I got help from Dr. Horn, Dr. Harding, and Dr. Allen. The doctors now have me medicated correctly – at a cost of five hundred dollars per month. This helps connect the wires in my head that are all screwed up due to the traumatic brain injuries.

Dr. Horn from NeuroRestorative was my savior. He helps me with rehab – helps me to take a look at the good versus bad side of things and reminds me that negativity doesn't help me and my condition.

I wouldn't be here without my wife and doctors. I was out of control. They sat me down and told me to take control of my life. I'm not a quitter. I instilled that into my five children. I'm a winner – I hate losing.

Roy Jefferson, Steelers Wide Receiver, 1965-1969:

I had carpal-tunnel surgery on my hand twice – though I think the need for the second time was the doctor's fault. I had hip replacement surgery and will be scheduling the first of two knee replacement surgeries soon. Medicare took care of all of the injuries – the NFL had to take care of none of it. They would have if I didn't have insurance – and the insurance took care of my surgeries in '75 and the 80s as well.

I also got some workman's comp for my back and knee. The NFLPA had assisted me financially when I had some issues dealing with depression when my mom died. They also helped when I developed Shingles – it was a mild form luckily. Then I developed hyper-thyroid issues and lost twenty-five pounds in two weeks. It turned to Graves Disease and the NFLPA helped with that too.

My thyroid's normal now. I'm playing golf again – my hip and carpal-tunnel are well enough now and I'm playing golf better than ever.

I'm not content at all. I received $15,000 from our lawsuit against the NFLPA for defrauding players. The attorney that represented us is now working for the NFLPA! They didn't take the advice of Larry Parish to go after the one hundred million dollars – they only went after seven million dollars. We should have gotten much more.

John Brown, Steelers Offensive Lineman, 1967-1971:

They [the NFL] couldn't help when I had the knee replacements – there was nothing they could do they said when I called. But there was a small subsidy for the hip replacement and I was glad to see that.

The new CBA agreement is now helping the older fellows. John Mackay's wife was going through a hard time and lobbied for more money for incapacitated players. Now players get $100,000 if they are incapacitated in an institution.

No one held a gun to my head to play, but it is a sacrifice. Young guys today – they are bigger and faster and I don't think their bodies will be able to take that stress over time. I worry they will have retirement problems too.

L.C. Greenwood, Steelers Defensive Lineman, 1969-1981:

During the season you're all banged up – you can't practice on skills during the season. You have to do that before the season. I used camp to get in shape. I didn't look at it like it was hard – though it was abusive at times. I took it as a challenge – I knew it would help me during the season – I knew I wouldn't have the energy to train during the season.

Terry Hanratty, Steelers Quarterback, 1969-1976:

Camp was real tough. I took my son a few years ago to see the Steelers camp – it was Tomlin's rookie year. I couldn't believe how little action there was. Players were complaining how hard it was under Tomlin too, no more Popsicle breaks like Cowher used to give them.

There's so little hitting now. We hit all the time in practice. When we were there all the hitting we saw was with the running back-linebacker drills. We ran all the time. Most of us went to camp to get into shape. Now those guys work out all year long. The only guy doing running was Polamalu doing wind sprints on his own.

Chuck's camps were brutal. People were knocking each other out.

Lee Calland, Steelers Cornerback, 1969-1972:

I asked Chuck to trade me....I knew it was coming to the end. I hurt my back and didn't want the team to suffer having to carry me. Soup (Mel Blount) was coming up, as was Anderson. They had great athletes coming up and I didn't want to hold them back, so they traded me to the Raiders.

Dennis Hughes, Steelers Tight End, 1970-1971:

Now, I'm unable to do much of anything. I'm a good bit disabled. My back is not in good shape. My knee was replaced. I had a disk taken out...screws in my back. I take it day-to-day...that's how I feel.

They are all football related, yes. A lot of them have to do with the field in Pittsburgh then. It was the worst field in the game, and then I went to the second worst stadium in the NFL after Pittsburgh in Houston. I played in the two worst fields in my two and a half years. I guess it wore me out.

There was no padding on that Pittsburgh field – there's nothing you can do about it now. And the NFL is not helping at all. All I have is three years and the way it's set up its five years you need to have. I pay $180-$200 a month out of pocket just for my medications. I'm helping to raise my granddaughter and need all the help I can give her.

Hubie Bryant, Steelers Wide Receiver, 1970-1971:

I didn't adjust to the turf at Three Rivers. I was a track guy and never pulled a hamstring until Three Rivers – the turf was crude – no cushion. I pulled my hamstring after seven or eight games and it really ended my career there. I was traded to New England and beat out their number one pick, but then got hurt in New England at the end of the Baltimore Colts game at Foxboro Stadium.

The offense had been sitting on the sideline for a long time when the Colts scored with less than a minute left in the game. I wasn't really warm and I had to go in and return the kickoff. I got the kick and hit the hole to the left and just as I was about to break it for six, Rick Volt grabbed my ankle; I tried to kick my leg free and popped my hamstring. I hobbled as fast as I could to the sideline where I was met by about five dudes, "Boom!"

On Monday as I'm sitting in the whirlpool, Head Coach Myzer asked me if I was alright because if so he was going to start me that Sunday. I had beat out the number one draft pick Jon Sekllers from Florida State, but I couldn't play! That is how my NFL experience ended.

Mel Holmes, Steelers Offensive Lineman, 1971-1973:

Like most players, I had my share of injuries, however none that were major. Only a knee injury that I can recall was serious. I injured it above all, in practice, on the artificial turf we had at the time called poly-turf. This stuff was not perfected during that time. I think quite a few injuries happened to players as a result of playing and practicing on this artificial turf.

Reggie Harrison, Steelers Running Back, 1974-1977:

I'm nursing a lot of injuries. I had back surgery and have been declared disabled. I fell down some steps that collapsed on me while I was working and have fought this injury for five years. I finally had to be cut on and had the surgery in the early 90s.

The type of running back I was got hit in the head a lot. Now I regret it. I used to get on Franco for running out of bounds. He told me that the way I run, I won't last. Taking lots of hits and giving hits out. Either way, you are taking hits he said. He told me it was like a bag of marbles. Say you have ten marbles. Every hit you take or give takes one away. Until you have none left.

Cullen Bryant, Earl Campbell, me…all of us backs that ran like I did have problems now. Guys that look for contact have issues. Look at Earl.

They say you should stop at three concussions. I had three before the NFL.

Now, I'm suffering from head and back injuries, taking my daily regimen of Methadone and Oxycontin.

I'm also dealing with the headaches from the various concussions I've received over the years playing football.

Dick Conn, Steelers Cornerback, 1974:

I actually left the league because of a spinal injury but have managed to put off that surgery so far. Our league and players association have not done much to help older players with insurance and pension benefits, but that's another story!

Neil Graff, Steelers Quarterback, 1976-1977:

I have had both of my knees replaced in the last two years. Prior to the replacements I had had five surgeries to correct cartilage damage. These surgeries were the result of former football injuries. The surgeries and the related damage limited the recreational activities that I could engage in, but I would not have given up my NFL experiences for anything. I had personal health insurance that paid for the majority of my surgical costs, but the NFL did reimburse me for my co-pay costs and deductibles.

The NFL has a program that does pay for joint replacements for players that do not have health insurance and that has been a blessing for a number of my peers who have not been able to afford a health insurance program.

Robin Cole, Steelers Linebacker, 1977-1988:

A lot of these guys today wouldn't make my team if I could pick one. We got beat up in practice before every game. You practice hard, you play hard.

I used to wrestle to get ready for games. There are other things you can do to get used to the physicality of the game. Coaches today don't understand that. Karate, Judo, wrestling – some of these coaches can't even scratch their own backs. There are other things guys can do after practice that can help them get used to the weight of other players and the contact without crushing each other.

Tom Beasley, Steelers Defensive Lineman, 1978-1983:

Things were fast in college, but at this level – it was all cranked up a notch.

The second was the length of the season. It went from twelve to twenty games. Physically and mentally it was tough – by November my body and mind were saying time out. Plus, playing in the North, the cold weather added another dimension to the game. We didn't have indoor facilities then. We practiced in the elements. There was a time the weather was so bad we flew to Oakland for a game on Tuesday just so we could practice.

Marvin Cobb, Steelers Safety, 1980 and Independent Retired Players Summit Director:

I became involved in advocating for better pensions and medical benefits for pre-1993 retired football players about five years ago after reading more and more stories of players committing suicide, being homeless, struggling to make ends meet, etc.

It turns out there's enough money in the NFL to provide a measure of dignity to all who played the game, and that is the mission of The Summit. We are aiming to educate and motivate as many retired players as possible to join the advocacy movement for better pensions and access to our disability benefits.

Truthfully, my biggest desire is for a change in the pension plan so that each vested man would have a vote in selecting the three "player representatives" on the pension board. Currently, we have no say in how our pension is managed and distributed, and we feel the NFLPA has not done an adequate job of representing the pre-1993 retirees.

I believe that on most issues, the NFL and the NFLPA are partners, so they both are responsible in many respects. However, the NFLPA has claimed to represent retired players, and many of us have relied on that claim to our detriment.

Craig Bingham, Steelers Linebacker, 1982-1984, 1987:

Ah, the knee injury. That happened in a game against the Packers. I was spinning out of a block, my whole body turned while my foot remained planted in the grass. I heard and felt the pop. I asked the person blocking me to call the trainers. Gotta tell ya, it did hurt.

I was able to get through the surgeries and rehab by grace of the good Lord.

Secondly, I was motivated by many who said that I would never play again. In fact, my knee was not fully repaired until I was finished playing. I played the later years without an ACL, or should I say, a very few strands. Thanks to Dr. Richard Steadman, Lake Tahoe, who helped to give me the motivation to get it done and get back out on the field. I was the second person from PA...the other being the Senator, and the first pro football player he had operated on.

After I made the team again in '84, one of the trainers came to me and said they had written me off a being finished and that I proved both he and them wrong. They did not think that I would have recovered from the injury.

Rick Woods, Steelers Safety, 1982-1986:

I remember playing the Giants my rookie year in mid-December. We practiced Saturday – did our walk-throughs as it was raining. The field would mush up as we ran through the infield and make footprints. That night it froze. It was like playing on knives. Me, being the dumb rookie, I cut the sleeves off of my jerseys and Coach Parker would not allow anyone to wear anything under their uniform. I learned my lesson the hard way!

The next time I cut off my sleeves I kept them and sewed them on when I needed them!

Chris Kolodziejski, Steelers Tight End, 1984:

We were playing in 1984 against the San Francisco 49ers who were the eventual Super Bowl Champions that year and at the time of my injury, they were undefeated. My injury occurred in the fourth quarter with just about three minutes left in the game. We were down by seven and needed a score to tie and we had a first and twenty on about the 49ers' thirty yard line.

Chuck Noll had called a timeout and I ran over to the sideline where Chuck, Mark Malone and Stallworth were huddled together discussing what play to run. I jumped in and called my own play. I told Chuck, "I got this guy, throw the ball to me and I will get the first down." Chuck looks at me and says, "Ok, let's run the play." The play put Stallworth and Louis Lipps out left where I knew their defenders would double up on them and leave me one on one on the right side with man to man coverage.

I beat my guy off the line and was wide open. Unfortunately, something happened on the throw and I think Mark got hit and the ball was badly underthrown. I had to try and stop and back pedal about three steps and caught the ball off of my foot just before it hit the ground. As I did a 180 to try and get headed back to the end zone, I turned and planted my left foot in the turf and by that time free safety, Dwight Hicks had now had time to adjust and make his way over to tackle me. His helmet hit me right on the kneecap as my foot was planted. My kneecap was partially shattered and my leg hyper extended to the point that my foot hit my helmet. I had also suffered two severed ligaments. I did however, hold onto the ball, made the first down and that gave us the ball on the five yard line.

Stallworth caught a touchdown on the next play and Brian Hinkle intercepted a Joe Montana pass and ran it back for a game winning touchdown. It was in one play, a career ending catastrophic injury. I think we all need to remember football is a brutal game and we leave not because we want to, but because we are generally injured.

Steve August, Steelers Offensive Lineman, 1984:

I actually left the team during the pre-season of the '85 year. I started training camp and was hurt after the first week in camp and was out for a week or so, then was placed on waivers and was picked up by the Jets.

The saying in the NFL is you get hurt you lose your job. Yes, leaving the Steelers was really hard for me. I had played for seven and a half years in Seattle and missed one game due to injury and then when I have this great opportunity to play in my hometown in front of family and friends I get hurt not just once but twice with the Steelers.

Ray Snell, Steelers Offensive Lineman, 1984-1985:

I had a good first season. After my second year I had a blowout fracture of my right eye. It happened in practice – on a trap play I collided so hard with David Little it broke my facemask. They fixed the helmet but I said, wow, I couldn't feel my face.

We thought it was just an open wound – but I later learned my eye was ruptured. I was a debilitating injury and I couldn't recover from it. I was placed on injured reserve, then released.

Detroit asked me later if I could play. I tried – I didn't know yet that it was a fracture. I made the team and played, but in the game against Chicago it got worse. I could not feel the right side of my face from my eye to my teeth. After that, I retired.

Ownership doesn't take responsibility for the injuries we have. They have to see it from our side. I have a dislodged bone in my optic nerve and will have surgery Monday. The NFL is not taking any responsibility for it. The surgeon said I made the right decision to get out of the game when I did.

I accepted my role and moved on. But I'm disappointed every time I see my teammates who are suffering from injuries from the game and who can barely walk.

I just wonder about the next athletes. These young guys – wait until they are forty or fifty – if they even make it. I feel lucky when I see my former teammates and pray to the Lord every day for myself and them.

Mark Behning, Steelers Offensive Lineman, 1985-1987:

You like to think you're in control. What you can control you can exploit and use it in your work. A reporter wrote that, on paper, I was superior to Bill Fralic, but on the field I couldn't hold his jock strap. I relied on strength – I guess you can say I was a brute. Nebraska wasn't a passing school so we didn't practice a lot of pass blocking. I went back to Nebraska my first two offseasons to practice my pass blocking. But, the injuries played a big deal. I broke my arm my first year, and when I got out of the cast I had my right elbow operated on for some loose cartilage. Then I had the other elbow operated on. I had six surgeries on my elbows and had my right elbow replaced five years ago. That didn't take and it has failed three times so far. Carrying around your arm like that doesn't work. I need another replacement – it gets expensive.

Preston Gothard, Steelers Tight End, 1985-1988:

In '86 I had a broken bone in my heel. I played through the season with it – I'm really not sure when it happened. I tore my PCL in practice in '87. It's an odd ligament – it's in the back of the knees and inoperable really. My knee kept moving and it sheared off cartilage. That and my Achilles tendonitis was the worst pain in the world.

It all caught up with my career. I was slow enough that the injuries compounded and shortened my career. Still, I got further than I was supposed to.

John Rienstra, Steelers Offensive Lineman, 1986-1990:

My shoulders are shot, one has been replaced and I can't run because of it and my back – had hernia surgeries on that. So now I mountain and road bike a lot. I can't run and can't lift anything because a couple of my rotators are gone. Running does more harm than good – so I'm looking into doing some swimming to strengthen those muscles.

I never got hurt in a game. The camps were brutal – the two-a-days were rough. Smashing into people every day. Chuck had us doing two-a-days even in January during the playoffs.

My only injuries were in camp, so the rules for camps I like. Noll used to have on some Fridays a "Rise and Blow" rule to protect players from hitting each other with their helmets on those days. I loved those days. It took the heavy hitting out of practices.

Delton Hall, Steelers Cornerback, 1987-1991:

In 1988 I broke my right wrist – I hit some guy on the thigh and it just crumpled the wrist. I played with a cast the entire year. In 1989 I broke the other wrist overcompensating for the right one and wore a cast that year too. So I deal with those issues from those broken wrists too.

Gerry Mullins, Steelers Offensive Lineman, 1971-1979:

We cut blocked all the time. There are a lot of rules now that weren't in place in the 70s which protect the players better. It was open season back in the 70s.

Craig Veasey, Steelers Defensive Lineman, 1990-1992:

You didn't whine. I was just happy to be there.

I tore ligaments in my left wrist and found out right before the combine. I thought my career was over. In fact it was the Steelers' doctor that told me. Well, Delton Hall had that same surgery that offseason so they knew it would be okay and that's why they drafted me.

After my first preseason game, in pregame, Tunch Ilkin poked me in the eye and I had to go on IR. I thought it was all over for me – that after I was off IR they'd let me go. So, after all of that, I was just happy to be there.

Todd Kalis, Steelers Offensive Lineman, 1994:

Over the last ten years, the NFL has created some new programs for the retired players. The NFL Alumni focused on advocacy especially during the CBA negations, pushing for improved benefits, increases in pensions, healthcare for players…I'm an optimistic guy. I think the NFL is trying to make the players happy. A number of prominent players have surfaced which brings more attention to the issues being discussed.

I appreciate their efforts because I also left the game with injuries I will deal with for the rest of my life. I have plates and screws in my knee and ankle and have had other injuries as well. We all have something – in every sport, we suffer injuries. But the NFL is different – it's a more gladiator style of game, I'm not sure how much the NFL can reduce the wear and tear of the game without making major changes

Any injury at that level is tough. I got injured in the preseason – on grass no less. My left knee was taken out on a play and it was a very difficult to return, I won't lie. I snapped two of the three ligaments in my knee in half. There's always pressure to come back and perform. If you can't…well, it's a business, your days are over if you can't.

There are always after-affects. Luckily, I was able to play another three years after the injury. It was tough though – physically and mentally. I wore a brace, but you have that worry that it could happen again, though the chances of it really doing so were pretty slim.

Nolan Harrison, Steelers Defensive Lineman, 1997-1999:

There were many players around the league who were having their careers put in jeopardy or cut by the chop block. I decided to take action and reach out to all the defense of players around the National Football League to sign the petition to ban the block. Once I got the signatures I also obtained film showing the type of devastating injuries that occurred from this block. I was able to get a hearing in front of the competition committee and Commissioner Paul Tagliabue to argue my case.

I was supported by The Leadership of the NFL Players Association. I successfully argued the case and the block was made illegal and also a fineable offense that will go up incrementally for repeat offenders.

This was one of my crowning achievements during my ten year pro football career.

Will Blackwell, Steelers Wide Receiver, 1997-2001:

I had lots of injuries playing that held me back. Broken foot, separated shoulder, broken ribs, torn ACL, dislocated fingers…after my second year I stayed in Pittsburgh to spend time rehabbing and getting healthy. I wanted to rehab in front of [trainer] John Norwig – I wanted them to see and chart what I was doing. I wanted to do it the way they wanted it done – I didn't want to go elsewhere. I felt I handled myself the right way. I had a rookie card that said, "They put their trust in me by drafting me, so I would do everything they asked me to do."

And that's what I did.

Chris Fuamatu-Ma'afala, Steelers Running Back, 1998-2002:

No doubt – injuries pile up because of all the different things I had to do. I had to do it all – special teams, scout team and the regular offensive plays, every day. That was like seventy plays a day – that's like playing a regular game.

The vets only had to do the offensive plays. The wear and tear in practice was brutal. That had a big part in cutting my career short.

Other guys had the same issue. Verron Haynes was always physically in great shape. But the wear and tear got to him too. Guys like that never get hurt, but he did due to that wear and tear.

Dewayne Washington, Steelers Cornerback, 1998-2003:

I was there when Hines was a rookie. Hines was a different player, you could tell. I'm not sure if he'd remember, but in his first practice, he lined up against me and I was playing bump and run. The first snap he came off the ball and knocked me down on my back. It threw me for a loop – I saw his strength. He came at me even though he was a rookie to prove himself. That tells you about the guy's mentality. He figured it out day one.

Jeremy Staat, Steelers Defensive Lineman, 1998-2000:

Steed, Strelczyk, Ward, Townsend…all were awesome. I enjoyed hanging out with them and being on the team.

Steed was one of the coolest guys I ever met. I'd watch him in his last season walk out with bad knees, bad shoulders…dog, I didn't want to be like that when I got older. I shake hands with some of the older vets and their mangled fingers…I was fortunate to get out healthy.

Shar Pourdanesh, Steelers Offensive Lineman, 1999-2000:

I destroyed my LCL, PCL, and ACL. It was the end. What was sad is that I was playing the best football of my career. As for now I feel great. I am in great shape. I am 310 pound with little body fat and I feel like I am twenty-five years old.

Ainsley Battles, Steelers Safety, 2000, 2004:

I stopped playing after I tore my hamstring in '04. It required surgery to re-attach it. Due to the severity of the injury, it was one of those things – it damaged my speed and ability and the team had to make a financial decision to not keep me. I wasn't a starter, they wouldn't pay me after that injury to be a backup.

Mike Logan, Steelers Safety, 2001-2006:

If I can complain about one thing in my career it would be injuries. I feel like I cheated my fans because they never really had an opportunity to see me play at one hundred percent. I was able to make the roster every year because I worked hard in the offseason to get in tip-top shape, but the continual process of beating down my body eventually caught up to me with age.

I've had five football-related injuries that required surgery. I still have three metal plates in my forearm and ankle. I had two total posterior knee reconstructions. At thirty-eight years old now I have arthritis in my hand and wrist and tendonitis in my knees. I also suffered from depression after I retired. It's hard to adapt without the game that you played for so long. I also had four documented concussions. The long-term effects of them have yet to be determined.

I don't think even after seeing the long-term effects of injuries and concussions that it will deter many athletes from playing this game. However, I'll personally say this. After your playing days are over you get a heavy reality check. When your health coverage is up and you need medical attention, you look back and think about the sacrifice you put yourself through and it hurts. The life expectancy of professional football players is going down. Someone once told me, "You take a year or two off your life expectancy for every year you play in the league." Well I played ten years and I'm a black male. Black males' average life span is sixty-nine years old. So when I think about my life possibly being over at fifty-nine, I ask myself was it worth it?

As I look at my Super Bowl ring I struggle to answer that question. I don't want to seem selfish. I have children and I need to be here for them to leave a legacy that helps them live a righteous life.

Jeff Hartings, Steelers Center, 2001-2006:

I don't think fans relate. People come up to me still and say to me that it was good I got out before I got too banged up. I don't know what they mean. Before I am paralyzed?

Fans forget that we play football in high school, college then the NFL. At forty years old your body feels like you are sixty. You have to do all you can to maintain your health now – to avoid having to use painkillers. In my era, we weren't educated on the effects of concussions and the pounding a body takes, but we're getting there now.

Steelers Quiz

1. Who did Bruce Arians ask to be his go-between between he and the wide receiver corps when he was the team's wide receivers coach?

2. Who did Gary Dunn tackle into a car on the Pittsburgh Turnpike?

3. Who was taken out to dinner at the age of ten by Art Rooney Sr. then drafted by him?

4. Who started the "Dress Off" competition?

6. What player did the beat impression of Bill Cowher?

7. Where did the 60s teams practice on bad weather days?

8. Who kept putting water in Jack Lambert's shoulder pads?

9. Who wheeled a tied-up Rocky Bleier into the locker room in a shopping cart on his last day as a Steeler?

10. What Steeler used to dress in a rubber suit in training camp, and why?

11. What Steeler was later blackballed from the NFL?

12. Who was "Big Play Ray"?

13. Who did **L.C.** Greenwood call "His Rookie"?

14. Name at least three Steelers that left the team to return in later years?

15. What former Steeler has a passion for knitting?

16. What scares Jack Lambert most?

17. Who ran a name your favorite sportswriter ad in the Post-Gazette?

18. What Steeler intercepted Joe Namath three times in one game?

20. What OL refused to accept a pass play call because he wanted to get to the bar before closing time?

21. How did Art Rooney do for Brian Blankenship after he notified **Mr.** Rooney of his injury?

22. What prompted Roy Jefferson's trade to Baltimore?

24. Which Steeler was the original target for the play that turned into the Immaculate Reception?

25. Who was "Boobie"?

26. What Steelers quarterback consistently talked so fast in the huddle he was frequently told to calm down by his linemen?

27. What Steeler was one of the first ten players to sue the NFL for Anti-Trust issues?

28. Who was the Steelers' player rep during the '87 strike?

29. Who stranded John Banaszak at the Super Burger?

30. Name at least three Steelers that played in the USFL?

32. Who ran out of the Steelers dorm yelling "The mongoose is loose!", and why?

33. What Steeler knocked Mike Ditka into a goalpost?

34. Who was Mad Rad?

35. Who established the Steelers' first weight-lifting program?

36. What was "The Crab"?

37. Who replaced Jack Lambert for the entire second half of Super Bowl IX?

38. Who caught Terry Bradshaw's last pass?

39. Who did the Steelers play in the first ever Monday night game?

40. Who stuffed Matt Bahr in a shopping cart while in his boxers and wheeled him into the Steelers lobby?

41. What Steelers coach put alarms on the dorm room exits?

42. Who put baby powder in Mike Kruczek's helmet?

43. Who was the most superstitious Steelers head coach?

44. Where did Chuck Noll coach before he joined the Steelers?

45. What former Steeler currently has two sons playing in the NFL?

46. Who was the first radio announcer for the Steelers?

47. Who was "Knotty Pine"?

48. Who did Hines Ward knock on his back in his first practice as a Steeler?

49. Who was called "**Dr.** King?"

50. What was "The Snakebox"?

51. What did Chad Brown see at Carnell Lake's house that changed his approach to football?

52: Name two Steelers who played wide receiver but never did so in college?

53. Who wanted to leave a game early to get to the bar before closing time?

54. What is the "Mind Gym"?

55. Who broke Levon Kirkland's hand in Tae Kwon Do class?

56. What former Steeler is now a VP of the Church of Scientology?

57. Name at last three former Steelers who are now on the radio or TV as broadcasters?

58. Name two former Steelers that played against the Steelers in a Super Bowl.

59. Who was Vaughn Nixon and why was he important to the Steelers?

60. What Steeler player was actually shot in the head in high school?

61. What Steeler player was a regular on a TV reality show?

62. What Steeler player was a professional wrestler in the offseason?